AN INTRODUCTION TO FENG SHUI

Feng shui has been known in the West for the last 150 years but has mostly been regarded as a primitive superstition. During the modern period, successive regimes in China have suppressed its practice. However, in the last few decades, feng shui has become a global spiritual movement with professional associations, thousands of titles published on the subject, countless websites devoted to it and millions of users.

In this book, Ole Bruun explains feng shui's Chinese origins and meanings as well as its more recent Western interpretations and global appeal. Unlike the abundance of popular manuals, his *Introduction* treats Chinese feng shui as an academic subject, bridging religion, society and culture. Individual chapters explain:

• the Chinese religious–philosophical background
• Chinese uses in rural and urban areas
• the history of feng shui's reinterpretation in the West
• environmental perspectives and other issues.

OLE BRUUN is Associate Professor at the Institute for Society and Globalization, Roskilde University, Denmark. He is author of *Fengshui in China: Geomantic Divination between State Orthodoxy and Popular Religion* (2003) and editor with Michael Jacobsen of *Human Rights and Asian Values: Contesting Identities and Cultural Representations in Asia* (2000).

AN INTRODUCTION TO
FENG SHUI

OLE BRUUN

CAMBRIDGE
UNIVERSITY PRESS

CAMBRIDGE UNIVERSITY PRESS

Cambridge, New York, Melbourne, Madrid, Cape Town, Singapore, São Paulo, Delhi

Cambridge University Press
The Edinburgh Building, Cambridge, CB2 8RU, UK

Published in the United States of America by Cambridge University Press, New York

www.cambridge.org
Information on this title: www.cambridge.org/9780521682176

First published 2008

Printed in the United Kingdom at the University Press, Cambridge

A catalogue record for this publication is available from the British Library

Library of Congress Cataloguing in Publication data
Bruun, Ole, 1953–
An introduction to feng shui / Ole Bruun.
p. cm.
Includes bibliographical references and index.
ISBN 978-0-521-86352-0
1. Feng shui. I. Title.
BF1779.F4B79 2008
133.3'337 – dc22 2008026921

ISBN 978-0-521-86352-0 hardback
ISBN 978-0-521-68217-6 paperback

Contents

List of illustrations   *page* vii

1 Introduction   1
    Feng shui as popular religion   2
    Three themes   3
    Western receptiveness   5

2 A brief history of feng shui   11
    The classical age   14
    The imperial age   17
    The colonial era   35
    The communist era   47

3 Feng shui in the context of Chinese popular religion   49
    Family ritual and the yearly festivals   52
    The Chinese almanac, or the Know All Book (Tongshu)   55
    Feng shui for building   59
    Feng shui for burial   67
    Other common applications   71
    Feng shui and belief   77
    Feng shui and other strands of popular divination   82

4 Feng shui research   84
    A new turn   85
    Studies in ecology and nature perception   94
    Studies in architecture   97

5 Cosmological principles, schools of interpretation and the
   feng shui compass   100
    The Book of Changes   101
    The five elements (wu xing)   106
    The concept of qi (ch'i)   108
    Schools of feng shui   110
    The feng shui compass   115

6 Feng shui in the Chinese cityscape: China proper
   and overseas   118
   Cities in China proper   118
   Taiwan and Hong Kong   129

7 Modern feng shui interpretations and uses   144
   A new perspective on an old subject   145
   New schools of feng shui   149
   Renewed exposure in China   156
   New feng shui uses: western, Chinese or global?   158
   Manual authors   168
   Global exchange   170
   Corporate feng shui?   171

8 Environmental concerns   173
   History and environment in China   174
   Some fieldwork experiences   176
   New Chinese environmentalism   183

9 Feng shui as cultural globalization?   191

Bibliography   196
Index   208

Illustrations

2.1 The Chinese national symbol, the dragon. Photographs by
Ole Bruun, with permission from the Luoyang Museum of
Ancient Tombs, Luoyang, China   *page* 13
2.2 Title page from *Dixue dawen* [Questions and Answers in
Geography] (1744). Collection of the Royal Library,
Copenhagen   36
2.3 Title page from a Chinese work on geography/feng shui
(1627). Collection of the Royal Library, Copenhagen   37
2.4 Illustration from *Dixue dawen* [Questions and Answers in
Geography], (1744), Collection of the Royal Library,
Copenhagen   38
2.5 Instructions for layout and use of buildings around a
traditional courtyard. Chinese manual from 1915   39
2.6 A series of feng shui situations at front gates. Chinese manual
from 1915   40
2.7 Drawing from a traditional feng shui manual indicating
placement in landscape. Chinese manual from 1627   41
3.1 A rural feng shui master using a large Hong Kong-produced
compass. Photograph by Ole Bruun   60
3.2 Example of a family grave. Photograph by Ole Bruun   68
3.3 A client seeking advice from feng shui Master Wang.
Photograph by Ole Bruun   80
6.1 New office buildings towering above older ones. Photograph
by Ole Bruun   123
6.2 Buddhist monk. Photograph by Ole Bruun   126
6.3 Feng shui-inspired, waving rooftop design on new apartment
buildings. Photograph by Ole Bruun   141
6.4 The postmodern architecture of South Chinese cities.
Photographs by Ole Bruun   142

6.5 Chinese property buyers viewing a model of a new housing
complex. Photograph by Ole Bruun   143
7.1 The eight trigrams of the *bagua* and their Chinese names   150

CHAPTER I

Introduction

Chinese feng   sed art of
placement. (ines have
introduced ii   roliferate
and the inter   ces to the
subject. The   USA and
shortly after   n interest
in Buddhism   century,
can compare   les. From
the first few   feng shui
book market   s. Today,
several thous   es, while
spreading fur   l parts of
the world.

Feng shui l   uch as to
redecorate or   ality and
interior desig

... ance, focus
on simple living, achieve harmonious relations with the environment or just
install quick changes to increase the quality of life. Increasingly, however,
feng shui has been applied professionally, such as to expand businesses,
increase sales, improve the health and performance of employees, renew
principles for architecture, better the performance of clinics and hospitals,
treat illnesses in children's institutions and so forth.

Despite the great interest it has created in the western world, people
tend to have only vague notions of its origin and meaning, and even less
understanding of the controversial nature of feng shui practices in their
home country. Obviously, this is not a manual of feng shui techniques
but an effort to explain the feng shui tradition in its various aspects and
contexts. The feng shui tradition is a piece of Chinese history, inseparable
from Chinese cosmology and popular religion and deeply intertwined with
the social and political processes of Chinese history. Many great Chinese

thinkers have written on the subject, though by and large being as sceptical and divided between believers and non-believers as Chinese society in general.

This does not mean that feng shui was unknown outside Chinese communities prior to the 1980s; the interest was limited to a few academic disciplines, mainly Chinese studies and anthropology. Several subsequent chapters in this book will show that feng shui had sparked off both curiosity and debate in the West since the mid nineteenth century, giving rise to a rich catalogue of interpretations.

Comparison with the spread of Buddhism may be instructive. While Buddhism gave inspiration to new philosophies of life (that is, in the realm of ideas), the interest in feng shui has been far more practical. Many users see in it simple techniques for achieving harmonious relations with the environment, for redecorating their homes, for curing various illnesses and ultimately for improving their lives. Yet this difference is not so pronounced in the respective uses of Buddhism and feng shui in their original Asian settings. On an everyday plane, people may leave philosophy to Buddhist monks and lamas and just ask from them simple advice on practical matters, just like how people approach a feng shui specialist. Similarly, taken in its entirety, feng shui has a large body of literature that connects with the entire range of Chinese cosmological thought as well as with popular religion and ancestor worship. Rather than the two traditions being radically different, this seems to indicate that their modern users, at least in the western world, tend to belong to different groups of people. Buddhism appeals, perhaps, more to those seeking spiritual depth and to academics; feng shui has a greater appeal to the everyday person. These differences may not persist; as new applications of feng shui unfold, new groups of professionals will take up the challenge to further develop and refine its tenets.

FENG SHUI AS POPULAR RELIGION

Feng shui differs substantially from world religions, enjoying continuous recognition and backing by state powers, perhaps even making up their ideological foundations. Feng shui is a broad contested field of knowledge and practice, consisting of several different elements. There is a large body of Chinese feng shui literature, which is rather diverse and for a large part belongs to a popular genre. There is a tremendous variation of practices, both historically and geographically, and many common uses of the feng shui tradition have little connection with the literature: Chinese popular religion has its own independent life. Then, of course, there are a great number of feng shui practitioners, clients and believers, who constantly interpret and reinterpret feng shui in accordance with the context of their own lives. Most recently, an exploding number of western studies have added to the existing literature and introduced a range of novel ideas and applications. New schools of feng shui have sprung up, mixing elements of Asian philosophy and religion with western outlooks.

Feng shui has often been introduced as an exact system with consistent concepts and ideas. Hence, most of its modern users have the impression that it can provide definite solutions to common problems; yet nothing could be more mistaken. The standard considerations for placement in space are but a diminutive part of the entire tradition, which was never thought to work as independent of human agency. Chinese feng shui is of very little exactitude and a huge mass of subjective interpretation by a specialist or feng shui master. While a small collection of rules applies to all situations, the feng shui master may draw on the entire Chinese cosmology, on popular symbolism and on local lore in his interpretation of the specific situation. This is what has turned feng shui into such a powerful drift in Chinese history: any aspect of everyday life and common concerns may be connected with any strand of Chinese tradition by the skilful practitioner. Of similar importance is the fact that every single specialist, whether in China or abroad, tends to develop his or her own speciality and style. From the fact that feng shui cannot be applied independent of its subjective interpretation by a specialist, it follows that the personal encounter between specialist and client is essential to any remedy – it is its mode of operation. What will hopefully be made clear is that feng shui means different things in different societies and to different people.

THREE THEMES

Three broad themes have guided the creation of this book. These are the common interest in Chinese culture in the West, the fragmentation of ideology and everyday life and the tendency towards religious or spiritual revival in the world today. They are briefly discussed below but remain explicit throughout those parts of the book dealing with feng shui in contemporary society.

First of all, a genuine interest in Chinese culture and society has persisted from the earliest contact; in fact, from antiquity, when civilization in Europe and the Mediterranean became aware of China. The nature of this interest has changed tremendously over the centuries, expressing the internal processes of development in the West as much as China's own course of development. It seems fair to say, however, that for a very long time China has stood out as the major alternative to civilization in Europe, primarily due to its formidable size and historical continuity. In terms of language, philosophical traditions, technology and organization of society, China represented a unique and separate formation, which both wondered and inspired western observers. Intensified in the recent centuries, however, China has stood out as both the positive and the negative example of a range of issues such as the secular state freed from the church, early technological advances, collectivism, socialism, human rights issues, economic stagnation, cultural conservatism, Marxism, unprecedented economic growth, etc. Each era has viewed China differently, and quick changes have followed ideological currents in the West. How the interest in Chinese feng shui fits into this picture will be taken up in Chapter 7.

The second broad theme indicated above is of an equally complex nature. With the coming of industrial society and modernity, and work processes becoming increasingly specialized, people were drawn away from small communities with intimate contact into cites with entirely new lifestyles and social relations. Thus, from lives in organic units with a great measure of coherence, people experienced a growing fragmentation of both their working and social life. That was already the theme of early sociology, vividly represented in the writings of Max Weber, Emile Durkheim and Georg Simmel in the early twentieth century. With the coming of the post-industrial or 'post-modern' society, these processes were further accelerated, and did so to an extent challenging human biology: individual work procedures are atomized to an extent that the individual cannot see the meaning of the whole, social life is further fragmented with the ongoing rupture of conventional family and morality is divorced from everyday life and monopolized by experts (Bauman 1995): in sum, 'life in fragments'. The new knowledge society, which all nations now compete to install in order to gain comparative advantages, further demands flexibility and creativity within still smaller segments of ever larger manufacturing, service and entertainment machines. As human beings, however, we are not merely passive subjects in this vast drama of revolutionizing everyday life, but persistently strive to hold on to meaning, values and people. When old forms of social life break up, new ones are established; when conventional outlooks are swept away, people search for new overarching perspectives to be able to sense connectedness.

The third broad theme may be said to follow logically from the second, but consists of many different elements without clear consistency. There is a growing sense of spiritual revival in the world today, expressed both in the backing of world religions and in a vastly growing significance of new independent churches, non-institutional religion and spontaneous religious movements, although Europe may be an exception (Casanova 2003). Fundamentalist religion has caught the interest of the media, but a more common characteristic is perhaps that this new religiosity is turned against simple rationality – understood as scientific rationality applied to everyday life (scientism) – and very often against modern education. Important writers from diverse fields such as philosophy, science and sociology have noted this: a return to 'reason' as opposed to technical rationality (Stephen Toulmin), the need for new perspectives that allow unity (David Bohm) and the general orientation towards de-secularization – that is, the returning prominence of religion (Peter Berger).

These three themes, as merely outlined above, are, of course, not randomly selected in the vast literature on recent changes in the human predicament. They are, in fact, what we see as the main impulses in the formation of feng shui as a global current of thought and practice. On this background, it is my sincere hope that this book will contribute greater knowledge about feng shui as well as meet the general interest in Chinese culture and thinking.

WESTERN RECEPTIVENESS

Learning about our adoption of feng shui is also learning about our selves. The following pages will be dedicated to establishing a frame of meaning for the rise of feng shui in the western world. Readers unconcerned with this question may simply jump to the core chapters of the book.

Since the West has known Chinese feng shui for at least a century and a half, but has only adopted it during roughly the last two decades, it is straightforward to consider changes within western societies as instrumental. These changes concern both the place of religion in, and the structure of, our societies. Since Christian churches previously functioned as the main bulwark against other religions as much as against all those currents of 'heretical' belief and popular magic previously termed 'superstition', when encountering Chinese feng shui in the mid nineteenth century, western missionaries, administrators and sojourners consistently used that label. The Christian churches were already under pressure from modernity, but social and political forces in the industrial society that had developed since have effected their further retreat from public and daily life. Today, there is still some correlation between formal religion and new currents of belief: feng shui is apparently strongest where Christianity is weakest, such as in US coastal cities as opposed to the mid-west, and in northern Europe as opposed to southern Europe. Similarly, feng shui tends to be stronger in Protestant communities than in Catholic communities, the latter often having a stronger sense of personal affiliation to the church.

Nonetheless, while Christian religion may be in the retreat, 'spirituality' appears to be on the rise. The emergence of feng shui in the West has followed that of a broad range of other religions, cosmologies and belief systems, which, according to some observers, is mounting to a spiritual revolution, a new age. Let's see what the sociology of religion can contribute to understanding this phenomenon.

Many writers have commented on the demise of religion in Europe, which shows in declining church attendance, membership and rites and even to the extent that the Christian god is dead (Bruce 2003). Most notably, a 'massive subjective turn of modern culture' is perceived as underlying a range of changes in our relationship with society and religion. It is a turn away from living according to prescribed roles, conventions and obligations, and a turn towards living by reference to one's own subjective experiences. Paul Heelas and Linda Woodhead (2005) thus argue that people increasingly search for the heart of life, living in full awareness of one's state of being, something easily converted into useful experience and practice. They distinguish between two different life forms: 'life as', which indicates living according to the external roles and duties given by established religions, and 'subjective life', which means living according to the unique experiences of a new age, essentially becoming your own master. The subjective life form focuses on the individual state of mind, including feelings, passions, bodily experiences, inner consciousness, dreams and compassion. Along with these two life forms, very different understandings of the sacred emerge: while religion has a transcendent source of significance and authority to which individuals must conform, the new 'spirituality', although an ambiguous term, emphasizes the inner sources of significance and authority, allowing the individual to sacralize its own unique life experiences. The possible outcome is a spiritual revolution.

These changes are evident in the rise of feng shui in the West. Yet it is less evident that people give up established religion entirely for the sake of new spirituality. In the fast moving and rapidly fragmenting society, they may as well combine and contextualize them, there being no dilemma in both going to church and using feng shui for spiritual home improvement.

Many important writers have emphasized that religion is on the rise globally. Starting with Samuel Huntington's concept of the 'clash of civilizations' along lines of religion (1993), more recent writers link the growth of religion to the effects of modernization – that is, as a counter-current to fragmentation. For instance, Peter Berger (1999) uses the term 'de-secularization' as the outcome of a shattered modernity. Modernity had certain secularizing effects, but on the individual level, religious beliefs and practices lived on and now take new institutional forms. Berger argues that apart from a global elite culture which adheres to secularization, the secularization thesis was false, and experiments with secularized religion have generally failed: the world is experiencing a religious revival of colossal dimensions. As modernity tended to undermine the taken-for-granted certainties of everyday life, religious movements promised new overarching perspectives, while 'dripping with conservative supernaturalism'.

Another relevant perspective is that of José Casanova (1994), who argues that the differentiation and increasing complexity of the modern society drives religion away from the central stage without, however, driving it away as such. Instead, centralized and controlling religion is giving way to religious pluralism, with many new groups competing for public attention. In that sense, religion has been privatized and differentiated, with a ready market of spiritual consumers zapping between new and trendy options.

Much international attention is devoted to the role of religion in the Middle East, while religion in other places is simultaneously neglected. Today, most developing countries across the world have powerful new religious movements (China included) that gather people locally while addressing issues like social differentiation, unemployment, meaninglessness, modernity and globalization. In the broadest sense, the sociology of religion ought to be less concerned with the decline of old congregational religion and more sensitive to new forms, whether individual, communal or transnational (Casanova 2003: 27).

So what are the societal conditions for the growth of new spirituality, including feng shui? Certainly, relentless and pervasive changes now occur in all societies across the globe, uprooting traditional life forms and identities and reaffirming the 'subjective turn'. Let us see how a selection of prominent sociologists from across the West depict these changes.

For the German sociologist Ulrich Beck, one of the most profound changes is individualization, now no longer a choice but radically institutionalized as a condition of society. He distinguishes between the first modern period up until World War II and the present 'second modernity'. In the first modernity, people were set free from repressive social structures and religious dogmatism and integrated into new collective life forms such as class, nation state and nuclear family. In the second modernity, however, previous social structures dissolve. New radical demands are put on the individual in education and career, to the extent that the ideal working subject is the unrestrained, fully mobile single. Yet Beck describes the 'self-culture' of the second modernity as one of considerable control and standardization through market forces. A massive responsibility for global risks are placed on the individual, forming a series of risky freedoms, a privatization of collectively produced risks, where the individual is constantly required to find personal solutions to systemic contradictions, such as between family and career. He phrases these conditions as the 'risk society'. Beck argues that in order to avoid insecurity and compulsory choice, people increasingly enroll in closed subcultures, radical political groups or new religious movements, which may provide ready-made solutions to existential problems (Beck and Beck-Gernsheim 2002: 92ff.).

Another equally important aspect of Beck's work is the changing concept of nature. In the first modernity, nature was viewed instrumentally as a resource, separate from society. In the second modernity, however, one of the fundamental processes of change (along with globalization, individualization, a gender revolution and a new technological revolution) is the global ecological crisis, which has undermined the assumptions and the concept of nature of the old industrial society. Nature is politicized and becomes subject to debate: a new concept of nature and society as mutually dependent develops, while science loses its monopoly on truth and rationality. Ecology and feng shui fit in nicely here, attempting reinterpretation of the conventional nature–culture divide; several later chapters will deal with this.

The observations of the American sociologist Richard Sennett, like those of Beck, pinpoint the insecurities of fast-moving capitalism (1998). The conditions of time in the new capitalism, he argues, have created a conflict between character and experience, the experience of disjointed time threatening the ability of people to form their characters into sustained narratives. Demands of extreme individual flexibility – against the background of a hyper-dynamic job market and constant business restructurings for the sake of stock market indices – have created a generation of highly successful employees, yet with fragmenting personal lives and corroding characters. Uncertainty was known to previous generations, but today it exists without any looming historical disaster; instead it is woven into the everyday practices of a vigorous capitalism. Instability is meant to be normal, anxieties breed in the new capitalism and its victims cannot hold up their own lives as tales to their children as characters and ideals dissolve. In the culture of the new capitalism, Sennett (2006) shows that the individual must manage short-term relationships, constantly develop new talents and learn not to dwell on past achievements as they are no longer honoured. It is a culture of pervasive consumption, far from setting people free.

Can we recognize the contours of short-lived cults as mere flickers on the spiritual horizon, before giving way to other even more radical aberrations from our common past? If so, it entails a more critical view of feng shui as filling the vacuum from the break-up of past ideals, values and institutions with a heedless search for quick changes and new potentials to fit in with the hunt for a consistent personal narrative, like the instant stimulation of a short-term relationship. As shown in Chapter 7, many feng shui manual authors advise cutting bonds to old objects, pictures, acquaintances, etc. As fragmented lives tend to be lived in episodes (in a series of unconnected events), currents of new spiritual inspiration may likewise form disjointed chance patterns. The rise of feng shui in the West may not be rationally explained, and nothing as yet indicates its enduring significance.

The French sociologist Pierre Bourdieu (e.g. 1999) also points out how our insecurity and vulnerability are the most painful features of contemporary life conditions: insecurity of position, entitlement and livelihood – and lack of safety of one's self and extensions in the form of family, neighbourhood and community. A number of constructionist sociologists, including British Stuart Hall, see our identities as ongoing and never completed constructions, always conditional and yet never in a proper fit with the conditions of life, never forming a totality. Identities operate across difference and as discursive processes requiring what is left outside in order to consolidate themselves. Perhaps playing with difference – radical difference such as feng shui – helps us to explore what we are (Hall 2004: 2–3).

Lastly in this tour of sociology, we shall pick a few points from the massive work of Polish-born Zygmunt Bauman. To him, fragmentation of meaning, identity and ethics present new moral choices. Far from pointing towards a care-free life, our modern predicament becomes acutely uncomfortable, as both meaning and identity only take shape as projects. In the post-modern society, Bauman uses the allegory of stroller, vagabond or tourist to depict the individuals' movement in space and time as fragmented into episodes. Expressive of common sentiments in a fast-moving world without givens, branded by uprooting, contingency and mass migration is the metaphor of human waste: 'wasted lives' (Bauman 2003a). Our search for meaning becomes still more acute and hopeless as we rise above nature, while our finitude becomes ever more visible and painful; from madness there is no escape but another madness. Knowledge of morality triggers the desire for transcendence, the search for transient life experiences stronger than death (Bauman 2003b: 3). The main business of culture, Bauman states, is to supply ever new untried and un-discredited variants of transcendence strategies as its explorers stumble from one disappointment to another frustration: the trade in life meanings is the most competitive of markets!

Is this a fatalistic caricature of the believer of instant feng shui, having just stumbled upon it like a new brand on the shelf, or does Bauman here capture our joint predicament as victims of a grand techno-economic experiment, that of modern capitalism? Undeniably, leaving our roots, however frail, is facing us with unseen dilemmas of meaning. Individualization, mobility, the break-up of traditional family forms and the denying of formal religion (conventionally linked to family ritual) take away the meaning embedded in family life and ritual, and rules out the following of long-trodden life trajectories. We shall return to these perspectives in the last chapter.

CHAPTER 2

A brief history of feng shui

Forms of divination, which in theory and practice had much in common with feng shui, date back to the earliest Chinese historical records. In the early literature, however, they are referred to as *zhanbu*, *xiangzhai*, *kanyu* (Heaven and Earth), *yin-yang* and *dili* (earth principles/geography), while the term 'feng shui' only became common during the Song dynasty (960–1279). Accounting for the evolution of feng shui through the entire Chinese history would take volumes, and the subject would in any case be too difficult to sort out from general cosmology and divination. Instead, this chapter will describe the rise and significance of feng shui in relation to some crucial themes in Chinese history such as the general importance of divination, the continuous interaction between elite and popular culture and the gradual trickling down of the ways of the royal court to commoners. But first, a few points:

- The further we go back in Chinese history, the less feng shui becomes separable from general cosmology such as that contained in Daoism and expressed in imperial divination.
- We cannot determine whether divination of dwellings for the living or for the dead came first. In the course of Chinese history, however, divination of houses, temples, palaces and other constructions for the living became more orthodox than divination of graves for the dead.
- Imperial divination, burial rituals, taking omens and symbolism linked to the Mandate of Heaven were increasingly popularized, siphoning down from the royal court and elite to the lower echelons of Chinese society. Feng shui was an important element in this process, a form of spiritual struggle with political metaphor.
- Some Chinese emperors believed and used feng shui while others shunned it. In countless incidents, however, feng shui was used and abused in imperial power struggles.

- Chinese scholars remained divided on the issue of feng shui; some held on to a rationalistic outlook while others built on popular religious trends. Being a controversial subject, it lurked at the sidelines of Chinese history, sometimes denounced in public while passionately used in private.
- Among common people, there was also a great measure of scepticism; although commonly used in rural areas, some clan organizations were known to warn their members against belief in feng shui.
- It was quite late in Chinese history, more specifically during the Early Song period (960–1126) – when the court patronized popular religion – and the Late Song period (1127–1279) that feng shui was constructed as a separate branch of study. A new profession simultaneously emerged from its practical uses. Feng shui became increasingly popular in the later dynasties, while at the same time the Chinese state grew ever more sceptical of its popular uses.

Some elements of feng shui, notably the white tiger and the azure dragon (see Fig. 2.1), are among the oldest known symbols in China, especially in the Yangshao Neolithic culture (5000–3000 BC). Depictions of these totem animals pieced together in shells have been found in graves of shaman chiefs dating back approximately 6,000 years, respectively placed to the west and the east of the skeleton (Yu and Yu 2005: 50–1). Some feng shui authors have taken this as evidence of the pre-historic roots of feng shui, which is indeed forcing the evidence. Dragons and tigers are constant elements in Chinese art objects of later dates, such as those depicted on pottery and bronze vessels from the Shang dynasty (1600–1046 BC), and they play a part in the *Yi jing* divinatory text (described in Chapter 5) from the Western Zhou dynasty (1046–771 BC). Most often and more widespread, however, the symbol of the dragon is found together with that of the phoenix (both in early crude versions), being mythological creatures linked to ritual and religion in the early agricultural society.

It has been much debated exactly when feng shui rose to become a separate branch of theory and practice, pitting adherents and manual writers against historians and anthropologists. While the former tend to associate feng shui with a primordial force such as that represented in the concept of Oriental Wisdom and expressed in the *bagua* and *Yi jing*, the latter are inclined to place its evolution in several stages, where some of the concepts were brought together during the Han synthesis (see below), and the art itself only rose as a separate activity after the emergence of Neo-Confucianism in the Song period. The explanations given by Ernest J. Eitel over a century ago still appear to be valid:

(a)

(b)

(c)

Fig 2.1 The Chinese national symbol, the dragon, is developed from an ancient totemic symbol and did not find its present form until around the Song dynasty. These early forms are from the Shang (a), Han (b) and Sui (c) dynasties. Photographs by Ole Bruun, with permission from the Luoyang Museum of Ancient Tombs, Luoyang, China.

The system of Feng-shui is of comparatively modern origin. Its diagrams and leading ideas are indeed borrowed from one of the ancient classics, but its method and practical application are almost wholly based on the teachings of Choo-he [Zhu Xi] and others, who lived under the Sung [Song] dynasty. (Eitel [1873] 1984: 5)

The leading principles of Feng-shui have their roots in remote antiquity, and it would not be exaggeration to say, that, though indeed modern Feng-shui was not a distinct branch of study or a separate profession before the Sung dynasty (AD 960–1126), yet the history of the leading ideas and practices of Feng-shui is the history of Chinese philosophy. (Eitel [1873] 1984: 51)

THE CLASSICAL AGE

The classical age consists of the three north-China dynasties of Xia (ca. 2070–ca. 1600 BC), Shang (ca. 1600–ca. 1050 BC) and Zhou (ca. 1050–256 BC), all centred at the bend of the Yellow River in north-central China and partly overlapping in time and territory. The three dynasties also constitute the Chinese Bronze Age until ca. 600–500 BC, during the Eastern Zhou, when the Iron Age begins. Until the early twentieth century, the Xia and Shang dynasties were merely considered legendary, only known from historical texts of the later Zhou dynasty. Gradually, however, archaeological and historical evidence began to coincide, and our knowledge has been continuously pushed backwards in time. One remarkable source was the findings of a total of 150,000 'oracle bones', mainly from the late Shang cult centre near Anyang. They testify to the divination practices of the Shang kings of attempting to communicate with spiritual forces: cattle shoulder bones and turtle plastron were poked with heated objects to produce fine cracks, and these lines were interpreted by diviners. The topic and the result of the divination ritual were then engraved into the bone in early Chinese writing. In addition to the oracle bones and general archaeological evidence, other early sources of Chinese civilization include bronze inscriptions; classics such as the *Book of Documents*, the *Book of Changes* (*Yi Jing*), the *Book of Songs* and the ritual classics; and several other historical texts, essays and recorded sayings of philosophers. In outline, the Zhou dynasty is well documented in historical records; the Shang dynasty is known for its superior bronzes, its many cities and the practices of its kings and diviners; while the cities and contours of the Xia dynasty may begin to appear in a series of more recent archaeological findings.

What emerges from these various sources of information is a civilization based on sedentary agriculture and crafts, and with high degrees of cultural originality, homogeneity and continuity. It is also an autocratic and highly stratified society in which kings and local ruling elite lived in walled cities and towns with great palaces, much like today's Forbidden City of Beijing. Strongly centralized and consolidated through lines of kinship and lineage, the central power was able to install a strong legal code as well as mobilize mass manpower for planned cities, royal tombs, public works or warfare among the peasantry. Already, in the classical age, Chinese civilization had acquired its basic characteristics (Fairbank 1992: 29–45).

Among these was the crucial importance of divination for the royal court. Shamans, diviners and priests assisted rulers in interpreting the will of Heaven and the spirits of ancestor kings. Elaborate centralized rituals, including animal and human sacrifices, underpinned central authority. From the Shang dynasty onwards, we have ample evidence of the immense importance of divination for government, agriculture, military campaigns, building projects, avoidance of disasters and a host of daily affairs of the royal court (Ebrey 1993: 3–5). By such means as oracle bones and shells, kings would receive advice, frequently presented in pairs of opposites (indicating the early roots of the *yin-yang* terminology). An example:

[A] Crack-making on *renzi* [day 49], Zheng divined: 'If we build a settlement, Di [the high god] will not obstruct.' Third moon.

[B] Crack-making on *guichou* [day 50], Zheng divined: 'If we build a settlement, Di will approve.' (Both from Ebrey 1993: 4–5)

Presumably from the Shang dynasty, and certainly from the Zhou dynasty when better historical records appear, ancestor worship implied notions of the ancestors' spirits being active agents capable of influencing the fortunes of their descendants. However, the earliest archaeological evidence also shows that ancestor worship played a prominent part in political organization. With a hereditary system of rule within patriarchal lineages, the royal family had placed their relatives as local lords and higher officials, who again ruled by means of their lineages. Ancestor worship commonly serves as a theocratic underpinning of this form of rule. Divination and shamanic rituals were particularly used by regents to learn about the will of their ancestor kings and dynasty founders; like other important aspects of Chinese civilization, the ways of kings and emperors seemed to gradually be emulated by lower strata and eventually adopted as the practice of common-ers. Throughout Chinese history, human interaction with non-human or post-mortal beings such as gods, ghosts, demons, spirits and animal spirits remain influential in the perception of reality and interpretation of daily life.

In a society based on kinship, ancestor worship supports a hierarchical order. Younger generations are ruled by elder generations, who in turn are subjugated to the ancestors. Also, paternalistic ties between lords and peasants are evident at an early date, evolving into feudal relations. These are evident from the Zhou dynasty and into the Spring and Autumn (722–481 BC) and Warring States periods (403–221 BC). Into the imperial age, however, city development, new technology and professional specialization tended to break down class barriers.

It takes but little imagination to connect the potency of ancestors with the appearance, locality and other qualities of their tombs; this step was already taken in the early dawn of Chinese history. Already, in the Zhou dynasty, the elementary principles of grave divination seem to have been applied (de Groot 1897: 983). At this time, commoners were reportedly buried in plain ground, princes in low hills and emperors under mounds constructed on mountain tops. The *Book of Rites* (*Li ji*) indicates that ancient graves were oriented so that 'the dead have their heads placed towards the north', since the north was conceived as ruled by the female principle, while 'the living face the south', which is ruled by the male principle (*Book of Rites*, Chapter 30, line 20).

Thus the fundamental male and female principles as well as the compass points are already indicating distinctions between the living and the dead. The still commonly held assumption that houses should face south, which repeats itself in feng shui (as well as in countless other folk traditions across the world), refers to this and other passages of the *Book of Rites*. In the course of time, the mound over the grave, originally maintained for the rulers, was adopted by all strata in mostly symbolic forms; even today, a mound 2 to 4 feet high is the most common form of a peasant's grave.

Many original philosophical ideas and concepts of Chinese civilization are apparent in the Shang period and are certainly established in the Zhou period. These include the *yin-yang* dualism, the Five Elements, references to the mythical beings of dragons and tigers (see Chapter 5), a solid belief in the power of ancestors, a centralized bureaucratic power supporting itself on divination, the Chinese calendar (see Chapter 3) and a political philosophy of Heaven conferring its authority to the emperor, who became the link between Heaven and Earth.

The rise of the three learnings: Daoism, Buddhism and Confucianism

A number of traits of Chinese pre-historic religion are assembled and refined in Daoism, which arose in the Warring States period. Two texts in particular from this period form its basis: they are the *Daodejing* (*Tao te king*) of the third or fourth century BC, and the *Zhuangzi*, composed shortly afterward. Daoism only rose as a religious movement in the Han dynasty (206 BC–AD 220) and gained official recognition in the Tang period (618–907). Daoism preached the return to Dao, the Way of Man, which had been lost in the process of civilization, and argued for detachment, individualism and the relativism of human ways of life. Although the philosophical aspects of Daoism clearly engage in the dialogue of civilization of its time, its religious aspects include the recognition of a range of supernatural beings that constantly interact with humans. There are ancestor spirits, gods and ghosts, of which the last are particularly dangerous and which demand offerings. Chinese feng shui can be said to draw on Daoism's multitude of beings as well as its ways of keeping a positive relationship with them through divination, rituals and offerings. Daoism is polytheistic, recognizing a range of deities, which in the popular tradition serve to strengthen local identities: a particular area may worship certain gods and local historical figures. Another interesting trait of Daoism, which repeats itself in feng shui, is the imperial analogy. Its deities are arranged in a heavenly civil service of ministers, administrators and comptrollers, which clearly mirror China's imperial bureaucracy.

Conflicts between popular cosmology, such as embedded in Daoism, and Chinese convention, such as promoted by the elite, is an underlying theme in much of China's history. By the time of Confucius (551–479 BC), we have ample evidence of conflicts over the construction of graves and the role of popularly held beliefs connected to ancestor worship. The Confucian philosophers were focused on social and political stability by means of preservation of tradition and moral cultivation. They were much concerned with the firm hold superstitious notions had on their countrymen, but chose to remain neutral and instead concentrate their efforts on moral reform modelled on the pattern of the ancient sages in order to reach a new golden age. Their cautious position clearly indicates the limits of their own power over people's minds, as illustrated by an anecdote: Confucius, after some difficulties locating the grave of his father, finally had it opened and the remains of his mother buried together with those of his father. On this occasion it was suggested that, in accordance with the custom of the time, a mound should be raised over the grave. Confucius did not oppose it, though he remarked that this was not in accordance with the rules of the ancients, but – it is said – soon after the mound had been raised, a sudden fall of rain washed it away and levelled the ground to his satisfaction (Eitel [1873] 1984: 55).

Many new strands of thought blossomed in this period called 'One Hundred Schools'; in addition to Daoism and Confucianism, important contributions were made by the Mohists and Legalists. Yet, rather than seeing them as independent and comprehensive philosophies, we may evaluate them in terms of a dialogue over man's inherent condition and his relationship with society and nature.

Confucius' followers observed what has been called 'a studied' neutrality. They allowed the application of diagrams for divination, although they did not believe in such themselves. They quietly accepted that polytheistic popular beliefs supplanted the monotheism of the ancient sages, and even though they disapproved of the cosmogonic speculations of their contemporaries, they offered no alternative explanations of how the world came into being. The *Book of Filial Piety*, purporting to be the recorded conversation between Confucius and a disciple, contains strong admonition against improper attention to ghosts and ancestors:

A filial son . . . divines to choose the burial place where the body can be placed to rest. He prepares an ancestral altar, so that the ghost can receive sacrifices. Spring and autumn he offers sacrifices thus thinking of the dead once every season . . . With the man's fundamental duty fulfilled, relations between the living and the dead are complete, and the filial son's service to his parents is finished. (Ebrey 1993: 68)

Also, Mohism, although speaking of salvation through doing good and in principle believing in ghosts' and spirits' power to reward and punish men, maintained a sceptical attitude in the pursuit of facts:

If there are ghosts and spirits, then our sacrifices are offered to feed and feast our own (dead) fathers, mothers, brothers and sisters. Is that not a fine thing? And even if there be no ghosts and spirits, we are at most spending a little money on our offerings. Even so, we do not waste it in the sense of throwing it into the ditch. We can still gather our relatives and neighbours and participate in the enjoyment of sacrificial victuals and drinks. Therefore, even if there be no ghosts nor spirits, this may still enable us to enjoy conviviality and give pleasure to our relations and neighbours. (Hu 1960: 75)

Despite the impact of Confucianism, Mohism and other pragmatic philosophies, early geomantic philosophy appears to have enjoyed considerable popularity during the Han dynasty (206 BC–AD 220). After the book-burning mania and suppression of ancient classics under the despot Qin had ceased in 190 BC, Confucianism flourished anew. Under imperial auspices, all remaining pieces of literature were studied and the classics were reconstructed. But despite its privileged position, Confucian learning again found itself impotent in the spiritual field. While Confucian scholars became absorbed in literary criticism and the meticulous study of the ancient classics, Daoism readily seized the opportunity that the reawakening national interest for literature offered. An immense, speculative Daoist literature arose as a result, abounding in alchemist, astrological and cosmogonic mystics. As far as the development of feng shui is concerned, the combination of the Twelve Branches (denoting compass directions as well as years, months, days and hours) and the cycle of the Twelve Animals (also denoting elements) is evidently used for divination at this time (de Groot: 987).

It is also from the Han dynasty that we have the first recorded incident of imperial opposition being eliminated by geomantic means. The Confucian scholar Liu Xiang, who successfully re-edited the lost Confucian classics, reported to the throne that a certain family's grave showed such remarkable features that it indicated a descendant would become emperor. Such a hint clearly intimated the extinction of the entire family in question (Eitel [1873] 1984: 57), while showing the conscious use of popular cosmology in the court as opposed to the Confucian *Book of Filial Piety*.

Historical records suggest that a substantial literature of grave divination existed under the Han dynasty (Song 2000). Among a large number of titles on divination mentioned in these records are one book called *The Golden Kan-yu Thesaurus, in Fourteen Chapters* and six works of 'authors on the rules concerning forms', of which one is entitled *On the Configurations of Grounds for Mansions and Houses, in Twenty Chapters* (de Groot 1897: 995).

Thus historical texts and records suggest that the literature on site divination coincided with the gradual rise of Daoism. Under Daoist influence, a first attempt to bring popular geomantic notions together into a unified scheme was made under, or shortly after, the Han dynasty. The book entitled *The Yellow Emperor's Book on Dwellings* (*Huangdi zhai jing*), which for purposes of authority was ascribed to the legendary Yellow Emperor, is a true exponent of early geomancy. On top of an outline of the theories of earlier ages, the book provides a new theory of geomantic influences based on the concept of male (*yang*) and female (*yin*) dwellings, thereby for the first time explicitly distinguishing between feng shui cosmology for the living and for the dead. Similarly, the book divides the diagrams, formerly used for divination, into male and female diagrams, and applies them to determine the geomantic characteristics of male and female dwellings. Of the eight trigrams, those of the west to the southeast were said to work in accordance with the female energy, and those of the east to the northwest were said to work in accordance with the male energy.

During the following periods of the Three Kingdoms (220–265) and the Six Dynasties (ca. 300–600), we find numerous references to the connection between favourable grave sites and high position for the descendants. Furthermore, geomancy became infused with Hindu astronomy – giving rise to the concept of twenty-eight constellations – and Buddhist cosmology.

Especially during the Six Dynasties, when Buddhism spread across China and was soon adopted by the state power, divination received a new impetus from the Buddhist cosmological concepts of ceaseless cycles of construction and destruction of the material world. While China was in a state of disunion, divination philosophy rose to a golden era and gave birth to many renowned figures in the various arts of divination, including the prophet Guan Lu, the historian and writer on supernatural powers Gan Bao and the outstanding scholar Guo Pu (276–324), the last commonly credited as the founder of modern feng shui. One of the principal classics on geomancy, the *Book of Burial* (*Zang shu*), which has a strong orientation towards topography, is commonly ascribed to this distinguished master.

The story of the *Zang shu* is itself intriguing. Although authorship is commonly attributed to Guo Pu, we have no way of finding out whether the book was really his work, a later construction attributed to him to gain authority or even an older classic already circulating in a variety of versions at this time. Guo Pu was himself born into a period with great attention to divination, mythology, supernatural powers, ghost stories, dream interpretation and so forth. In addition to being a scholar with great knowledge of the classics, and a distinguished writer of mythology and folklore, Guo Pu developed skills in Yin-yang theory, Five Elements, astrology and various arts of mystical divination such as divining burial sites for the success of descendants. His powers of divination became legendary: according to the official history of the Jin dynasty, he was credited with over 60 events proven true. The first historical record of him, written a hundred years after his death, thus cites several instances. One story goes:

Emperor Ming of the Jin Dynasty wanted to understand divination of residences for the living and the dead. He heard that Guo Pu helped people with burial. He then went in disguise to the site and asked the master of the family, 'Why is the grave pit at the dragon's horn? This way of burial will diminish the whole family clan!' The master said, 'Guo Pu says, "This burial at the ear of the dragon is not visible, and will lead to the arrival of the Son of Heaven within three years."' The Emperor asked, 'How shall it produce a Son of Heaven?' The master replied, 'It possesses the faculty of causing a Son of Heaven to come hither to ask questions.' The Emperor stood, stunned. (J. Zhang 2004: 20–1)

Guo Pu was even known to have foreseen his own death. When the notorious usurper Wang Dun asked him to foretell the success of his attempt to overthrow the ruler, Guo Pu refused to divine for him, but was soon again urged to reply. He said, 'No success.' Wang Dun was outraged and asked, 'How long will I live?' 'You will die within this very day', was Guo Pu's answer. Wang Dun was so furious that he ordered Guo Pu to be executed. Thus he was killed because he refused to lie about the outcome of his divination. The story of his immortalization further goes that three days after his burial, people saw him on the street in Nanzhou, wearing casual clothes and talking to acquaintances. Wang Dun did not believe this and had his coffin dug up, only to find it empty. Guo Pu had learned the technique of transcending corporeal existence. He was later deified and became known as the God of Water as well as the founding patriarch of feng shui.

Several different versions of the *Zang shu* are at hand, but none of them may be dated exactly due to unclear authorship and processes of transmission: the book became subject to competition among feng shui masters writing imaginative additions to it in the name of the old master Guo Pu. The only translation into English (by J. Zhang 2004) is taken from an imperial edition: the *Complete Library in Four Branches of Literature* (*Si Ku Quan Shu*), a compilation of pre-modern Chinese texts prepared by edict from the emperor Qianlong during 1773–82. In the preface to this version, the Chinese scholars in charge of the compilation write:

Guo Pu once studied with a master Guo of Hedong, who gave Guo Pu nine books in a dark-blue bag. Guo Pu gained thorough insights into the arts of astrology, Five Elements theory, and divination . . . However, there was no record that Guo Pu wrote the Zang Shu. By the end of the Tang Dynasty [618–907], there appeared books entitled Zang Shu Di Mai Jing in one volume and Zang Shu Wu Yin in one volume. They did not mention that they were written by Guo Pu. Only in the Song Shi [*History of Song Dynasty, 960–1279*] was there a record of Guo Pu as the author of the Zang Shu in one volume. Therefore the book originated in the Song Dynasty. Afterwards, practitioners of various divining arts competed to elaborate on the book and thus formed a book of as many as twenty chapters. (J. Zhang 2004: 10–11)

To sum up, a simple proclamation of Guo Pu as the founder of feng shui and the *Zang shu* as the original book on the subject – such as was seen in the popular literature – is either merely ritual or, if taken at face value, impermissibly naive. The tradition of divination is much older, following Chinese civilization as far back as any historical or archaeological record, while the concept of feng shui tends to be of a younger date. The *Zang shu* is formally the first work to define feng shui, but since we cannot date precisely the available versions of the *Zang shu*, this has no value. Some scholars argue that the older versions of the *Zang shu* do not use the term 'feng shui' other than in a single passage (Gao 2005: 73), while the version mentioned above tends to use the term 'feng/shui' as a comprehensive term for influence of these two elements, considered to be the most vital. It is during the Six Dynasties that references to divination grow substantially in numbers in the official annals, to remain prominent in the dynasties to follow; many such references allude to the potential of auspicious graves to produce emperors, kings and ministers. While feng shui-related philosophy was apparently promoted during this period, and imperial annals contain special sections on blissful geomantic influences, it is also seen to gradually become an issue of political significance. The official histories of the fourth to tenth centuries relate many instances of geomantic prophecy coming to pass when exceptional tombs and omens lead descendants to wealth and dignified state positions. One such story from the official histories of the sixth century tells of a man who 'attained to the highest dignities of the State':

> Wu Ming-ch'eh was a native of the district of Ts'in. His father, who bore the name of Shu, was a general in the right division of the armies of the Liang dynasty. Ming-ch'eh was still a lad when he lost him, and yet he proved himself possessed of filial devotion of the highest order. When an auspicious hour had been fixed for the burial, a person of the surname I, who was proficient in the art of discovering burial sites by means of divination, said to Ming-ch'eh's elder brother: 'On the day on which you commit the corpse to the earth a man will pass by the burial place, riding a white steed and hunting a stag; this portents a high and influential position for a filial youngest son'. There was indeed such a prognostic when the hour of burial arrived; and Ming-ch'eh was Shu's youngest son. (de Groot 1897: 980)

It is also reported, however, that Wendi, the first emperor of the Sui dynasty (581–618), argued against the truth of grave divination while fighting for the throne. His enemies then violated the tombs of his ancestors to inflict misfortune upon him. He nevertheless ascended to the throne although he lost a brother on the battlefield. The imperial historiographer credits him with the words: 'If the tombs of my ancestors are not in a felicitous position, why did I attain to the throne? but if their position is felicitous, why was my brother killed?' (Eitel [1873] 1984: 60). Later elaborations of grave divination have perhaps considered this legend when they came to the conclusion that the same tomb may give blessings to one and cause misfortune to another among the descending family members. The Tang dynasty (618–907), particularly in the later centuries, marked a further propagation of the doctrines of Daoism and Buddhism, which again created a favourable environment for geomantic philosophy. Literature, both of philosophy and poetry, flourished during the Tang period, and also a large body of Buddhist literature was translated from Sanskrit into Chinese. Again, new concepts and ideas were transplanted into divination literature, not to replace the existing ones but to supplement them in an agglomerative pattern. From Sanskrit literature the notion of the Five Planets influencing the earth and its inhabitants was borrowed; in addition, some works adopted ideas of the Nine Stars influencing the auspiciousness of dwelling sites. Important works on divination arose from this new influx of foreign ideas. Three books are ascribed to the geomancer Yang Yunsong, who in particular developed those aspects referring to the symbols of the dragon and the tiger, as well as the direction of watersheds and influence of watercourses. These classics are the *Book of the Moving Dragon* (*Han long jing*), which, in addition to the influence of the Five Planets, develops a theory on the influence of the Nine Stars on the dwelling site; the *Book of the Blue-Green Bag* (*Qing nang jing*), which speculates in numerological correlations between Heaven and Earth; and the *Book of the Doubtful Dragon* (*Yilong jing*), which develops theories as to which land-forms and outlines of nature may accommodate the dragon and tiger.

Both recurrent criticism of 'unauthentic' geomancy during the Six Dynasties and an imperial initiative to curb such during the early Tang period testifies to growing imperial concern over the popular beliefs in divination. Divination literature increasingly takes the appearance of a comprehensive cosmology. In the sixth century, the scholar Yan Zhetui wrote the following, representing well the ambivalence of the literary class:

The art of utilizing the two breaths of nature having sprung from up within Heaven and Earth themselves, confidence must be placed in the indications of that art with respect to good luck and ill, weal and woe. But a long time has elapsed since the ancients lived. Therefore the writings on that art, transmitted from one generation to another, are altogether the product of unsettled popular notions, and contain gossip of a vulgar and superficial kind; little therein is trustworthy, much is pure nonsense. Yet, by contravening the art in question, by deviating from it, or by refusing to utilize it, calamity might finally be incurred. Infelicitous results cannot be always eluded by attending to it with anxious carefulness or by entirely relying upon it; but advantage is just as little to be secured by sticking to it with very great anxiety. (de Groot 1897: 1005–6)

Then, in the seventh century, emperor Taizong (reigned 626–49), the famed co-founder of the Tang dynasty who was recorded as one of the greatest emperors in Chinese history, appointed a commission to screen a large number of popular works on divination and geomancy to sort out the orthodox and useful elements from the unauthentic. The commission, consisting of over ten scholars under the leadership of the famous scholar Lü Cai, passed a harsh sentence on the existing literature. Lü Cai's statement is the earliest scholarly critique of the theory of good fortune emanating from graves. Lü Cai condemned in particular the selection of auspicious graves and lucky times for burial for violating tradition and misinterpreting the classics. According to these (the *Book of Changes*, the *Book of Rites* and the *Book of Filial Piety*), he argues, people turned to divination in order to protect the graves and secure them as places of worship: good or bad luck had nothing to do with it. Then, only recently, he goes on, grave geomancy has appeared, predicting fortune or disaster, while diviners, for the sake of profit, recklessly add new theories on how to avoid this or that. As a result, he claims, 'there are now about one hundred twenty schools of geomancy. They all have their own theories about what brings fortunes and misfortunes' (Wang C. 1993: 120–1). Instead, he writes, people should behave themselves and follow the way of the sages: high positions depend on human agency, not burial. He concludes:

Ordinary, ignorant people all believe the geomancy books. The diviners cheat them by making up tales about fortunes or disasters they are going to experience, leading these ignorant folk to feel themselves lucky. As a result, even during the mourning period, they are eager to choose a good site for burial in the hope of an official position. They also select Indian summer as the date for burial in the hope of getting rich. Some mourners will smile when greeting funeral guests because the day of the burial is said to be improper for weeping. Some believe taboos on relatives attending the burial and so do not accompany their parents' bodies to the grave. No sage ever taught such ideas. Geomancy books have ruined customs. (Wang C. 1993: 122)

Although this was obviously an official attempt to curb the booming trade in divination, its effect was doubtful; the literature on the subject continued to grow over the next centuries, from a dozen in the catalogue of the Sui period to over a hundred in the Song period. Instead, he founded a long state tradition of attempts to control folk religion and to curb its unorthodox elements – this is simultaneously the history of the growing rationalization of the Chinese state and the gradual outlawing of alternative cosmologies.

It was not only the Chinese state that felt compelled to take action. From around 900 onwards, there is ample evidence of efficient and determined clan organizations establishing meticulous clan rules to prevent their members from playing with geomancy and other 'superstitious' activities (Eberhard 1962: 40–4; Yen 1968: 204).

It was not until the Song and Late Song dynasties that all the previously mentioned elements, and the multitude of independent theorizing, were synthesized into a single scheme for interpreting the exhaustive influence that Heaven and Earth may exert on humans and their society: this is close to what we now know as feng shui in its more literate form. It is also during this period that the printing techniques made the spread of books on popular divination possible.

While previously the imperial court's Directorate of Astronomy carried out the Three Methods of Divination (*san shi*), it was not until the Yuan dynasty and onwards that the government ran district schools of divination (*yin-yang xue*) to train functionaries in this specific discipline in order to 'divine auspicious days, and related matters of topography and orientation' (Huang Y. 1991: 4). With a philosophical basis in the writings of the great Neo-Confucian thinkers of the time, such as Zhou Dunyi, Chang Mingtao, the Cheng brothers and particularly Zhu Xi (Chu Hsi, 1130–1200), the feng shui tradition was infused with a single scheme for applying a great variety of originally independent notions.

The Song dynasty was a period of stable government and administrative refinement. Expanded and improved rice growing in the south allowed great population increase, presumably doubling the population in a relatively short space of time. Urban development was intense, and China had some of the largest cities in the world, with very complex professional specialization and rich social and cultural life. Advances in technology were apparent in agricultural and other production, construction, printing, economic management, shipbuilding and warfare. The Song period was a golden era in which China was among the most prosperous and advanced countries in the world.

Great changes in social organization as well as in religion and ritual also occurred up until the Song period. At the same time, Buddhist influence was felt in many areas of life. Previously, graves had been of great significance, but to individuals more than to groups, and the greatest emphasis was on the graves of recent ancestors. Under Buddhist influence, offerings to ancestors expanded to include seven generations as compared to the Confucian four generations; Buddhism competed with Confucian values and held that its ways of caring for the dead were the most filial.

The Qingming Festival (see Chapter 3), previously a 'cold food' festival, became an occasion for visiting graves only in the Tang dynasty. While visiting graves to make announcements to ancestors was mentioned in the classics, sacrificing to them there was not. By the Song, it is evident that graves had become places for sacrifices rather than altars, shrines and tablets (Ebrey 1986). The popular Buddhist festivals were also occasions for visiting graves. Along with the inclusion of early ancestors in rites, and the practice of everyone visiting the grave on the same occasion, a stronger association between grave rites and descent groups developed. Grave rites became popular for both social and religious reasons and further created motivation for burying all ancestors of a descent group near each other; grave rites to an increasing extent would mark group identities. The making of kinship genealogies and attempts to trace old family graves were commonplace.

During the Song, descent groups such as lineage and clan became increasingly important for local community organization. It may be argued that a key element in their emergence was a change in religious ideas and ritual practices related to graves and ancestors (Ebrey 1986: 29), although disagreement will prevail as to the primacy of religious or economic or political factors. Along with the growth of lineage organization and land ownership, ancestor halls of the recent type (emphasizing lineages) also became common. Many other ritual practices of late imperial China took shape in this period. And of special relevance in the present context, a new profession of burial specialists emerged, presumably very similar to the later feng shui masters.

Zhu Xi's philosophy and Neo-Confucianism in general was both a consequence of and a response to the increasing dominance of Buddhist, Daoist and *Yin-yang* studies at the time, often in highly popular forms. Old-style Confucianism – keeping a scholarly distance from ghosts, spirits and metaphysics while emphasizing education, ritual and etiquette – was simply losing out to the more colourful, speculative and emancipating philosophies of the alternative traditions. Zhu Xi himself was influenced by

Buddhism and Daoism, and was deeply involved in divination, including both the *Yi jing* and feng shui (Smith *et al.* 1990). For instance, he was known to have moved his father's grave, and had graves for other family members selected according to feng shui (J. Zhang 2004: xi).

Zhu Xi's philosophy, mainly in the form of commentaries on the *Four Books of Confucianism*, provided the necessary synthesis to reinstall convention, albeit contested by many of his contemporaries. He incorporated the Principle of the Great Ultimate, the theory of Celestial Breath (*tian qi*) and Terrestrial Breath (*di qi*) (which by uniting produce and reproduce everything), the distinction between Principle (*li*) and Ether (*qi*) and the distinction between the Way (*dao*) and 'instrument' (*qi*). The distinction between *li* and *qi* has been interpreted in terms of modern science as one between structure and mass/energy (Needham 1969: 251).

In addition to the above, the very premises of Zhu Xi's teachings, that man and cosmos are bound together and human nature therefore derives directly from cosmological principles, had strong appeal to feng shui advocates; according to him, all men's capacity to speak, move, think and act was entirely a product of *qi*.

As the Neo-Confucian philosophy was adopted as state orthodoxy and sanctified as the national faith in the state examination system, greater coherence between literary learning and popular religion was achieved. The feng shui masters of the time closed the gap by systematizing the leading ideas and adapting them to the new terminology developed especially in Zhu Xi's philosophy. By adopting everything that was appealing to common people and making it directly applicable to the routines of daily life, feng shui rose to a new golden age. Competition between individual writers could never be ruled out, however, and each one had his own scheme of interpretation. Moreover, what is usually termed a 'synthesis' might as well be depicted as a confusing array of disparate theories without common consistency. Thus, the diversity and fluidity of site-selection theories allows for a wide range of practices, and, in any case, the human factor remains decisive (Bennett 1978: 21).

The two major schools of feng shui draw much of their philosophy from the Neo-Confucian learning of Zhu Xi and his contemporaries. Still, these two schools developed on top of an existing division between competing factions in Chinese divination: *Hong fan* Five Phases (Fujian) and Orthodox Five Phases (Jiangxi) (Huang Y. 1991: 19). One school, namely the one usually termed the 'School of Forms', show greater continuity with the earlier divination philosophy. This school is primarily concerned with the 'influence of forms and outlines' (*jing shi*), including mountains, hills and water courses, and recognizes as its founder the famous ninth-century geomancer Yang Yunsong. Yang was attributed authorship to several books, which are still regarded as classics on feng shui (see p. 23). Another work of his, the *Method of the Twelve Lines*, remained a standard work through the imperial era. Yang even held the office of Imperial Geomancer during the reign of Ji Zong (874–88). The School of Forms is also termed the 'Jiangxi School' or *kanzhou*, after the department in Jiangxi Province where Yang Yunsong worked.

Zhu Xi's metaphysics, combined with the development of the magnetic compass, gave rise to a new school of feng shui. It granted principal importance to the *bagua*, the Branches and the Constellations, and derives its name – the School of Orientations or 'directions and positions' (*fang wei*) – from the use of the compass. It is also termed the 'Fujian School' after the place of work of its principal representative, Wang Ji, to whom several works are ascribed, including the *Canon of the Core and Centre* and *Disquisitions on the Queries and Answers*. These two schools prevailed without any significant competition from other denominations.

Historical texts mention a great many schools of divination that may have competed in Chinese history. The *Book of Burial* (*Zang shu*) at one point indicates three different schools – Forms, Compass and Direction – but which all are components of the same practice (J. Zhang 2004: 140). Thus, giving too much importance to one of the schools or their distinction – as is often seen in western works – may lead to misinterpretation. Many Chinese classical texts combine theories supposedly unique to one denomination, just as late classical literature often attempts to include them all (Bennett 1978: 4). In the practice of contemporary Chinese feng shui masters, the division of schools tends not to be of great importance (see Chapters 3 and 6).

To some extent, geography has determined which school or aspect will predominate regionally; the School of Forms may be better adapted to the mountainous regions of south and west China, where people cannot all possibly face their dwellings towards the south, whereas the School of Orientations obviously fits better into the flatter land.

A golden era for feng shui philosophy is not at all synonymous with a prosperous society, however, and in the larger perspective we may see them correlated in an inverted fashion. Although this is only one side of divination, the growth of feng shui philosophy must be seen in conjunction with a growing destitution of the Chinese peasant; a massive drive from north to south due to population pressure, famine, invasion and unrest;

and increasingly despotic state power in the later dynasties (Wittvogel 1957; Gates 1996).

Both western and Chinese texts support the assumption that very little happened in the evolution of feng shui philosophy during the entire period after the Song dynasty, comprising the dynasties of Yuan (1271–1368), Ming (1368–1644) and Qing (1644–1911). Many texts suggest that the number of poorly versed diviners grew, to the dismay of both government and the literate class. One example is an anonymous text from Late Song to the Early Ming period called *Twenty-four Difficult Problems*, which deplores the scores of practitioners who 'absurdly match longevity, the receiving of favours, becoming an official and imperial prosperity with good and evil spirits and good and ill fortune, consequently causing the lucky not to be buried and those buried not to have good fortune'. These men 'conduct the art of swindlers' (Paton 2007).

Large numbers of new manuals, mainly drawing on the classics mentioned above, were produced and reproduced, and commentaries on the old works were made. Also, the imperial court had a long row of standard guides made, trying to sort out orthodox from unorthodox divination. One such guide from the seventeenth century is the *Qin ting xie zhi pian fang shu*, which still remains the basis for popular almanacs on Taiwan (Huang Y. 1991: 17).

But is it really true that cosmology was stagnant, or is it partly owing to common prejudices against the intellectual production in late imperial China? It is a matter of fact that Zhu Xi's learning remained authoritative in the state examination system throughout most of this period, and that little foreign influence could be detected in the indigenous cosmology throughout much of the same period, but such facts accounted more for stability in the outer framework than for the inner dynamics of the tradition; we know very little of how and on what types of occasion it has been applied or the social contexts it has addressed during this vast expanse of historical time.

In the Qing dynasty, lasting contact with the West was established as a consequence of European and, later, American seaborne expansion. A number of confluent factors in Chinese history relatively unrelated to colonialism account for the growing significance that we may attribute to popular cosmology in the Qing dynasty, particularly the divinatory practices. First of all, in the long-term perspective, divination lost some of its political functions after the Song dynasty (960–1279), and increasingly became a private practice during the Yuan and Ming dynasties. It was privatized in a double sense: while it became open to individuals, growing numbers of private diviners served the public as a means of subsistence. The Qing heterodoxy and anti-rebellion law bears witness to the intense state vigilance against popular divination, and derived forms of 'deluding the people'. Second, the destitution of increasingly large parts of the peasantry, particularly during the course of the Qing period, is a factor of intrinsic importance to the role that folk-religious practices may have played in local communities, and to the number of rural specialists attempting to extract a living from such practices. Yet, we must be aware that the relationship between poverty and beliefs in supernatural forces is a complex one. Third, and intimately connected with these other trends, was a sharply rising number of rebellions in the Qing, met with increasingly intolerant state power. While military operations in the early part of the dynasty were targeted at non-Chinese peoples, after the middle of the eighteenth century they were turned against internal religious rebellions. During this period, nearly all rebellions had religious gathering points, and most were staged by blacklisted sectarian organizations with religious emblems (C. K. Yang [1961] 1970: 207, 219).

Much evidence points to divination becoming increasingly powerful in late imperial China, particularly during the Qing period. A massive Qing encyclopaedia from 1726 devotes over 2,000 pages to fortune-tellers and mantic techniques (R. Smith 1991), while another index is Yuan Shushan's monumental *Biographies of Diviners* (quoted in Smith 1991), of which about one-third are from the Qing period. Western sojourners constantly commented on the prevalence of divination in the Qing dynasty. Despite their hostility to all kinds of 'superstition' and possible exaggeration of the situation to justify their civilizing mission, the general picture may hold. Richard J. Smith concludes: 'where evidence exists from the Chinese side, whether in the form of official documents, letters, anecdotes, proverbs, popular fiction, or scholarly indictments of fortune-telling, it almost invariably confirms the accuracy of Western accounts' (R. Smith 1991: 6). A seventeenth-century manual for local magistrates, for instance, advises feng shui considerations in the construction of ditches for defending cities against bandits, but at the same time it strongly recommends action to rectify people's beliefs in heterodox religions and 'their charlatans that promise riches, power and long life' (Huang L. 1984).

Taken together, Chinese and western sources indicate that divination became a social phenomenon of extraordinary importance. Throughout the grand course of Chinese history, divination was of crucial importance. Yet it may be said to have evolved from a privileged practice performed on behalf of kings, emperors and nobility to a practice performed on behalf of everyday people; a simultaneous trend was the change from a more passive practice to avoid disaster to an active practice in search for good fortune (J. Zhang 2004: 7).

Feng shui for cities

Given the facts that Chinese civilization rose on centralized rule, and that divination played a crucial role to the maintenance of power, Chinese capital cities would be expected to be ritually ordained. Both archaeological evidence and the earliest written records show cities to be designed by bureaucratic rulers conscripting public mass labour and using divination for placement and orientation.

China's 'four great ancient capitals' – Beijing, Nanjing, Luoyang and Xian – are, in classical tradition, all known to be chosen because of their auspicious location. In all four cities, the central palaces, city wall and gates were laid out according to a strict north–south axis. This, however, is not a consequence of feng shui considerations as such, but a convention with reference to the classic *Zhou li* (*Rites of Zhou*).

The *Zhou li* itself formulated a range of conventions with regard to city construction, which may be said to predate feng shui. First of all, it indicated the precise north–south orientation of the city as consonant with the cosmological order. Astronomical specialists should make successive observations of the shadow of the sun at noon and of the North Star at night in order to make accurate calculations of the four directions. The city walls should form an exact square, with three gates placed in each of the eastern, southern and western walls, thus arriving at the cosmological number nine. Similarly, the streets should form a grid of nine lines, while a large open line should run north–south as its central axis. The placement of the royal palace in front and markets behind were also precisely indicated in order to achieve the perfect ordering of the city as a coherent cosmological symbol (Biot 1851).

Thus, the application of feng shui may figure more in the retrospective writings of later scholars than in the original choice of a city site. While from the late Zhou, Qin and Han dynasties there are references to specialists interpreting the flow of *qi* at a site (*wang qi zhe*) to determine its favourable character, the application of *qi* flows and feng shui theory to the placement of cities is only partially and uncertainly reflected in the sources (Wright 1977: 54). Arguments referring to such ideas are brought up from time to time in debates of proper placement of cities, but never appear decisive. It is only after feng shui is maturing in the Song dynasty that it is consistently applied to entire cities and the geography of China as a whole.

In an account of the building of the capital city of Daxingcheng (later known as Changan and now Xian) (the last Chinese capital to be built on an unoccupied site) during the Sui dynasty, Arthur F. Wright has evaluated the use of feng shui and classical cosmology. The city was planned at an unprecedented scale, and at its height accommodated over a million people. The founding emperor, Wendi, did perform the ancient oracle-bone form of divination for timing and placement, but nothing of the sort linked to feng shui. The principal guiding lines for the city were drawn from the *Zhou li*, thus having the city face south, the outer walls forming a square (although in this case a rectangle), the central north–south street forming a principal axis, and the east, west and south walls having three gates each. Yet the *Zhou li* was not followed in full; the placement of the royal palace was not in the front but the back of the city, the number of streets exceeded the prescribed and the placement of markets was practically chosen. Another source of inspiration was the numerological symbols in the city's division into wards, representing the harmonious relation between Heaven and Earth. When it comes to topographical placement, however, nothing indicates the use of feng shui. Ideally, the city should be protected by tall mountains to the north, lower hills to the east and west and a river to the south. Yet the Wei River lay to the north of the city, and mountains lay to the south. Wright concludes that 'planners used selected elements of the classical cosmology to reiterate the claims of the Sui to be the heirs of the long-vanished Han and thus the new and rightful rulers of a reunited empire' (Wright 1977: 56–60).

During the last century, archaeological excavations have revealed the location of other historical capitals, so that the list now includes Kaifeng, Hangzhou, Anyang and Zhengzhou.

The history of Kaifeng, which was made the capital by the emperor Zhu Wen of the Later Liang dynasty (907–23), shows a different development. Kaifeng was presumably the first Chinese capital that was a naturally grown city, based on industry and commerce in a period of intense population growth and economic activity. It was a multi-functional urban centre, probably unsurpassed by any metropolis of the pre-modern world. In this haven of commerce, cosmology received scant attention from the rulers: the layout of streets, gates and markets conformed to practicality rather than ritual. Yet the stance of each individual emperor put its mark on the city. The emperor Hui Zong, who was clearly influenced by Daoism and feng shui cosmology, introduced during his reign (1101–26) a number of changes to the city to enhance its cosmological symbolism. Most radically, in 1117, under the influence of Daoist experts, he began the building of an immense complex of hills northeast of the city, which stood 450 feet high and over 3 miles around when completed. Covered with rare rocks and plants, and dotted with pavilions with names of cosmological symbolism, the complex clearly drew from folk religion and feng shui (Wright 1977: 62).

With the increasing influence of popular cosmology in the Song and later periods, while at the same time population growth and spontaneous city development in China left fewer options for fresh city construction, the stance of each individual emperor became dominant in the choice and cosmological allegory of the capital. This resulted in immense variation from one emperor to the next.

Beijing was first established as the all-China capital by Khublai Khan, the founder of the Mongol-ruled Yuan dynasty. Some sources speak of feng shui considerations in the design of the city. Then, in the Ming dynasty, the Yong Le emperor began the process of moving his capital from Nanjing to Beijing (completed in 1421) after discussions had gone on from the beginning of the Ming era. Among a wide range of arguments for and against the move were also feng shui considerations, without anything indicating that these in any way should be decisive. Still the city demonstrated a wide range of cosmological symbolism. The city walls from the Yuan had the three gates in three walls as prescribed by the *Zhou li*, but had an additional two gates in the northern wall – yet not a central northern gate, which would have meant malicious *qi*. In the Ming era, the northern wall was moved and the total number of gates was reduced to the conventional nine. The layout of the imperial city as a walled compound displayed the increasing influence of feng shui cosmology. Three artificial lakes, surrounded by pavilions and temples, were placed in the western section of the complex, while an artificial hill lies to the north (Wright 1977: 66–73).

Feng shui for individual constructions

While popular forms of grave divination from an early date were surrounded by controversy, even continuing today, geomantic deliberations for constructions such as palaces, temples, walls and individual houses tended to be matters of orthodoxy (feng shui for ordinary houses is described in Chapter 3).

The distinction between orthodox and illegitimate uses of feng shui in the eyes of the state can be seen from countless official documents, law making and court cases. In a manual for local magistrates from the seventeenth century, the scholar Huang Liuhong clearly draws the line. He complains that 'there is no lack of charlatans who take advantage of human psychology and hoodwink people by saying they can bring riches, power, long life and blessings to believers by some magic formula' (Huang L. 1984: 552). At the same time, however, he stresses that good government must take due precautions to the feng shui of an area when starting public works:

Wherever people congregate there is a concentration of 'the spirit of the dragon [*qi*].' A locality with a large population is endowed with a huge amount of the spirit. Digging indiscriminately without considering the contours of the land can break the dragon vein, which is inauspicious for the inhabitants. It is advisable, then, to make a survey of the topography from a high place to see where the dragon vein is . . . The important thing is never to break the dragon vein, lest the spirit disperse, thus auguring ill for the inhabitants. (Huang L. 1984: 483)

During the Song, Ming and Qing dynasties, we have ample evidence of the great cosmological importance attributed to temples, pagodas, wall and canals by gentry, local magistrates or local communities. A common theme among the gentry was the influence of these constructions on the ability of local candidates to pass the imperial examinations. Here are two examples from a Late-Ming gazetteer:

Some time after 1573 people recklessly excavated a hole in the eastern wall of the prefectural capital, built a bridge, and altered the flow of the water in the moat. In 1597 the prefecture did not have a single success in the imperial examinations. In the winter of this year, Zheng Zhenxian, the country magistrate, had the bridge demolished and the gap filled in. In 1600 eight candidates were successful, so that all at once we could be said to have been doing well.

At that time the school of Confucian scholars was located in an out-of-the-way spot. The 'aether-energies in the human and physical atmospheres' [meaning forms of *qi*] in the western part of the prefectural capital city . . . were not concentrated, and so successes in the examinations for the second and third degrees were few and far between. (Both from Elvin 2004: 199)

When reports of such ideas were first presented in missionary and other China journals in the nineteenth century, they brought great wonder to western readers. One of the first English language accounts of feng shui from 1838 sums up the supposed influence of pagodas on agricultural production and the prosperity and success of the people. It has a translation of a placard posted in the same year by the gentry in Canton:

Fellow-countrymen! The region of country southeast of the provincial city, on account of its water-courses, has an important influence on the fortunes of the inhabitants. From an examination of old records it appears, that the pagoda on Pachow, and the adjacent temple dedicated to the monsters of the sea, were built in the twenty-fifth year of Wanleih (1598); and that the pagoda of Cheihkang, and the temple there consecrated to the god of letters, were founded in the reign of Teënke (about 1621); all these structures have had a most happy influence on every thing around them, causing the number of literati to be very numerous, and the productions of the soil most abundant. Recently, however, the winds and the rains, driving furiously, have broken down the tops of the pagodas, and laid the temples in ruins, and injured even their foundations. Their appearance is now very unsightly; they ought to be repaired, in order to secure the return of happy and prosperous times. (Chinese Repository 1837–38 6: 189)

THE COLONIAL ERA

Western discovery and exposure

After European seaborne expansion began in the 1500s, the first Europeans to come into contact with Chinese philosophy and divination were Roman Catholic missionaries. Most important among them were the Jesuits, deliberately schooled in the revolutionizing disciplines of mathematics, physics and astronomy in order to penetrate a civilization that they found to be obsessed with celestial analogies.

Under the leadership of Matteo Ricci (1552–1610), the Jesuits in 1583 founded a mission near Canton in south China, beginning a long engagement with the Chinese empire. During his 27 years in China, Matteo Ricci learned to master the Chinese language and engage in dialogue with the finest Chinese scholars, as well as continuously report back to Europe. His journals reveal that he came into contact with popular diviners and religious practitioners, who at that time appeared to abound everywhere: 'This obnoxious class is a veritable pest in the capital cities and even in the court.' With specific reference to feng shui, the practitioners of which he called 'geologists', he comments: 'Many of their most distinguished men are interested in this recondite science and, when necessary, they are called in for consultation, even from a great distance' (Ricci 1953: 84–5).

The Jesuits' intrusiveness and calculating use of the new sciences brought them closer to power than any other Westerners before or after. During several decades leading up to the anti-Christian movement in the Kangxi era (1662–1722), the Jesuits Adam Schall and Ferdinand Verbiest controlled the imperial Chinese Directorate of Astronomy. Their work brought them

Fig. 2.2 Title page from *Dixue dawen* [Questions and Answers in Geography] (1744). Collection of the Royal Library, Copenhagen.

into the intricate political games relating to the interpretation of omens and divination. After seizing control over the Directorate, they introduced modern European astronomy for the sake of precision, but used it entirely for traditional purposes of divination for the imperial court in order to optimize their political influence (Huang Y. 1991: 1–20).

The Jesuits' and Franciscans' writings on China and translations of Chinese classics inaugurated the subject of sinology back in Europe, and served as a great source of inspiration for a new breed of thinkers during a time of groundbreaking transformations in science, theology and philosophy. Among the most prominent examples, the philosopher and mathematician

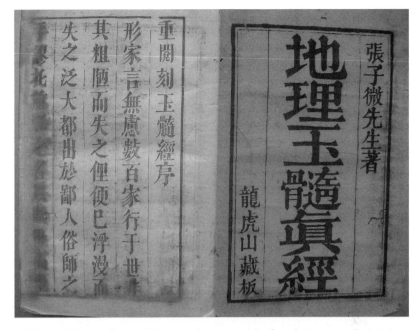

Fig. 2.3 Title page from a Chinese work on geography/feng shui, in ten vols. (1627). Collection of the Royal Library, Copenhagen.

Gottfried Wilhelm Leibniz (1646–1716) was much devoted to the study of Chinese philosophy, especially during the latter part of his life. He wrote introductions to the works of Jesuits, countless correspondences and a small book, *Discourse on the Natural Theology of the Chinese.* Apart from discussing issues of theology and morality, this work also salutes the *Yi jing* for its ancient discovery of binary arithmetic as given in its use of full and broken lines in the trigrams (Leibniz 1977).

During this period, European interest concentrated on the classical tradition, which was seen to surpass by far the contemporary Chinese philosophy as well as the popular tradition; a standard work on China from 1736 devoted one page to 'Fong choui', termed the 'most ridiculous invention' of an otherwise rationally disposed nation (du Halde 1736 III: 48–9).

The Anglo–Dutch–German–American 'discovery' of feng shui not only came much later than that of the south-European missionaries, but also tended to see it in a different light. Moreover, the Germanic speaking observers appeared unaware of the abundance of experience and writings of the Jesuits. Europeans had been expelled from Chinese territory for

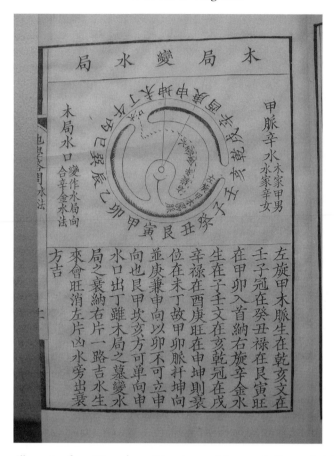

Fig. 2.4   Illustration from *Dixue dawen* [Questions and Answers in Geography] (1744).
Collection of the Royal Library, Copenhagen.

more than a century leading up to the Opium War (1840–2), but were now coming back with the unprecedented might of the north-European nations. The self-confidence and chauvinism that bolstered the new Industrial-Age European identity produced a view of China as backward, obscure and inaccessible (Bruun 2003: 38). Revolutionary writers such as Karl Marx and Friedrich Engels embodied this spirit when depicting China as an 'embalmed mummy at the end of the world' (Hamilton 1985: 187).

Contemporary writers on China, such as Charles Gutzlaff (1833), described mostly the established religions, while John Francis Davis in 1836 has a short description of the 'superstition of *foong-shuey*' (original

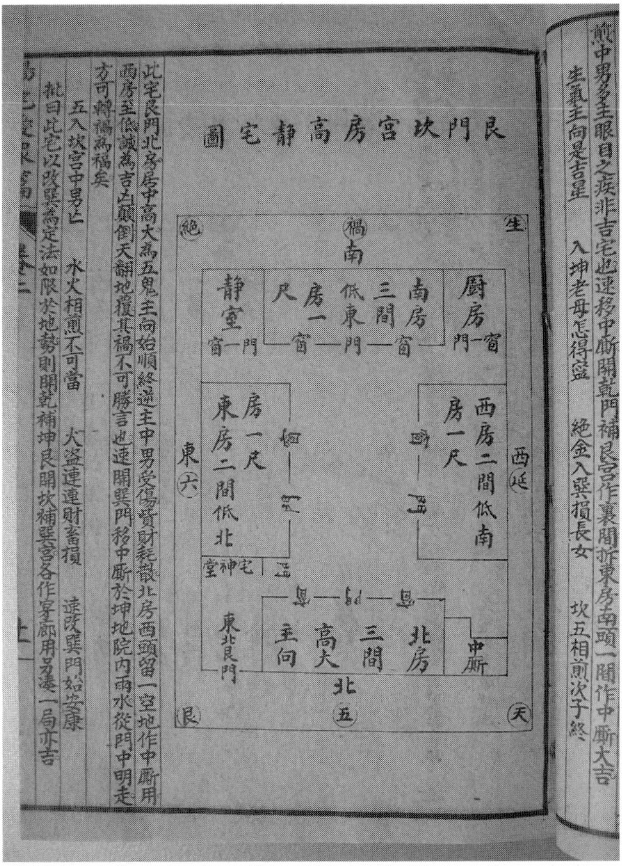

Fig. 2.5 Instructions for layout and use of buildings around a traditional courtyard. Chinese manual from 1915.

emphasis). References to the use of geomancers or necromancers in funerals were occasionally found (e.g. Fortune [1847] 1979). Small essays on the subject occasionally appeared, such as the one on the Chinese belief in the influence of pagodas on local communities according to *'fungshuy'* (original emphasis), published in the Chinese Repository in 1838 (see p. 35).

Few individuals had stayed in China long enough to learn the language and become acquainted with Chinese popular cosmology. In a careful account of Chinese religion from 1848, Wells Williams mentions how burial places are selected by geomancers according to the 'doctrines of the *fung shwui* . . . as ridiculous a farrago of nonsense, superstition, and craft, as

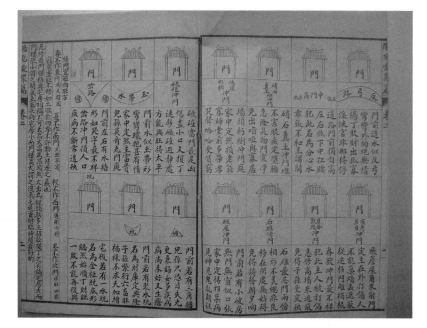

Fig. 2.6 A series of feng shui situations at front gates. Chinese manual from 1915.

have ever held sway over the human mind in any country or age' (Williams 1848: 264).

It was the missionary outstations, which slowly spread inland in the late 1840s and early 1850s as a result of the opium war, that brought attention to feng shui. Many of them encountered feng shui-related resistance as one among countless obstacles. There were popular opinions that the presence of foreigners disturbed graveyards, increased the number of deaths, brought general misfortune or otherwise affected the feng shui of individual people. From detailed accounts of the cases, however, it appears that other factors were involved. Locals wanting to extort money from the foreigners played a leading role in some cases, while the local gentry and elite often fanned the fire against foreigners. Anti-foreign sentiments increasingly surfaced, for instance in placards stating that foreigners and Chinese could not live together, that Chinese who rented to foreigners would be treated as traitors, or placards threatening foreigners with death if they entered certain cities (Carlson 1974: 38, 117).

Though feng shui had not become a dominant theme in the encounter of the Chinese with foreigners, the seeds of popular protest

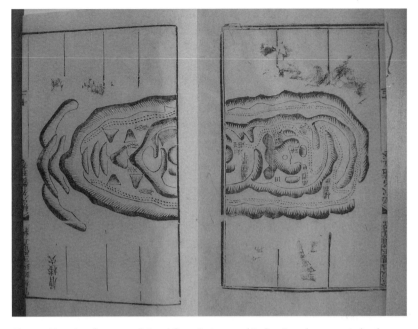

Fig. 2.7 Drawing from a traditional feng shui manual indicating placement in landscape. Chinese manual from 1627.

had been sown. Still in the 1850s and early 1860s, there was little awareness of the subject among foreigners. In a two-volume work on *The Social Life of the Chinese* from 1865, for instance, the American missionary Justus Doolittle devoted just a few pages to 'geomancy', which he describes as one out of the six distinguishable methods of fortune-telling, albeit the 'dearest and most tedious' (Doolittle 1865: 339). After devoting two pages to describing the geomancer's work and consideration as to determine a good site for a grave, Doolittle comments: 'The above remarks . . . show how willing the people are to deceive and delude themselves, and at their own expense. All of these kinds of fortune-tellers are very fluent in speech . . . They all have a very patronizing manner' (Doolittle 1865: 339).

It was only after the foreign occupation of Beijing (Peking) in 1860–2, however, that feng shui increasingly became an issue in the Chinese–foreign encounter. Foreign interests in opening the Chinese interior to traders, travellers and missionaries, as well as competition among the foreign powers, contributed to rising tension. The revolutionary impact of steam power in Europe served as a model for the foreigners' vision of progress for China. Another great invention of the day, the telegraph, which was about to revolutionize long-distance communication, had changed the prospects for enterprise in the Chinese interior. It was exactly this potential for irreversible and foreign-dominated change throughout China that many Chinese reformers and intellectuals sensed and attempted to counter by internal mobilization. Feng shui was inflated in the tense field between the foreign drive for the interior and the Chinese self-strengthening movement, searching for new national symbols that were easy to read for the general populace.

At the same time, Catholic and Protestant mission stations spread into every province of the empire, and their scope of activity also expanded rapidly, including churches, residences, schools, orphanages and small hospitals. Although their converts were too few to matter in the colossal Chinese population, they could still form small communities, enjoying certain social privileges and turning away from the Chinese order under some degree of foreign protection. The missionaries in China were reformers at heart; they called for the reform of Chinese thought and institutions through the adoption of what they saw as the salient elements of western civilization: science, technology and Christianity. By engaging in aggressive dialogue with the Chinese elite, publishing books and journals and challenging the social order, they set out to revolutionize the inherently conservative Chinese society.

Apart from numerous attacks on missionary stations in which feng shui accusations played a part, it was not until 1867–8 that, quite suddenly, feng shui arguments were introduced in the imperial government's policy towards foreign enterprises. In the next few years, things developed quickly, and soon every foreigner involved with Chinese affairs, either through missionary, commercial or diplomatic activity, would become intensely aware of the importance that everyday Chinese citizens evidently attributed to the matter. Rather than a product of the western world's late discovery of feng shui, the escalation of conflict must be seen as a consequence of feng shui being adopted in a rising anti-foreign discourse, which in turn gave new vitality and support to the feng shui tradition (Bruun 2003: 43–55).

The many accounts of foreign building projects declared impossible on grounds of feng shui, which have circulated in later publications, mainly date from this period. One such project was the building of the Gap:

When the Hong Kong Government cut a road, now known as the Gap, to the Happy Valley, the Chinese community was thrown into a state of abject terror and fright, on account of the disturbance which this amputation of the Dragon's limb would cause to the Feng Shui of Hong Kong; and when many of the engineers, employed at the cutting, died of Hong Kong fever, and the foreign houses already built in the Happy Valley had to be deserted on account of Malaria, the Chinese triumphantly declared, it was an act of retributory justice on the part of Feng Shui. (Eitel [1873] 1984: 2)

In the late 1860s, all foreign-language journals in China (most of which were run by missionary societies) had queries and comments on feng shui. Here is a time-typical comment from the journal *Notes and Queries*, dated 31 January 1867:

Most of the residents in China, particularly those who have any knowledge of the language, are aware of the importance attached by the Chinese to the Doctrine of Fung-shui, or the spiritual influence of wind and water. In traversing the country the traveller sees Pagodas and on enquiry as to their origin and title is told – that the first is unknown, and the second has reference to Fung-shui . . . Most of the Chinese have very hazy notions on the subject. Many, however, not professionals in the art, but who study Geomancy as a science, have some distant inklings of the truth, and after repeated conversations, enquiries on the subject, and on inspection of the Geomantic books, which, indeed, I could make little of, I have come to the conclusion that Fung-shui is simply terrestrial magnetism . . . Perhaps some of the contributors to 'Notes and Queries' could throw some further light upon the subject. (*Notes and Queries*, 31 January 1867)

It did not take long before other observers answered the call. In 1868, the *Chinese Recorder and Missionary Journal* (CRMJ) printed a seven-page speech on 'ancestral worship and fung-shuy' by Reverend M. T. Yates (1868), one of the first attempts at an exhaustive account in English. Yates gave a sympathetic account of feng shui, with several examples of its extraordinary power of explanation among the Chinese, ending with a proclamation of the malicious influence of western constructions in the eyes of the Chinese, for which he saw the gospel as the only antidote. Then came a series of articles by Joseph Edkins in 1872, also in the *Chinese Recorder and Missionary Journal*, and in 1873, Ernest Johann Eitel (a German missionary and linguist serving in Guangzhou and later having several posts in Hong Kong) wrote his monograph on feng shui, the first of its kind in a western language, as well as the first western publication not entirely dismissing feng shui as plain superstition. Then, in 1892, the outstanding Dutch sinologist J.J.M. de Groot (1854–1921) started publishing his monumental work, *The Religious Systems of China* (1892–1910, 6 volumes), which included the first comprehensive study of Chinese feng shui (see Chapter 4).

Chinese official policy

Against the background of continued foreign intrusion, it was only natural that the Chinese imperial government was terrified, particularly at the prospect of telegraphs and railways spreading into the empire. Much of its ruling elite feared the foreigner. As much as the ruling elite feared the foreigner's technology and culture, they feared his zeal to revolutionize the world in the image of a western liberal-democratic society.

The imperial government extended to all printed media its monopoly on worshipping Heaven and on interpreting its will in the future of the empire – and there were no printed news media other than the central government's gazette. Any prophecy concerning state affairs was an open challenge to authority, whether expressed by a geomancer or a journalist. As if the printed Chinese language media were not enough, several foreign missions ran specific programmes for reaching the Chinese mandarins. By their aggressive and provocative style of work, missionaries of all denominations certainly made their contribution to the increasing awareness of an alternative social order, which just a few decades later was heard as a strong call for reformation across the empire (Cohen 1978: 586–8).

Previously, it was mainly the Chinese gentry that took advantage of popular cosmology in the struggle against foreign interests. A continuous trend throughout the nineteenth century, which might have stimulated the growth of popular cosmology, was the spontaneous militarization of the countryside (Kuhn 1970). The Qing government strove to maintain control over both local militia and a growing and recalcitrant rural populace capable of political revolution: the White Lotus Rebellion from 1796 to 1804, the Eight Trigrams Uprising in north China, including an attack on Beijing in 1813, and the Taiping Rebellion of 1851 to 1864, nearly overthrowing the imperial government, all conveyed the hopes of millions of destitute peasants. The period 1850 to 1875 was particularly marked by a long series of rebellions, affecting most parts of the empire; in addition to the Taiping, there were also Muslim rebellions in the west, the Miao rebellion in Guizhou and the Nian rebellion in the northeast. Rebellions had drained the resources of the state and could only be put down by the establishment of local militia forces throughout the country. The gentry played a crucial part in organizing these part-time soldiers, not because this was an ideal solution in the eyes of the imperial government but because it was the only solution.

Also, at the political level, this period saw substantially changing relations. While colonialism in the early period, termed the 'first phase' by John

K. Fairbank, was signified by 'imperialism of free trade', a second phase was begun in the 1870s (Fairbank 1992: 205). The Anglo-Qing dominion of the China coast gave way to imperialist rivalry among the great industrial powers of Britain, Russia, France, Germany and Japan, who all invaded Chinese territory. While establishing an alien hegemony in their possessions and granting extra-territoriality to their citizens, the foreign powers placed the native Chinese elite in the situation they most abhorred: ruling under alien hegemony, reminding them of both the Manchu-dominated Qing rule and the Mongolian-dominated Yuan dynasty. The imperial government's reaction to foreign domination was the movement for self-strengthening and restoring 'wealth and power' (*fu-qiang*).

Feng shui cosmology thus appeared a convenient means of manipulating popular sentiments and particularly aggression towards foreigners. Particularly in the 1860s and 1870s, in a series of incidents, the Chinese authorities obstructed mining operations, railway and telegraph construction and road building with reference to their disturbance of the local feng shui situation. The Qing government in general attempted to check the art of geomancy, and Qing law was very restrictive about geomancy and all sorts of magic. In 1871, however, it issued a memorandum on foreign missions, in which one article proposed to legalize feng shui as a justified veto against the opening of foreign mission stations (Bruun 2003: 52). In the years following the 1871 memorandum, on countless occasions both Chinese central and local government authorities would refer to feng shui disturbance to postpone undesirable matters or simply oppose everything foreign with diversionary issues and bureaucratic obstructionism. They argued that local people were worried about feng shui interference and that the missionaries had to consider public opinion. Similarly, they held that officials could not change the opinions of the people (Carlson 1974: 117), although for centuries the persecution of heretic sects had involved rectifying the beliefs of the people. The Qing rulers exhibited great skills in sensing contradiction among their enemies; in this matter they could play on the common criticism of missionary activity among the missionaries' own governments and in the foreign communities in China.

One out of many incidents of Chinese feng shui-related resistance in this period was the famous destruction of the Shanghai-Wusong railway in 1878. Ambitious railway schemes for China, including a line from Calcutta to Canton, had been suggested by foreign merchant interests in the 1840s, but had been abandoned because of rebellion and western exclusion from the interior. In the 1860s, a new comprehensive railway scheme for China was drawn up by a British company, but a Chinese government official replied that: 'Railroads would only be beneficial to China if undertaken by the Chinese themselves and constructed under their own management' (Fevour 1970: 107). Foreign enterprises insisted, and Jardine organized a company to build a little tramway from Shanghai towards the Wusong port (completed in 1875) in defiance of the Chinese authorities. Despite the first section being only a few kilometres long, it was given tremendous symbolic value since its proprietors, who included Chinese shareholders, hoped that once the little railway had proven its worth it would end the Chinese reservations about railways. It had been built with an oddly winding track to avoid accusations of interference with the feng shui of the region and disturbance of graves and spirits. The imperial government on the surface chose not to get involved. The railway operated at a profit until 1876, when the death of a Chinese person on the line was announced by the Chinese authorities in Shanghai; this was followed by a number of official protests and disturbances along the line, openly supported by the local gentry, who accused the line of ruining feng shui. As part of the Chefoo Convention of 1876, the Chinese government agreed to purchase the line. But instead of continuing its operation, the line was dismantled in 1878 and the rails and rolling stock sent to Taiwan, while the Chinese officials supervising the destruction work moved about in sedan chairs 'as an expression of their abhorrence of mechanical locomotion' (Chang 1943: 24).

As an increasing number of Chinese reform-minded officials advocated railways, mining and telegraph lines as inevitable means of moderniza- tion and national defence, following the advocacy of, for instance, Li Hongzhang, Zuo Zongtang and Ding Richang, the Qing court gradually eased up. In 1881, it permitted the construction of a 10-kilometre railway line from a coal mine near Tianjin to the river, but using only wagons drawn by horses and mules. The American engineer in charge of the line secretly built a locomotive from scrap materials and ran it on the line. Again, the court officials protested on the grounds that the rumbling locomotive disturbed the ancestral spirits and that the smoke polluted the rice fields. After a lengthy discussion, the locomotive was finally sanctioned and, as it proved its worth, China soon entered a phase of native railway construc- tion; public opinion was quickly diverted from the theoretical issue of the benefit from railway construction to the practical question of which rail- way to build first (Chang 1943: 25). As a matter of greater importance here, however, since it seems to confirm the argument, feng shui-based protests to railway and telegraph construction apparently died out soon after their nativization. Local magistrates resolutely handled public protests and, by 1890, objections had been overcome everywhere (Morrison 1895: 157). Dyer Ball wrote in 1893:

[I]t is not an insuperable obstruction, for whenever the Chinese government has made up its mind to the introduction of any of the inventions of Western science, Fung Shui is not allowed to be an obstacle, for, while pandering to its absurd ideas as far as is practicable without hindering the feasibility of their scheme, yet the populace, if obstructive, is soon made to feel that the will of the rulers has to be obeyed. (Ball 1893: 206)

THE COMMUNIST ERA

Much has been written on this gloomy period of Chinese history, and we shall not go into detail here but just point out the overall trends.

Atheism had been on the rise in China for decades, and general modernization had taken a firm grip on most Chinese elite and intellectuals. There had been a growing divide being urban and rural lifestyles and outlooks, to the effect that folk religion primarily thrived in the countryside. Successive governments attacked the 'superstitious beliefs' of rural people, which they saw as obstacles to progress. When the communists under Mao Zedong came to power, they merely extended the policy on religion of the previous regime, only the means were harsher. Deteriorating foreign relations and severe obstacles in implementing the communist social order contributed to a hardening policy through the 1950s. Simultaneously with the establishment of people's communes in the late 1950s, all religious denominations and sects were again persecuted. Attacks on Buddhist and Daoist temples and monasteries, Christian churches, Muslim mosques and all local religious institutions followed. Religious specialists of all kinds, denigrated as a common category of 'religious and superstitious practitioners', were generally persecuted and killed in the thousands. Ancestor worship and folk-religious practices were discouraged or forbidden but appeared difficult to stamp out (C. K. Yang [1961] 1970; Bush 1970). Failed development policies of the Great Leap Forward led to the Three Hard Years from 1960, the greatest famine in human history, which eliminated tens of millions of people.

During the Cultural Revolution of 1966–76, when the Red Guards were sent into the rural villages, policy hardened still. Traditional religious practices came under renewed attack, this time accompanied by the frantic destruction of everything of the old society, including furniture, personal belongings, books, images, porcelain and whatever could be found in people's homes. All other objects relating to popular religion were smashed, including tombstones, tablets, pillars, statues, pagodas, gates and so forth. Fanatic beatings, killings, parading of social enemies of all kinds and constant sessions of self-criticism turned this period into a living nightmare. Western missionaries, travellers and sojourners were gone, all foreigners were kept out and China was closed off. Few sources on these events were available to the outside world.

Rural feng shui specialists were persecuted in this period, often senselessly beaten up but rarely put to death like the monks and priests of the established churches, which were seen as a more direct threat to the state. Most were forced into other professions while some practised clandestinely. Ancestor worship as such could never be stamped out, however, and except for brief periods there was a steady demand for feng shui-related services. Many stories indicate that leading party officials in the rural areas wanted traditional burials for their own family members.

It is even plausible that the regime used feng shui-related means to punish and inspire fear. The peasants' links to their ancestors and clans were broken when graves were wrecked and ancestor halls, shrines and tablets demolished. The Red Guards would scatter the bones in the graves or even burn them. Particularly, people belonging to the 'four stinking categories' (capitalists, landlords, rich farmers and anti-revolutionaries) were punished by the public destruction of their ancestors' tombs and the burning of the bones to symbolically wipe out their family lines (Bruun 2003: 102).

With the economic reforms of the Open Door Policy, declared in 1979, popular religion slowly revived. The remaining rural feng shui specialists resumed their practice, first clandestinely and later more openly. The demand for their services exploded with private agricultural production and economic growth (see the following chapter). Still today, even though the old generation of specialists is gone, feng shui specialists will, out of historical experience, rarely advertise their trade.

It was quite late in the reform process, around 1990, that new books on feng shui cautiously began to be published in China. Yet they suffered occasional setbacks, such as during the surge on FalunGong in 2000. Into the 2000s, and not least inspired by the international popularity of the subject, new books have appeared at an accelerating pace.

CHAPTER 3

Feng shui in the context of Chinese popular religion

In contrast to modern views, Chinese folk wisdom says that no matter how skilfully and dedicatedly you work, there are independent factors involved in determining your success: 'Destiny and human effort both play their part.' These independent agencies include the cosmological resonance of *yin* and *yang*, the *bagua*, the Five Phases and the flow of *qi*. They also include astrology as a separate repertoire, as well as the workings of various invisible beings. Similarly, symbols and rituals may have their effects, as may other matters.

Such autonomous and unpredictable agencies may seem inconsistent with the idea of a fundamentally undivided world, which is characteristic of Chinese cosmology. It is nevertheless symptomatic of an anthropocentric worldview. Each of the above phenomena may derive from the same basic cosmological processes, but they still have their own power and will. Compared to modern notions of a world divided into various domains of, for instance, the natural, the social and the psychical, to which specific laws of causality may apply, anthropocentrism tends to invert domain and agency. There is only one domain, the world that matters, but multiple agencies exercise their influence on it. As compared to a monotheistic rationalism, such as Christianity, there is no incentive to reduce them into a common formula.

To some extent, these agencies may be manipulated, if the pertinent knowledge and techniques are at hand, but they must be confronted one by one. So when people almost customarily express uncertainty in terms of 'maybe', this or that aspect of cosmology may be at work, rather than they adhere to a positive 'belief', it is first and foremost an indication of the fundamental assumption that the given world includes an endless number of truly independent forces or agencies, which bridge the physical, the social and the psychological domains. There is an uncertainty factor built into every human activity, and a pervading assumption that good luck works autonomously – it is not distributed meaningfully according to morals or other forms of personal merit. Rural people may have ideas of how the various forces and beings interact with their own lives, but tend to rely on diviners and religious specialists for interpretation.

This was also the case for feng shui. Throughout Chinese history, the vast majority of its users were the millions and millions of farmer households, to whom it was an integrated element in popular cosmology and religion. In contrast to newly developed western forms, traditional Chinese feng shui is inseparable from ancestor worship, beliefs in influence of ghosts and ancestors and burial rituals. It includes an organic perception of reality refusing distinctions between Heaven and Earth as well as between the material conditions of life, the social life of the family and kinship group and the inner feelings of the individual member.

Chinese popular religion is a vast repertoire of ideas, practices, life-cycle rituals and ceremonies, connecting the basic condition of agrarian production to social life and local place. The common Chinese values are, above all, materialistic, and the focus of life is this-worldly. Yet they expand the immediately accessible material plane with a huge repertoire of invisible aspects of this one-and-only world. Some aspects are impersonal, such as those accounted for above, while others are personalized.

A plethora of gods and local deities are recognized and worshipped. Some common ones are the Kitchen God (*zaoshen*), Door Gods (Qin and Yuchi), Goddess of Mercy (*guanyin*), Jade Emperor (*yudi*), Eight Immortals (*baxian*) and the Sea Goddess (*mazu*). It is important to note, however, that territorial cults presumably were always as important as ancestral cults and their deities worshipped separately. Previously, a huge range of local-area and occupational deities were honoured, but both the images and their worship were forcefully abandoned in the communist era. With the overall religious revival and reconstruction of rural temples in China, they are coming back at a rapid pace, including deities transposed from temples in Taiwan, Hong Kong, Malaysia and elsewhere, along with the return of emigrants and descendants to their native areas. The demarcation of local identities by means of festivals, processions and temple fairs is unmistakably rising and has territorial facets. Territorial protector gods and locality gods were focal objects in the past for prayers, offerings and incense burning to avoid calamity and bring good fortune (Feuchtwang 1992: 61–3). The rehabilitated correlation between lineage and territory in south and south-eastern Chinese towns especially, and the 'coming home' from exile of local deities, offer a new range of possible forms of identification, while at the same time challenging existing political authority.

The relationship between Chinese popular religion and economic enterprise is a fascinating and increasingly pertinent topic. In China since the 1980s, economic liberalization has created wider scope for religious activity (Weller 2000; Bruun 2003; Goossaert 2005), and continued popular religious revival has coincided with rapid economic development. Entrepreneurial groups eagerly embrace feng shui and engage in new religious cults while spending lavishly on funerals, banquets, festivals and the hiring of religious expertise. Since ancestor worship is still strong, funerals tend to be the most important among life-cycle rituals; higher local officials and leading businessmen in particular may spend senselessly on the burial of their deceased family members, not least to demonstrate their status and local influence. But also the sponsoring of new temple constructions, festivals and fairs results in huge amounts of money changing hands. Mayfair Yang has argued that this 'ritual economy' is not merely a result of privatization, and it does not imply that funds are being wasted on useless purposes, as implied by the Chinese state. There is no opposition between religion and economic development, she argues; in fact, the ritual economy has fuelled economic growth by providing organizational apparatus, site and motivation for economic activity (Yang M. 2000: 480). Economy and production may this way be perceived as part of Chinese ritual and religious practices, including the territorial deity cults, festival routines and pilgrimage centres. There are even Chinese classics such as the *Guanzi* (4th–2nd century BC) that recommend 'wasteful extravagance' on the part of the emperor in order to enhance production (Yang M. 2000: 492). Today, for sure, popular religion (and with that also feng shui) blends with global capitalism to produce new hybrid forms as easily as it blended with pre-modern Chinese capitalism under bureaucratic control.

Family altars were abandoned during the communist era because they were considered backward and against material progress. They are now again universally present in the homes of rural and overseas Chinese, constituting the focal point for worship of ancestors and a variety of deities, just as small altars and shrines are everywhere the hallmark of Chinese family businesses.

Popular religion incorporates rituals for finding spouses and performing weddings as well as including elaborate mourning and burial rituals, often stretching over several days and involving the entire village or surname group. It prescribes the worship and care of ancestors, such as in the yearly Qingming Festival (see below), where graves are swept clean, possibly restored, and adorned with colourful paper strips while food, drink and paper money may be offered to the dead.

Popular religion is furthermore linked to a range of domestic practices and rituals such as putting up posters, lanterns or red bands for good luck, gift giving with specific meanings, respecting traditional manners and forms of address and interpreting a host of traditional symbols.

For many or all of these activities, rural diviners offer their assistance, for instance by finding auspicious days for weddings, farming activities, travelling, building and burying. Or they may assist in fortune-telling, divining places for houses and graves, solving problems in the household, communicating with spirits, curing diseases, giving advice for careers, as well as finding lost people and property. In traditional Chinese society, diviners abounded, particularly in the later dynastic periods such as those described in the previous chapter, and this was often to the dismay of public authorities. They spanned, for instance, hand, face and ear diviners, other fortune-tellers, geomancers, and *Yi jing* and *bagua* diviners (see end of chapter).

Feng shui specialists were only one category out of many, albeit perhaps the most widespread and respected. After the great proletarian revolution of China in the 1950s and 1960s, feng shui specialists may have come out with a relative advantage: they were often the only rural religious specialists available when reforms opened for religious revival in the 1980s. The established churches (primarily Buddhism, Daoism, Christianity and Islam) and their monks, priests, ministers and mullahs were persecuted to a higher extent and more often subject to killings than the practitioners of popular religion, who lived in the villages and blended with ordinary villagers.

Below are described the common uses and understandings of feng shui in the Chinese popular tradition, and towards the end we shall return to the question of practice versus belief.

FAMILY RITUAL AND THE YEARLY FESTIVALS

Family and kinship played a crucial part in China as the basic – and in some localities the only – social organization. The traditional family, with the eldest male as the patriarch, may contain three or more generations under the same roof (also called 'extended' family), and forms a common household. Beyond the immediate family, local communities were in most places tightly knit into lineage and clan organizations, recognizing descent from a common ancestor and sharing a common surname, such as Wang, Zhang, Yang, Feng, Li, Xu, etc. The Chinese refer to the 'old hundred names' (*lao bai xing*) to designate ordinary people, at the same time indicating that there are relatively few surnames and that name groups are huge in size. All across China (yet more prevalent in the south and east), people lived in clan-based villages, thus having common surname and ancestry. This still tends to be the case in many rural areas, shaping people's identities and sense of history. It is also relevant to the feng shui situation, since both competition and conflicts are played out within or between large surname groups, with intense awareness of the doings and achievements of each family.

Popular religion is often depicted as the religious aspects of the Chinese kinship system – a kind of family religion. Popular religion is the social glue, with meaningful roles created for all family members in a dynamic hierarchy including powerful positions assigned for ancestors, as much as it is the link between man, cosmos and a range of spiritual beings. Popular religion contains a huge mass of rituals, observances and festivals in which the honouring of ancestors takes a prominent place – many authors, both Chinese and foreign, have described ancestor worship as the real religion of the Chinese, even as the origin of feng shui (see Chapter 4). Feng shui is intimately linked to life-cycle rituals and ceremonies, agrarian production and the basic conditions of rural life, in which family and kinship organization always played a crucial part. Many writers have pointed out that Chinese family organization and popular religion really are synonymous; as long as one survives, so will the other (e.g. Jordan 1972: 177). The Chinese family has both sentimental and religious value; it could be added that publicly denouncing the family would probably be the closest anyone could get to blasphemy in a Chinese setting. Some plainly call Chinese religion 'familism', a religion centred on the family itself, with a focus on the dead (Paper 1994: 79), but without a stringent ideology or concept of truth. This religion is a distinctive institution, which connects family with clan, ritual, festivals, local territory and the greater cosmos, and which has in its centre the Imperial Metaphor (Feuchtwang 2001, and see Chapter 4).

With the family in centre position, every traditional Chinese home thus becomes a temple in itself and a shrine to its ancestors. In the centre room will be an altar with picture, name tablets, incense, wine cups and candles or red light bulbs. Food and drink may be placed as offerings in front of the altar.

It should rightfully be pointed out, however, that the Chinese term for 'religion' (*zongjiao*) is of recent origin, while in the Chinese tradition there is little distinction between various teachings of ideology, cosmology and world religion. Using the term 'popular religion' for Chinese values and practices associated with the family is therefore a western approximation. A further qualification is that while family takes centre stage in Chinese popular religion and Chinese self-identity, the relation between the individual and the wider community, polity and cosmos is equally significant in local and territorial cults, in the honouring of particular deities, in participation in religious associations and in the yearly festivals. Below are described some of the festivals with a direct bearing on ancestor worship and feng shui matters.

By far the greatest and most well-known of the Chinese festivals is the New Year, or Spring Festival, marking the new year according to the traditional lunar-solar calendar, itself a vital instrument in astrology, divination and feng shui (described below). Spring Festival is a time of family union and celebration with plenty of good food and drink, honouring the ancestors, setting off fire-crackers and watching lion dancing and other performances. In rural villages, it is also a time of elaborate rituals, including posting Door God pictures and a variety of couplets, wood-block printings and paper cuttings displaying a wealth of gods, spirits and mythical figures. Posting large pictures of the Door Gods on the main entrance is an ancient practice worth explicating in the present context.

One folktale relates that when Li Shimin, emperor of the Tang dynasty, once fell sick, he heard ghosts howling in his dream. The next morning he told of his dream to his court officials. Two powerful generals, Qin Qiong and Yuchi Gong, who were among the founders of the dynasty, buckled on their full armour and stood on guard outside the emperor's bed chamber at night. Thereafter the emperor dreamed no more of ghosts, but to have peace at night while relieving the generals he told a painter to draw images of the two fierce looking generals on pieces of paper, which he hung on the palace entrance as 'Door Gods'. When the incident became known to the public, the people eagerly did the same in order to suppress evil spirits around their homes (Qi 1988: 4). Whether based on historical evidence or not, this theme – the ways of the royal court diffused to become general practice in the homes of the Chinese people – permeates many folk religious practices, including those of feng shui.

Also, spring couplets (*chun lian*), bearing auspicious words and poems, may be posted on doors. They originate from ancient charms, consisting of rectangular pieces of peach wood with magic incantations written on them to 'exorcise evil spirits and ask for blessings'. Later, probably during the Song dynasty, paper was used instead of wood, and, again, legend has the will of emperors as a motivator: when Taizu, emperor of the Ming dynasty, made Nanjing his capital, he issued a decree requiring all officials, scholars and commoners to post a pair of couplets on their doors.

The second most popular of the long range of Chinese festivals is the Qingming Festival (meaning 'clear and bright', and usually falling in early April), translated as Tomb Sweeping Day or Festival of the Dead. The Qingming is ancient, according to folklore created by the Duke Wen of Jin during the Spring and Autumn Period. Before he became leader of the state of Jin under the name of Duke Wen, he was exiled for nineteen years under severe hardship. Only a man named Jie Zitui and a few others loyally endured the long exile. After ascending the throne, Duke Wen granted his followers titles and fiefs, but Jie Zitui did not want fame and instead retired to a secluded life in the mountains with his mother. When Duke Wen later went to search for him in the mountains to make him come back, but did not find him, he set the forest on fire to drive him out. But Jie, so the story goes, would rather die than accept a reward for his past deeds, and was burnt to death in the mountains together with his mother.

The day this happened was the Qingming (although historical sources suggest it has changed its meaning; see p. 26). On this day, people go to sweep the tombs of their ancestors and mourn the dead. Food and drink are offered to the dead (either placed on the grave itself, on family altars or elsewhere), and paper money may be burned for the dead to have enough of everything. The Qingming is also a day of family outings to enjoy the spring, as well as many kite-flying and sporting activities. Most important in our context, however, it is a day of intense focus on the wellbeing of ancestors, when many seek to make up for what they neglected during the year. Many graves are restored or even moved, and feng shui specialists experience their busiest season, giving advice on the proper arrangement of graves, showing respect for the dead or redressing the bad influence from forefathers unhappy with their lot. Like the wealth of other Chinese festivals, Qingming too is wrapped in rich imperial symbolism, allowing the masses to draw on the finest moments of China's history and the most gracious ways of its culture.

THE CHINESE ALMANAC, OR THE KNOW ALL BOOK (TONGSHU)

Although all Chinese societies officially use the common Gregorian calendar, the traditional Chinese calendar – a combined lunar and solar calendar of ancient origin – remains universally important. It marks all traditional festivals and holidays, is essential for Chinese astrology and is in itself an important medium of divination, as intricate almanacs based on it mark out auspicious and inauspicious dates for every kind of undertaking.

The traditional calendar goes by many names. The most common name is the farmer's calendar or rural calendar (*Nongli*), but it is also frequently referred to as the lunar calendar or Yin calendar (*Yinli*) due to its emphasis on the moon phases as compared to the common solar calendar (*Yangli*). Yet other names are the old calendar (*Jiuli*) or the Xia calendar (*Xiali*).

The origin of the Chinese calendar goes back into the remotest antiquity, being among the root conceptions of Chinese civilization, as of all other ancient agricultural societies. Its significance for ritual and cultural integration and state formation cannot be exaggerated. Chinese mythology commonly credits the legendary Yellow Emperor (Huangdi, 2697–2599 BC) with inventing the calendar to advise the peasants when to sow, plant and harvest. Historical evidence goes far back indeed, as the oracle bones of the Shang dynasty (see Chapter 2) describe a combined lunisolar calendar of years with twelve months and an intercalary thirteenth month to avoid drift. Documents of the Zhou dynasty testify to a complex calendar, including a sixty-day cycle (a combination of the Ten Heavenly Stems and the Twelve Earthly Branches, used in *yin-yin* or *yang-yang* combinations to produce a cycle of sixty named days). Along with the calendar reform of the Han dynasty, the sixty unit cycle began to mark years, and has been used continually since. A simple representation of this cycle is given by the twelve animals of the Chinese zodiac combined with the Five Elements (year of the fire-pig = 2007, year of the earth-rat = 2008, etc.). Despite some modifications, of which the latest was introduced by the Jesuits under the leadership of Adam Schall in 1645, the traditional calendar was in use in China until 1929.

Yearly calculated almanacs based on the traditional calendar have been produced by the Bureau of Astronomy/Astrology since ancient times, modelled upon the classic called the *Monthly Ordnances* (*Yueling*). The making of the almanac was the privilege of state power and a crucial function, by which the Son of Heaven would show his ability to read the cosmos and bring order to the empire. The almanacs were so precious that they were transported in sedan chairs and greeted with prostrations before being distributed to the highest officials; more simple versions were available to the public.

These almanacs remain immensely popular today in Hong Kong, Taiwan and Singapore. Each family may have a copy of the almanac, often termed the '*Know All Book*' (*Tongshu*), comparable in significance to the Christian bible. No diviner, priest or fortune-teller would be without it. In China proper, where almanacs were prohibited during the communist era while illegal copies circulated in rural areas, they are now again commonly available and are gaining significance. English versions are now also produced and widely distributed in the West.

The Chinese almanac, which is still printed in a string-bound format with ancient wood-block illustrations, contains an astonishing variety of information. It is the one solid guide to living 'correctly' through the year, making use of propitious universal forces while avoiding all bad ones or offending gods and spirits. The largest section of the almanac, however, is an ancient text that does not change from year to year, even though there are regional differences. It is useful for everyday life, in accordance with tradition, including instructions for health problems, lists of herbal medicine, notes and illustrations on baby care, help in choosing a child's name, knowledge on particular gods and deities and sections on the interpretation of dreams, of which there are many distinct types relating to the classical tradition of mountains, trees, silk and emperors. Both the Hong Kong and Taiwan versions include large sections on omens and their interpretation as well as on the writing of magic spells for every type of problem that may haunt mankind, secular and spiritual alike. There are spells for various forms of sickness and pains, for driving away evil spirits, for keeping away wild animals, for bad habits in the family such as drinking and gambling and for a host of other problems.

The almanacs also contain a long list of Confucian quotes for every occasion, in order to help people live their lives correctly, in accordance with tradition. Other sections of the almanac, however, seem even more peculiar to the western observer. For instance, a Taiwanese almanac from the 1980s offered a list of ancient advice under the heading 'How to choose the sex of your child'. One such piece of wisdom says that the way a couple makes love will influence the sex of the child: if they want a boy, the man should spend a long time on the foreplay and restrain himself; if they want a girl, the man should enter a climax as soon as possible. Another way relates to diet: husband and wife must eat the same food for seven days prior to intercourse. If they want a son, they must eat no meat during this period; instead they must eat plenty of beancurd, carrots, cucumber, lettuce and other vegetables, while avoiding sour foods. If they want a girl, they must eat plenty of meat, sour foods and pickles. A third way relates to numerology, encapsulated in a Chinese verse:

> Seven sevens are forty-nine
> Ask: Which is the pregnant month?
> Take away the mother's age
> Add nineteen

The calculation is this: you take the number forty-nine, add the number of the month in which the woman gets pregnant, subtract the woman's age and add nineteen. If the total is an odd number, it will be a boy; if it is even, it will be a girl (Bloomfield 1985).

Most almanacs also contain illustrated sections on physiognomy and palm-reading, aimed to judge people's character by their appearance, as done by the professional diviners. Similarly, sections on moles in the face may be used to judge a person's success in life. Other sections are devoted to numerology and the meaning of specific numbers, which are considered good or bad, mainly depending on the homophones in their pronunciation (there are countless of these in the Chinese language, though specific ones vary with dialects).

Yet several parts of the almanac, as conventionally printed in Hong Kong and Taiwan, contain many sections that are inaccurate transmissions or are entirely incomprehensible, even to those skilled in the classical tradition. Presumably this is due to the fact that, over the centuries, the book has been reprinted by people with little scholarly knowledge and in an environment where little such knowledge existed, while retaining an unswerving reverence for the ancient written word.

The almanac itself, containing the precise information for each day of the year, is a large section in the back of the book. It is written by someone skilled in astrology, very often also famous feng shui masters. It is divided into the traditional double-hours, thus indicating not only auspicious and inauspicious days but also double hours fit for specific activities. It may indicate times for prayer, rituals, ceremonies, trips, purchasing items, meeting friends, moving the house, holding funeral services or honouring the dead. Similarly, it may warn against haircutting, repairing the kitchen or digging the earth at certain times. Much information relates to agriculture, obviously reflecting the origin of Chinese civilization and the almanac itself.

Self-evident from the above, the Chinese almanac contains a long list of advice, divinatory techniques and interpretations that are very similar to what the feng shui master engages in. Laid out in a popular form and ready to use, ordinary people use it a lot and keep it for reference, yet when it comes to crucial matters such as serious illness, accidents, moving home, burying the dead or finding dates for marriage, they call on expert assistance. The *Know All Book* has nevertheless great significance as an exposition of the common cultural platform, and thereby provides a powerful backing to the work of feng shui specialists as well as of the other traditional diviners (such as those listed at the end of this chapter).

FENG SHUI FOR BUILDING

A house is a living symbol; it is the focus of the aspirations – social and spiritual – of the people who made it. It shelters the family, and it is here in the courts of prescribed portions, shaded by walls of prescribed heights, in its chambers for social intercourse, in its chambers for religious meditation and ceremony, and in its private chambers that occurs the slow elaboration of thought and ritual.

Such begins Ronald Knapp's account of China's 'living houses' (Knapp 1999: 1), and nothing could be a better introduction to the use of feng shui cosmology in Chinese family houses. In Chinese rural villages, houses were mostly simple constructions, being built, demolished and rebuilt at a fairly rapid pace. It was customary for each generation to build for itself in a highly dynamic relationship between the size of the family and its status, land tenure and wealth. In a situation of extremely limited land and resources, as well as intense competition, only those families with economic success had the means to grow bigger. Thus, bigger families wanted bigger houses, while at the same time a large family tended to indicate wealth. In the rural setting, building houses was narrowly connected with building wealth and reputations. As noted by Maurice Freedman in his celebrated essay on Chinese geomancy (Freedman 1969), building higher or bigger has always been regarded as a challenge to the rest of the community; or, as put by an elderly feng shui man with regard to pre-Liberation society: 'If you built bigger you should have the means to defend your wealth' (Bruun 2003: 128).

Having a specialist to 'see feng shui' (*kan feng shui*) on the building site is an essential aspect of building activity in rural China today as much as in the preceding several centuries (see Fig. 3.1). Family houses should fit harmoniously into the local patterns of *qi* resonance, and should be placed in an auspicious position so as to capture the most of the living-giving flows of *qi*. The concept of *qi* in rural feng shui tends to be as many-sided as in the philosophical tradition, with a range of possible subdivisions into specific forms of *qi* according to the specialization of the individual feng shui master as well as with endless manifestations in objects, relations and occurrences. It is commonly asserted that the benign flow of *qi* is a general condition for success in life, expressed, for instance, by the four individual concerns of feng shui work: prosperity (*cai*), happiness (*fu*), long life (*shou*) and procreation (*zi*). Conversely, a malignant flow of *qi* will ruin any human endeavour and cause boundless suffering.

As shown below, very different local traditions exist to interpret the flow of *qi* around homes, to some extent referring to the different schools of feng

Fig 3.1 A rural feng shui master, using a large Hong Kong-produced compass, checks the ground plan for a house before construction begins. Fujian, China. Photograph by Ole Bruun.

shui. Yet these popular traditions show remarkable continuity, depending on oral transmission more than books of learning, and following their own independent course rather than the dramatic changes in Chinese natural philosophy and intellectual thought over the last millennium (Weller and Bol 1998: 327). The contrast between popular practice and intellectual thought have never been greater than in the modern period, when rural villages follow centuries-old patterns of thought while urban elites have adopted a modernistic view of life. The modernizing efforts of consecutive regimes over the last century, including prohibition and persecution, have changed little. Only very recently, when feng shui has re-emerged in public in towns and cities, is the gap slightly narrowing.

Feng shui is seen to work around homes in various ways. First, the specific natural environment gives shape to flows of *qi*, for which reason all its features must be identified, including compass directions, topography, symbolic representation of the landscape, flows of water and vegetation. Second, human constructions impinge on each other in such a way that one building may block or pervert the flow of *qi* to another, making specific evaluations necessary. Third, the possible impact of a range of natural and man-made objects around the home must be evaluated, including trees, rocks, monuments, ponds, dams, pagodas and shrines. Fourth, but of great importance, the astrological data of the household leader must be considered, as well as symbolic interaction between, for instance, his animal sign or birth date and the surroundings. Last of all, in connection with building activity, a number of rituals and local customs must be respected, most commonly including marking up the intended building site for local inspection, the killing of a cock and the sprinkling of its blood on the site, setting off fire-crackers, hanging up strips of coloured paper or posters, inviting the feng shui specialist and offering a feast for all involved. Several such rituals have a common aim to expel evil and preserve good: in ancient lore, the blood of a cock is supposed to scare off demons, while firecrackers, at least since the Qing dynasty, have been used to 'keep away evil spirits, exorcise ghosts, suppress demons and seek happiness'.

The rural brick or concrete houses now commonly built still have much of the traditional layout, but the rooms are likely to be bigger. The main entrance is mostly facing due south where the compass school is practised, and in a southerly direction where the forms school is predominant, giving higher priority to facing open landscape. The entrance leads into the main room, which serves as a living room for the family. From ancient times, the main room, or main hall, has been the true location of good feng shui. There is always a table with benches or stools in this room, which otherwise is sparsely adorned. Here visitors will enter, usually without much formality or courtesy. Bicycles may also be parked here and vegetables or grain may be temporarily stored along the walls.

To the right of the main room is the bedroom of the married couple, and to the left either children or grandparents may sleep, depending on the age composition of the household. The kitchen is usually placed towards the back of the house, sometimes in a small appendix with an entrance from the main room. The kitchen has a delicate position in the feng shui tradition, and used to be placed in a separate building since the stove chimney is thought to have a bad influence.

Recent constructions are mostly considered modern, 'western style' (*xifang*) houses, not due to the fact that they are built in concrete, but that they tend to have two stories with a staircase in the main room. For larger families, having an extra floor containing two or more rooms can be a relief. Where everybody previously slept in one or maybe two rooms, generations may now be parted. The married couple will usually sleep in the ground-floor bedroom, and children will be placed upstairs or to the left of the main room. Elderly people are usually allowed to stay on the ground floor, both because they may not be able to climb the stairs and because they commonly refuse to leave the ground floor with reference to custom.

After the communist takeover in 1949, rural mansions were demolished or seized by public authorities, and small standardized housing became a political manifestation of equality. In the old established rural communities, very little building activity was performed at all, and only very basic repair work was done during the times of political turmoil. A frantic building activity in rural areas began in the early 1980s, with the later constructions becoming ever bigger and more conspicuous in exterior design. Along with the unfolding economic differentiation of rural families, increasing sums of money are involved in rural feng shui. Those with wealth and power will search for auspicious surroundings for their houses and graves. Now that private construction has been given free reign, an immense production of both houses and symbols is taking place: the family home is a means of demonstrating the position that a family thinks it deserves in this world. Since this quite naturally is subject to interpretation, feng shui has become an idiom for expressing social relations that are not easy to verbalize either in the village or in the society at large: private ambitions, social competition and manipulation of moral codes. While in the Chinese interior most private houses tend to be of moderate size and appearance, in the coastal areas in particular they may rise to spectacular proportions and grandeur. Individual houses of four or five stories and clad in coloured tiles may now be seen in many coastal localities.

Chinese villages are known for social vigilance and tacit community rules, for which feng shui thinking provides cosmological backing. Families building too big, too close or too dominant, especially in a southerly direction, may be faced with accusation of blocking the *qi* for other families. At the same time, however, once certain households move ahead and consolidate their position, the same principles can turn into a powerful cosmological backing to social inequality. Feng shui is itself a motivating force for building new houses: many people appear to think that other families building bigger houses will threaten their own life if they do not follow suit.

In the feng shui mode of thought, the flow of *qi* is influenced by all natural bodies and by human constructions. Moreover, the relation between one's own house and other buildings and constructions in the vicinity has a major impact on the common feng shui situation, since a larger house may catch more of the common *qi* at the expense of others.

As a parallel to material wealth, which comes from a limited source, *qi* is also regarded as a resource that can only be tapped at the expense of other people's share. But while access to material wealth is restricted by human politics, *qi* flows freely for everyone to catch and with considerably more room for manipulation. Material wealth and *qi* are two separate things, but people naturally want both. Yet they serve as each other's preconditions: if somebody has good *qi*, material wealth and a good life should come easy; and it works the other way around: if people get wealthy, they will immediately strive to get good *qi* in order to preserve their new-found wealth.

These are also part of the considerations behind the 'modern' type of family house. They are powerful symbols of the new wealth in many rural areas, immediately displayed to the local community. The desire to have a new and bigger home is shared by everybody, sometimes amounting to public hysteria. New wealth has flown to rural areas in the coastal areas and around cities, but for the poorer segments of the farming population who have no ability to make extra money on sidelines or wage labour, the goal can only be reached by pruning the common budget. The collective craze has literally made entire village populations tighten their belts to acquire this new symbol of family success and material affluence. Cutting down the home consumption of meat and selling the surplus on the market is one common solution. Countless families in the poorer areas are putting their health at risk when they are reluctant to spend medical expenses in the long haul of saving up, particularly because a number of diseases are still prevalent and public health service is inadequate.

A common feature of modern China is that villages are breaking up, and feng shui often plays a great part in this. Anywhere within the village confines, a new house towering above others is bound to influence other people's feng shui. Thus, when people living in crammed old villages want to build new and bigger houses, they must move to the village outskirts. Local governments usually allocate land for such undertakings, not least to avoid complaints and potential unrest; many local areas have known feng shui conflicts turning into physical violence.

It is important to distinguish between various types of village communities in China, however, since they rest on different schools of feng shui and have evolved differently over the last several decades. In those areas with a predominant forms school, the houses in the old villages are not placed according to a set pattern, but according to the individual features of that particular site, including smaller hills, rocks, vegetation and other constructions. The main entrance may deviate considerably from due south, giving much wider span for the feng shui specialist to orient the building towards wide spaces and openings between houses. These types of villages have now grown out of their original confines, scattering over a much larger area. They tend to rest on individual choices of type and size of house, giving them a diverse and casual appearance. Similarly, conflicts over feng shui matters are mostly individualized and tend to be solved in private, for instance by paying monetary compensation.

Many regions of particularly east and south China are politically and socially very complex, influenced by a large number of lineage or single-surname villages (*shicun*), to some extent functioning as independent polities. In each of them, one surname group has dominated village life entirely, either on a lineage basis when recognizing common descent from a given ancestor or on the basis of a number of large families with a common surname without clear notions of their inter-relation. Some villages have two or three surname groups, usually with each one dominating a section of the village. All villages used to have large ancestor halls and shrines, where tablets and lineage records were kept, until the new regime either demolished them or forced their conversion into other uses in the 1950s and 1960s. In both south and southeast China, these institutions are now being revived. Here, kinship organization in the villages has tied individuals together in a much closer texture of mutual obligations, and has accounted for attention to feng shui on a much larger scale, potentially involving more people and frequently effecting conflicts to be played out in public.

Stricter rules and less scope for interpretation will also result in greater competition among households, particularly when adhering to the compass school of feng shui. As every house wants to have its entrance facing the life-giving sun to the south, the layout of villages tends to be fixed and standard. Narrow lanes run east–west between several rows of houses, so that the entrances of the houses on one side of the lane face the backs of the houses on the other side. If all houses were of the same size and nobody wanted to build bigger, harmony could be perpetuated. This is not the case, however. In order to regulate the size of houses so that the *qi* is equally distributed and no household is left in the shade, a strict rule has been effective since 'ancient times', according to the villagers. It states that: 'East overlooks West and North overlooks South'. This implies that people may build bigger and higher towards the north and the east within the village, but never the other way round since this would cause feng shui to be blocked for those households behind. With reference to the historical development of feng shui, one may question the perseverance of this rule, but it has been effective long enough to regulate all existing structures in the villages. As will be shown in Chapter 6, it is also commonly referred to by feng shui specialists in the south-Chinese cities.

In general terms, the designs contained in the 'directions' school of feng shui are more orderly and predictable, allowing for less improvisation on the part of the geomancer. Since the directions of the compass are a primary concern when building a house, and the layout of rooms likewise follow a distinct pattern, the basic principles of feng shui are known to everyone. Thus it may be considered safe to build on a site already approved by a geomancer one or two generations ago, if only the basic layout and directions of the old house are respected. 'East over West and North over South' is zealously guarded and measured out in inches. In the old villages, where most houses have attached gables, the lines of the walls and roofs of houses along one lane will either be perfectly flush or will be broken to allow for slightly bigger houses towards the east. The logical consequences are, of course, that villages must either have flush lines or be quite small, since houses cannot vary indefinitely. In reality, the villages are mostly quite small, usually with two to five rows of houses and with a few to ten houses in each row. Political leadership in the individual villages may have determined that lines must be flush at least in some lanes to avoid competition and struggle, while in others, each lane will have its own shape with sharp edges and rooftops breaking the line towards the east. To allow for variation in household size according to the number of children and domestic cycles in general, the buying and selling of houses or sections of houses is common; a large family may be seen to own two houses either adjoined or separated by a lane, while a small household may occupy only a single room in a house.

Now that an increasing number of people want to build new houses, the old rule is felt like a straightjacket. It still stands, however, and struggle is commonplace when people attempt to manipulate the lines of the old houses or simply build bigger in the hope that neighbours will not respond. The result is that the traditional village layout tends to break up, since nearly every second family moves to another location when building a new house in order to build bigger and avoid complaints. In the modernizing villages along the main roads almost all new houses are built individually and spread out from the old village centres, since hardly anyone would be content with a new brick-built house the size of a traditional mud-built one.

It is the duty of the local administrations to regulate these matters, so that things do not get out of hand. Local governments tend to support 'tradition' to avoid public turmoil, since conflicts easily escalate, as in one particular case described below. In the villages where a lineage or a single surname group prevails, local organization and informal leadership will usually assure reconciliation when conflicts arise, but in the villages that accommodate competing surname groups, matters are more complicated. These are common occurrences, which may also involve geomancers. For instance, in a Jiangsu village, two neighbouring families belonging to different surname groups got into a row when one of them built a new house slightly exceeding the lines of their neighbours'. The house-builders argued that the doorway and rooftop of the neighbouring house had already broken the lines, so feng shui was not disturbed. By the intervention of the village leader, it was agreed that a geomancer should be consulted to settle the matter. Each family invited their own geomancer, however, and, as could be expected, the geomancers proved loyal to their clients and ruled contradictorily. A third geomancer was called in from another district, paid jointly by the two families, but when he heard that he had to rule against one of his own kind, he hushed away and the two families were back to square one. Finally, when the entire village was involved through lines of kinship and loyalty, it was agreed that the house-builders should pay a moderate sum of money as compensation to their neighbours.

Another case was reported by a local official in Jiangsu. In 1978, two neighbouring families named Feng and Luo, dragon and tiger respectively, started building new houses simultaneously. Since the two families' old houses had been exactly the same size, it was only natural that the new houses should also match. However, both families wanted their new houses a bit bigger than the old ones, and they agreed upon where to put the marking sticks in the ground, outlining the layout of the houses. Then the tiger family started digging the earth and putting down base stones, but simultaneously moving the marking sticks beyond the original layout. The dragon family was outraged; immediately they called in relatives 'from all four directions' to have a meeting. The crowd soon agreed to pull out the sticks and remove the base stones, which they did. The tiger family knew what was coming and had also sent for their relatives from all four directions. As soon as the tiger family's relatives arrived and saw what was going on, fighting broke out. They fought 'young against young, old against old, women against women', using sticks as well as odd farm-implements, and there was terrible bloodshed. The whole village was terrified at the escalation of events and called for a local official, Mr Chen. When he arrived, wounded and bleeding people were lying everywhere. Since there was no law that could resolve the matter, he used entirely traditional means. He commanded that the white tiger respect the green dragon, and that the family refrain from building higher or bigger than their neighbours. The whole village stood behind this command, so the tiger family withdrew their marking sticks and built exactly the same size as the dragon family.

In economic developing areas all over China, however, old villages are swept away by new industrial and urban development. Today, traditional villages tend only to survive in the poorest regions, where little industrial and urban development takes place. The most common picture is a rapid disintegration of village communities. This at the same time means the fragmentation of traditional kinship organization and, with that, many aspects of Chinese popular religious life: they lose ground to modernity, are being divided into various fragmented customs and tend to be individualized, not finding expression in public life. Yet, in a matter of time after transferring to a modern lifestyle, the human yearning for alternative reflection and explanation will produce renewed attention to old philosophies. As previously seen in overseas Chinese communities, and today in Chinese cities, feng shui in particular finds reinterpretation and unfolds in a new context, while a new batch of specialists will establish themselves.

FENG SHUI FOR BURIAL

After how to build for the living (*yang* dwellings, *yangzhai*), how to build for the dead (*yin* dwellings, *yinzhai*) remains the second most important strand of feng shui thinking. Historically, it may have had greater significance, pointing to the *Book of Burial* as one of the fundamental classics on feng shui. This classic originates from a period when official annals frequently refer to the potential of auspicious graves to produce emperors, kings and ministers. In the popular tradition, the ways of historical royal courts are adopted both symbolically and literally as a means to reap maximum benefit from buried family members into the life and careers of their descendants. Ancestor worship is practised as an exchange in the same way that exchanges take place among the living members of a family: if the ancestors are buried properly and looked after well in rituals and festivals, their spirits will bestow good fortune on their descendants.

Being a fundamental and terminal life-cycle ritual, marking the passing of a generation and transfer of responsibility to the next, burial is framed in a series of observances and in rich local culture. Feng shui specialists are commonly involved in several stages of it. Central to the geomancer's work is to locate the most auspicious site for the tomb, and in many cases the search begins long before the person has deceased, perhaps at their own initiative (see Fig. 3.2). The common principles for grave siting differ from

Fig 3.2 Example of a family grave in Anhui, China. Very often in rural areas, graves are prepared before the actual death of their inhabitants, only to be sealed after the final placement of the dead bodies or urns. Photograph by Ole Bruun.

those of house siting in several ways. Graves are, where possible, placed on higher ground facing open space, ideally with a view to misty mountains in the horizon. They must have solid backing behind and representations of the dragon and tiger on either side. Close flanking on the sides are preferred so as to form an 'armchair' position with good protection and support. Vegetation such as bushes and small tress may be used behind graves, but never in front. As a consequence, in hills dotted with many graves, the compromise is usually no high growth at all. On flat land, however, the common principle is a small mound, usually in a corner of a field or in places with some wild growth, such as behind houses.

Both Chinese and western literature is rife with references to family conflicts over the siting of graves, for example several brothers may compete over the best possible location of the grave according to its influence on their own households (Freedman 1969; de Groot 1897), indicating that honouring the dead may be less important than reaping the benefits from its influence. One such story tells of four brothers, of which two lived in a clan village and two outside. The brothers in the village decided to build a joint grave for their parents without consulting the remaining two brothers. The latter heard of it and arranged to steal their mother's bone pot. Thus the mother and father were buried separately. After a year, things began to go wrong for several of the brothers, experiencing sickness, death of domestic animals and so forth. In the common interpretation, the deceased couple was unhappy with living in separate dwellings and so punished those responsible (Ahern 1973: 187).

Feng shui specialists are also consulted for burial preparations, including the calculation of the right moment to put the body or urn in the ground according to astrological data and the projections of the traditional calendar. Preparations are meticulous and funeral processions lavish, usually involving the entire hamlet and relatives from outside. They begin in the early morning hours, well-advised by the geomancer so that, in the case of proper burial, the coffin may be taken to the tomb without official interference. Sometimes the coffin is even carried to its resting place before the procession starts. First to appear in the procession is a man with a basket, running ahead while generously spreading 'road money' (*malu qian*) – elongated sheets of plain paper – to appease the spirits and open the road for easy passage of the procession. Then follow a number of people carrying gifts and expressions of honour to the deceased, including paper wreaths and garments. Next may follow carriers of large paper constructions, for instance models of houses and automobiles, which will be burned and transposed to the world beyond to make life comfortable for the deceased. Finally come four people carrying either the coffin or a sedan chair with the urn, and after them follow the rest of the procession, easily numbering fifty to a hundred people. In recent years, with diminishing public interference with religious life, some funeral processions have developed to include thousands of people and the active involvement of local temples, broad kinship networks extending overseas and newly rebuilt ancestor halls in villages and towns.

Practically all rural households preserve family graves, either on their own contracted farmland or in the nearby hills. For decades, family graves were hidden or restricted to inconspicuous plots in vegetable gardens or insignificant corners of fields. Contrary to the argument raised by the government that graves infringe upon farmland, setting aside a few square metres for family graves rarely strains the budget, and it is not even remotely comparable to the burdens placed upon the peasants by the regime (in the form of taxes and grain quotas) at any time. After the 1980s, grave construction has followed the development in *yang* dwellings, with increasing demands on family savings. Still, graves in the Chinese interior tend to be quite humble in comparison with those in Guangdong and Fujian, but newly established graves or old restored ones are growing rapidly in size and grandeur in those areas with new-found wealth. In recent decades, people have searched for old family graves that were demolished during the Cultural Revolution, in order to re-erect them or to build new, larger graves for the entire family line. Some recent ones consist of a small, half-rounded brick wall protruding from a hillside, or are entirely built up in concrete as coffin-length arched chambers sealed up at both ends. These constructions are plainly meant for burying the dead body without cremation, although unlawful, but they tend to be hidden on private plots with lush vegetation.

Many different burial customs and grave styles are seen across China, depending on local culture as much as topography and population density. The most common form on flat farmland is, as already noted, a small mound of earth, marked with sticks, rocks or a stone slab. In hilly areas, the simplest graves are just holes dug horizontally into a hill in a north–south direction and sometimes covered with a stone. Where people can afford it, they tend now to use large engraved slabs of flagstone on the tombs, and small trees may be planted around the back where possible.

Previously, tombs built for the elite were either bigger earth mounds or stone constructions in the mountain areas with historical traditions for auspicious grave siting. Under the Guomindang rule, for instance, powerful generals had their voluminous graves built on hillsides near shrines and temples. Today, the rich and powerful may spend fortunes on buying sites in famous mountains and equip them with huge stone constructions, either private designs or ready-made traditional horseshoe designs, advertised on the internet by manufacturers in the southeast.

Since 1978, the Chinese authorities have enforced cremation in order to save farmland from the millions of small mounds that dot the fields, hillsides or spaces set aside for village graveyards. Cremation is against Chinese tradition and was, behind the rationalistic motives, part of a package of measures against rural 'superstition'. Cremation has been adopted as the common practice in many rural communities, but certainly not all. In most areas, the public authorities will control the dead being cremated. It still seems to be the case that when people have a real choice, they prefer proper burial. Corruption thrives in China, and this field is no exception. Instances of people bribing local officials to look the other way when traditional burials are taking place, or local authorities simply demanding a standard fee for circumventing the law, may be found all over China. So what was originally intended as a penalty to make people obey the law is now regarded as a levy by both parties involved. Even if people want to make the burial a public event and invite the whole village for the ritual, this levy is just an expense to be reckoned with along with the coffin, the entertainment of the guests and maybe professional mourners and musicians. Since convention prescribes that the coffin is placed in the grave pointing towards the centre of the hill, only a small opening in the hillside is required, and when the grave is closed it will be impossible to determine whether it contains an urn or a coffin. Usually, the local authority does not interfere with the placement of graves as long as only inconspicuous sites on privately contracted land are chosen.

Creativity may be great to avoid cremation. For instance, a recent media-reported case involving murder caused horror across China. Someone described as a 'sorcerer' (presumably a feng shui man) was detained by police for killing ten innocent people in his home town and selling their bodies to bereaved families to cremate instead of their loved ones, who were secretly buried. The man had strangled or poisoned the victims in his home next to a temple and sold the bodies for several thousand yuan apiece (*China Daily*, 20 February 2006).

OTHER COMMON APPLICATIONS

Apart from the conventional uses of feng shui for positioning houses and graves, feng shui specialists are used for a great number of purposes. They are either called upon in their own homes or 'invited' to inspect the client's home to solve a specific problem.

Specialists are often required to divine lucky or proper dates for funerals, weddings, travelling, building and so forth, for which they use a combination of the traditional lunar calendar and the individual's data relating to astrology. In this sense they compete with other religious specialists – such as Buddhist and Daoist monks – offering the same services. Within the confines of villages and towns, however, feng shui specialists traditionally are respected men with some measure of literary skills (often interpreted as mediating between the elite and the masses, or bringing the ways of the royal court and the elite to the people), to whom people can turn with any problem or grievance. It goes without saying that the successful specialist builds a tremendous knowledge of each household, which may be used professionally, such as to mediate conflicts.

The specialists usually receive their clients at home, using the common main room, which in the traditional rural dwelling is a space where people may enter without much formality. Some have small shops or even offices in connection with their homes, but it is customary for rural feng shui specialists to avoid any grandeur.

From historical times, Chinese feng shui men have developed their own line of specialities, which were guarded like trade secrets in their families and passed on from master to apprentice, ideally from father to son. This is quite similar to a range of other professions in traditional China, from simple artisans to medical doctors, who all guarded their knowledge against competitors and sought to pass it on within their own families. Feng shui specializations may include building, burying, writing lucky couplets (*duilian*), making charms (*fu*), chanting for the sick, communicating with spirits, spirit possession, searching for 'departed souls' (*hanhun*) in relation to disease, finding people and lost property, solving marriage problems, giving advice on how to achieve pregnancy with the outcome of having a son, offering advice on business matters and so forth.

There is really no limit to the matters for which people seek feng shui-related advice, arising from the everyday life of ordinary people. What follows are some examples of matters that were raised when I spent time in the houses of rural feng shui men: a woman complains of her husband's drinking habits and asks for advice; a young woman asks for advice on how to increase the possibility of a giving birth to a boy; a man complains of a series of traffic accidents while driving his new motorcar and asks why so many people want to strike him; a mother enquires about a lucky day for her son's marriage; a young mother brings in her baby daughter for inspection; a man asks for a lucky day for a business transaction; and several people invite the specialist to inspect their homes for various reasons. The most sought-after specialists are busy all day.

As noted above, by means of his intense local knowledge the specialist may act as a counsellor on affairs other than cosmological ones. For instance, in Jiangsu I witnessed a couple seeking advice on how to locate their fourteen-year-old daughter, who had run away from home. The specialist already knew that the parents were themselves to blame, however, as for several years they had pressed her to study hard and score good marks so she could enter university. They had very little education themselves and wanted her to do better than them 'for the sake of the whole family'. Many kids her age are pressed so hard that they consider taking their own lives, and in this particular case everyone knew her situation. The specialist simply advised the concerned parents to rest their souls and wait for her to come back, while arranging to check her astrological data for finding a suitable career.

Feng shui specialists are called out to solve all sorts of problems in the household, following the conventional expression: 'inviting a feng shui master to see feng shui' (*Qing feng shui xiansheng kan feng shui*). It should be pointed out that it is mostly women who invite specialists on behalf of their households, while, contrarily, the specialists are exclusively men. (Chinese women acting as feng shui specialists are unheard of in history and in present rural areas. However, it has recently emerged as an exclusively urban phenomenon.) It is a common saying that 'only the women believe in feng shui', while the men tend to be more sceptical, but when it comes to building houses, both sexes will support the invitation of a specialist.

Today, a common task is 'seeing' and 'amending' feng shui in households that suffer from poor health, disease and mental disorders or premature deaths. During my own fieldwork in Sichuan and Jiangsu, they accounted for nearly two-thirds of the total number of incidents where geomancers were sent for. Illness – affecting either individuals or entire households – is a common threat to people's happiness (*fu*). The most prevalent under-standing of illness in Chinese rural areas is neither traditional, nor modern, but a conglomerate of reasoning involving both plain physiological causes, metaphysical, non-personal causes and spiritual agencies, including ances-tors. Such co-existing aetiologies, or 'multi-causality', is also reflected more generally in Chinese medicine. In the popular tradition, however, people can never be sure whether a stomach ache is due to food poisoning, to malicious *qi* ruining one's feng shui, or to spirits pressing some message through. To the western observer, brought up with an expectation that a given phenomenon must be explicable along a single strand of reasoning to avoid anomaly, this may seem confusing. Yet a closer probe into pri-vate lives may reveal that also a great many westerners contemplate several possible causes of life-threatening diseases, including astrology, fate and own fault. In the Chinese context, these co-existing interpretations rather belong to explanatory domains within a single universe of great complexity. It is still very common that disease is understood not in terms of a singular cause but in relation to several 'possible' causes that should be addressed individually.

Obviously, feng shui developed in an environment of limited medical capability and small economic resources. Still, today, Chinese rural areas are plagued by a range of very serious health problems, which people may seek remedies for by consulting feng shui specialists. Here follow some stories as told by rural people themselves:

Some time ago my daughter got ill. She had a terrible pain in the left side of her stomach. On advice I went to Yinyang Master Fu, who is a geomancer specialized in driving out evil spirits. He poured water into a bowl (shengshui) and then stirred it slowly with his finger. Then he said, 'You have pulled out a beam from the roof of your house, your ancestors are very unhappy about it. You have to put in back in place and honour them properly.' I remembered that shortly before my daughter got sick I had pulled out one of the sticks supporting the thatched roof, because it had become loose and was sticking out so I was continually bumping my head into it. I went into town and bought plenty of wine, food, candles, incense and strings of coloured paper. When I came back the whole family, except my daughter, gathered to honour and pray to our forefathers to make my daughter well again. Soon after my daughter recovered. She was also taken to the hospital and got some medicine ...

My sister contracted some gynaecological problems and went to hospital many times. But the drugs she got did not help her. Then she invited a yinyang specialist to her house. He inspected it and found that a large tree stood right in front of the entrance. He told the family to cut it down. They did so and my sister soon recovered. (Both from Bruun 2003: 209)

Second in importance is another broad category of 'misfortune', including miscellaneous kinds of failure, mishap and lack of prosperity. Another story:

In the village of Woji people had felt unhappy for many years. The village was not prospering and there was much illness, many miscarriages, and a general uncomfortable feeling. At a public meeting the inhabitants decided to invite a specialist to inspect the feng shui of their village. Upon his arrival he started walking around the village for a very long time, just walking and walking without saying anything. Finally he told the villagers that the water in the village pond was still, which means very bad feng shui ... He told them to connect it to a nearby stream in order to increase the water flow and bring fortune to the village: 'After that was done people felt much better and more confident. Everybody could work much harder to improve their lives and the village finally prospered', a villager commented. (Bruun 2003: 204)

Another rapidly developing concern relates specifically to prosperity – that is, monetary affairs and business. It may be stated as a universal Chinese conviction that a good life has material satisfaction as a precondition – all positioning of houses and graves refer to this fundamental concern. Yet popular cosmology, moulded through centuries of hardship and distress, tends to indicate the confines of the Chinese world and the scarcity of its resources. Population pressure, hunger, political turmoil and social disintegration have been the common experience of passing generations, transmitted in the form of common appreciations of what to share and what to hoard. Feng shui thinking contains a deeply ingrained belief that one man's gain is another man's loss, a fact that boundless ancient and modern literature, proverbs, expressions and terms indicate. For these reasons, Chinese feng shui cannot be viewed separately from competition between households and individuals: it is in fact at the centre of this. Feng shui thinking elaborates on this theme and gives cosmological credence to individual pursuits of wealth as contrasted to communal enterprise. There is a close parallel between the flow of *qi* and the flow of wealth. A leading notion is the interconnectedness of the social and physical environments, commonly understood as the general arena where *qi* flows and creates. This world of mutually interacting human and natural agencies can be neither expanded nor deepened, and it contains a given pool of resources. From a personal standpoint, it may be further exploited, however, but the anthropocentric outlook does not differentiate between exploitation in the natural and the social worlds. In feng shui thinking, everyone is expected to care for his own household and optimise its potentials, while convention sets the rules for interhousehold competition.

But convention alone does not impede differentiation. When people build bigger houses in the village, for instance, and build far bigger than they need, in a common sense they appear to show off their wealth and indicate their social superiority. By contrast, in feng shui terminology, which is equally applicable, they build bigger to catch more of the fortune-bringing *qi* to improve all aspects of the good life. Inside the confines of villages and towns, where most people live, they inevitably do so at the expense of other people's *qi*. The two explanations above are clearly synonymous, but the former tends to be socially contemptuous in any respect, while the latter has cosmological backing and therefore can be posed as morally neutral. Incidents relating to accusations of 'broken' or 'stolen' feng shui are common all over China, seen in the smallest villages as much as in the largest commercial centres, described in Chapter 6. Examples of village skirmishes, even some evolving into bloodshed, were given earlier in this chapter.

Fatal illness and the occurrence of death are common stamps of horror and danger that feng shui masters are asked to address. In the Chinese folk tradition, longevity is invariably pursued, the causes of early deaths are looked into, burial arrangements are made, precautions are taken for the descendants and so forth, leaving little room for fatalism. Contrary to Chinese state ideology, which has customarily placed the strongest emphasis on a collective spirit as the basis for an orderly society and demanded that the individual submit himself to society's grand scheme and work for its common good, feng shui rather stands out as a celebration of the self. It depicts an anthropocentric universe in which everyone may place himself at its centre. Although it lays out rules for the competition for the life-giving *qi* in the local community, it would hardly recommend making sacrifices for others. Geomancers take great pride in having lifted their clients to wealth and power, while the rich feng shui allegories in Chinese literature provide powerful backing for the idea that humans inherently strive for ever higher eminence with only the position of emperor as the upper limit.

Feng shui ideology may therefore be seen to mobilize the powers of mind and body, and not least to suppress bonds, obligations and communitarian demands from an innately oppressive society. It stands for longevity (*shou*), activism until old age and rejection of fatalism, since any human condition may be amended. Once individuals and families in the local community rise to wealth and power, few restraining devices are found in feng shui ideology – on the contrary, it provides cosmological backing to inequality.

All significant human values are firmly placed in a this-worldly context, and human satisfaction is pursued unwaveringly, preferably enjoyed through a long life. Accordingly, feng shui thought really cares little about the afterlife, except for making the best of the departed. Ancestor worship is a different tradition, which feng shui cosmology may draw on, but the practice of ancestor worship is not an aim in itself, since the wellbeing of the ancestors may essentially be unimportant. It is only when the dissatisfaction of the dead has a direct bearing on the life course of the living that feng shui advises action to be taken. An example of such is as follows:

A family in Baoting buried a deceased family member in the public graveyard on the mountain behind the village. After the burial, however, the family's dog started digging in the grave. It went out there every day and nothing could keep it back. It was digging and scraping its snoot in the soil like mad until blood was pouring from its head. Then the family went to see Yinyang Master Wang, who had selected the grave, to ask his advice. He looked in his calendar and found that the direction of the grave was contradicting the mourning periods (*fan qi*, periods of seven days). He calculated a certain day according to the deceased's birth day and asked them to go out on this particular day and put sticks on the grave. On the calculated day they went out and did what they were told, and immediately the dog stopped digging in the grave. (Bruun 2003: 222)

A last category of common feng shui uses concerns the positive continuation of the family line – that is, procreation, education and, if possible, social ascendance in the next generation. In China, the birth control programmes installed after 1980 were critical in preventing the new wealth from being swallowed up by masses of helpless people. Obviously, for a population that attaches such overwhelming importance to family values, the prospect of a broken family line may be devastating. A similar concern is the schooling and education of young people, mostly being without opportunities in their home areas. A few stories may emphasize their significance for rural people:

A woman from a neighbouring village once came to *Fengshui* Master Li for advice. She had been married for nine years but still had not given birth to a child. Her husband, who was an army officer in Beijing, scolded her every time he came home for not being with child. Once he got so mad that he even tried to kill her, but other villagers interfered and saved the poor woman. She was so depressed that she did not know what to do and eventually went to Mr Li. He told her that he was not sure if he could help her, but that he would try. He checked the family grave sites and the birth dates of the man and wife. He found that the direction of the former household head's grave did not harmonize with their birth dates, and asked them to change the direction of that grave. They did so – and after only one year the woman bore her husband a son. After some time, another local woman, having heard about the sudden good fortune of the first, also came to seek advice. She had been married for six years and was still childless. Li told her that maybe he had only been lucky with his cure last time. Anyway, he found that also in her case a family grave had to be changed, and just a year later the woman gave birth to a boy. Yet another woman came, and after just three years she had two boys.

A new-rich family in Chendi village were about to send their son to university. At the same time the family were nurturing plans of building a new house for themselves. To show off both their wealth and the higher status they had attained now that their son was going to university, they intended to build both higher and bigger than the house to the west of them in the alley. The walls and roofs of the two old houses were exactly flush, however. The neighbouring family protested viciously against the plans and demanded that the lines of the new house did not deviate a single inch from the previous lines. After endless quarrels gradually involving the entire village, the wealthy family finally had to obey conventions and build so that lines were flush. At the same time the family had applied for their son's admission to one of the national key universities, but shortly after the new house was completed – so they said – they were informed that he could only be admitted to a mediocre university. The family was convinced that this was due to the average size of their new house and they continuously complained to their fellow villagers. (both from Bruun 2003: 223–6)

FENG SHUI AND BELIEF

The universal Chinese respect for ritual and convention should not be misread as blind conservatism or simple fatalism. Chinese popular religion has never been an impediment for material pursuits, and Chinese farmers throughout the historical period, the period in which feng shui rose, also developed highly sophisticated land-use patterns to optimise agricultural production, built water tanks and irrigation canals, cleared forests and levelled out hills to open new land. Feng shui concerns, such as placing houses and graves in auspicious ways, always followed farming activities, but they never hindered the progressive exploitation of the natural environment. In fact, as will be discussed in Chapter 8, in the Chinese context, feng shui beliefs never worked for conservation in the modern sense.

Yet it may be said that there is a built-in dialectic between the way of the cosmos (*tianming*), which cannot be changed, and human intent, which maximizes own benefits by means of divination. Hence both activism and fatalism have their place in popular religion.

It is a common observation that there is only a vague link between religious creed and the individual in China, to the effect that Chinese religion is not a question of belief, such as in the monotheistic religions of Christianity and Islam. In Chinese classical literature, Buddhist and Daoist monks frequently appear side by side, and in the popular tradition they may be used for interchanging purposes, depending on which specialist is available and the denomination of the local temples. For the vast majority of rural people, religious life and experience has not been limited by creed: there was really no contradiction in honouring all the Three Great Learnings, Confucianism, Buddhism and Daoism. These were the customary religions acknowledged by the Chinese state.

Can we at all characterize feng shui as part of Chinese popular religion? Perhaps the problem is not feng shui but the term 'popular religion' itself. We usually see as the core of religion a worship of superhuman beings such as gods, spirits and ancestors. Chinese popular religion, on the contrary, has no distinction between personal and impersonal matters of veneration, including, for instance, gods, sun, Heaven and the Five Elements. Instead of popular religion, we may well use the more neutral term 'popular cosmology'. Rural people tend not to differentiate purely cosmological thought referring to impersonal forces from religious creeds involving actual worship of gods and deities. Chinese feng shui, in its original setting, likewise contains no distinction between pure physical forces – such as represented by *yin-yang* and *qi* – and those forces deriving from the will of beings in the form of gods, ghosts and ancestors. They have been equally significant throughout the history of Chinese divination.

Chinese feng shui masters continue this long tradition by taking both into account, insisting on a comprehensive interpretation of the feng shui situation, while refusing any distinction between personal and impersonal factors, or between physical, social and psychological domains. Feng shui surely belongs to the active side of the equation more than professing fatalism: there are always remedies for both human and cosmological ills, and the feng shui situation may be considerably improved in nearly all circumstances.

Nineteenth- and early twentieth-century western missionaries were often bewildered by the mind-sets of the Chinese they attempted to convert, since these willingly accepted a new god but refused to give up old ones or ancestor worship. Belief is commonly associated with concepts of truth, faith, evidence, exclusiveness and so forth, all of which tend to have different meanings in China. We may say that belief in 'something' refers to an agent external to the human mind, a separation of human and external nature, or to an agent external to mundane life, thus belonging to a transcendental level. Chinese cosmology, on the contrary, tends to have an immanent order, meaning that all beings and forces are of a common kind. As a consequence, the distinction between human and external nature, as well as between human and non-human agency, is more plastic.

For these reasons, and because feng shui contains purely ritualized elements, people may widely use feng shui for building, burying and multiple other purposes without actively 'believing' in its direct effects. Some argue that Chinese culture is strongly ritualistic in the sense that properly performed rituals are essential in distinguishing between insiders and outsiders (Watson and Rawski 1988: 4). As a consequence, performance of rituals takes precedence over beliefs. Another way of putting it is that Chinese religion in general is experiential more than a matter of faith (Paper 1994: 81), meaning that the total experience of ritual and social life combined is what matters, rather than the individual elements in each domain.

Even though there tends to be no belief in a single, transcendental authority, there is still adherence to general patterns of order. Acceptance of the authority contained in orthodoxy and archaic rites is also acceptance of the idea of an ordered universe (Feuchtwang 1992: 9). A key characteristic of Chinese civilization is the conception of an organic universe, bound together by resonance and synchronicity and spontaneously arisen without external will or power.

When cosmic resonance takes priority over autonomous agency, every act of interference in the world will depend on how it is reflected in the grander order of things. In real life, this means that nobody 'believes' that feng shui alone will do the trick. This may be captured in a series

Fig 3.3 A client seeking advice from feng shui Master Wang. Jiangsu, China. Photograph
by Ole Bruun.

of common statements: 'you need good *qi* to build a happy family and to
become wealthy'; 'in order to have good fortune you need to work hard'; 'if
malicious *qi* flows into your house, mishaps will occur'; 'you can influence
your fortune by improving the flow of *qi* around your house'; 'you must
honour your forefathers and pay attention to their graves, or something
bad may happen'.

It is ingrained in Chinese religious life that cosmological and spiritual
forces must be balanced with the active interference of humans – and both
must be taken into account at any time. Basic knowledge is widespread,
such as that provided in the traditional almanac, but to judge exactly how
they impinge on another is not considered a matter for amateurs. It takes
a professional to have the sufficient knowledge of each domain, to know
the cosmological theory from the old books and to gather the necessary
experience for applying it all to a specific case; to know all the subtle
connections and to master the refined tuning to make all elements work
harmoniously together take a feng shui specialist (see Fig. 3.3). Hence it
may be said that the specialist both maintains a local tradition of knowledge
and, at the same time, monopolizes its interpretation.

The human factors imply that a common scepticism prevails, contradict-ing the alleged rule of superstitious beliefs. Chinese peasants are rational people who do their utmost to squeeze a meagre existence out of their plots, and travel long distances to sell their produce at urban markets where prices are higher; but at the same time they may honour their fore-fathers with increasing vigour at the Festival of the Dead (*Qingming jie*) if market prices drop. They employ modern farming methods with chemical fertilizers and pesticides to control production and increase yields, but will call in a geomancer if a sudden pest hits their crops or if their domestic animals inexplicably die from disease. They may spend considerable funds to send a son to town for secondary schooling, with a curriculum strictly controlled by the Chinese state, but if he fails his exams they may call in a geomancer to have their house checked. Young people may ridicule the superstitious practices of elder generations, but at their own weddings they will take great care to have their birth dates and wedding dates calculated and matched by a village diviner, and they may return to him if they do not fare well in matrimony. If seriously ill, people will see a doctor if they can afford to, but at the same time they will arrange for a geomancer to check their house and their ancestors' graves, or their family may call in a spirit medium to chant through the night at their bedside. These are not attributive to positive beliefs, but rather to a general acceptance of the wide range of cosmological resonance in people's everyday lives, such as given by the saying: 'Though fortune is governed by the Heavens, your fate is still in your own hands.'

It is for the reasons above that Chinese folk literature abounds with references to geomancers: they are common figures in family dramas and accounts of competition for wealth and power, often noted for playing with people's frustration when they are caught between the geomancer's potentially supernatural powers and his cheating character. The common ambivalence towards divination in general and its practitioners in particular is vividly expressed in Chinese literature, drama and proverbs. Diviners are assigned both fearsome powers and the disposition of charlatans. Many proverbs encapsulate feng shui in irony or paradox, such as: 'The fortune-teller dies in the prime of his life; the feng shui master has no burying ground'; or: 'If you invite those who inspect houses and graves, you may as well move your dwelling altogether.' Another one goes: 'He who has split firewood for three years is fit to inspect grave yards' (A. Smith 1902: 318–19). A folk story tells of a dead geomancer who punishes a little boy for falling into his coffin, but is himself punished by superior spirits and his bones eaten by a dog (Eberhard 1967: 31).

FENG SHUI AND OTHER STRANDS OF POPULAR DIVINATION

A range of divinatory traditions have been practised in China and remain in use this day, although some are more prominent than others (for traditional forms, see, for instance, Needham 1962, Chapter 14). It may be relevant to distinguish between sooth-saying and divination for a start, the former being practised in villages, at markets and fairs, in front of temples and in the streets, mostly at a simple level such as by itinerants and vagabonds. Common sooth-saying may draw on some of the established forms of divination, however, such as reading by hand, ear or face, or refer to the *Yi jing*.

The more established forms of popular divination, of which feng shui is part, often interact with one another and borrow elements. Justus Doolittle in 1865, for instance, distinguished between six different forms:

(1) *'By using the eight honorary characters which denote the year, month, day, and hour of one's birth'*. This is the most popular form, with constant references to the Five Elements and Twelve Animals (obviously astrology). This is often practised by blind people.

(2) *'By an inspection of the physiognomy'*. These diviners inspect eyes, eye-brows, nose, mouth, ears, cheek-bones, temples, lips, teeth, whiskers, fingers, hand and skin for a range of expressions, character traits and symbols. The diviners may decide the good or bad character of a man as well as his life course and fortune.

(3) *'By means of a bird and slips of paper'*. Like the others above, these are itinerants; they travel with a rattle to make peculiar sounds and draw attention. They carry a bird cage and sixty-four slips of paper, each with a figure of a god, beast or person and a small verse. The bird is let out and picks one slip for a given customer, which is then interpreted.

(4) *'By the dissection of the written character'*. These diviners carry a small box that contains a number of small sheets of paper folded up, each having one written character. The customer takes two sheets, the characters of which are then interpreted, both as a whole and in their individual strokes.

(5) *'By use of the tortoise shell and three ancient cash'*. This is most often practised in small shops, where customers may have their fortunes ascertained. The cash are put into a tortoise shell, which is shaken in front of a picture of the god presiding over this form of divination. The cash are then turned out onto a plate and it is observed which are heads and tails. This is repeated three times, on the basis of which one

of the eight diagrams of the *bagua* is constructed (this is most probably *Yi jing* divination, still practised today).

(6) *'By an inspection of the earth and scenery, in order to fix upon a fortunate burial site'*. This is obviously feng shui, which Doolittle terms 'the dearest and most tedious' (Doolittle 1865: 331–9).

CHAPTER 4

Feng shui research

This review of Chinese feng shui research can merely embrace a fraction of the studies that have been undertaken across the world. Furthermore, it deals mainly with social science and humanistic studies as opposed to those that may have been done in fields, such as science and medicine. It should also be noted that historical studies are widely used in Chapter 2 and elsewhere, rather than presented here.

Quite similar to other aspects of Chinese culture and religion, feng shui was first investigated by a number of missionary writers, eager to pave the way for the gospel in China. An account of the writers M. T. Yates, Joseph Edkins and Ernest J. Eitel is discussed in Chapter 2 (p. 43). In 1892, the Dutch sinologist J. J. M. de Groot (1854–1921) published his monumental work, *The Religious Systems of China* (1892–1910), which included the first comprehensive study of Chinese feng shui. In contrast to other contemporary writers, who employed theological perspectives or merely common sense, de Groot's work offered sophisticated ethnographic analysis based on systematic fieldwork combined with study of the classics. J. J. M. de Groot also specifically sets out to answer the familiar question 'what is feng shui?', since it 'holds the nation in its grip and reigns supreme in the empire, through its whole length and breadth'. He identified the roots of feng shui in two different areas of thought: first, veneration for nature, and second, ancestor worship – both being inherent patterns of thought in Chinese civilization. He also suggested a definition: 'a quasi-scientific system supposed to teach men where and how to build graves, temples and dwellings, in order that the dead, the gods and the living may be located therein exclusively, or as far as possible, under the auspicious influences of Nature' (de Groot 1901: 935).

His exemplary fieldwork and immense ethnographic detail raised his account to a timeless authority, still widely read and quoted. Yet his analysis was somewhat hampered by two conflicting sets of ideas. One was the evolutionary perspective on religion and culture, according to which he saw ancestor worship as the origin and root form of Chinese religion. Another was the common standpoint of sinology that China had degenerated from antiquity; through his career he gradually moved from viewing China as an alternative civilization on par with Europe to regarding the Chinese as a semi-civilized people: 'Many rites and practices still flourish among the Chinese, which one would scarcely expect to find anywhere except among savages in a low state of culture' (de Groot 1892: xii). Accordingly, his study of feng shui had an uncompromising tone:

Fung-shui is a mere chaos of childish absurdities and refined mysticism, cemented together, by sophistic reasoning, into a system, which is in reality a ridiculous caricature of science. But it is highly instructive from an ethnographic point of view. The aberrations into which the human mind may sink when, untutored by practical observation, it gropes after a reasoned knowledge of Nature, are more clearly expounded by it than by any other phenomenon in the life and history of nations. (de Groot 1892–1910: 938)

A NEW TURN

After the publishing of de Groot's monumental work on Chinese religion, not much happened in the study of Chinese feng shui during the first half of the twentieth century, which was dominated by wars and international hostility. The present account of feng shui research will therefore only cover roughly the last half-century, taking its outset in the 1960s. Some other writers commenting on feng shui from various perspectives are mentioned in later chapters.

At the time feng shui began to spread in the West, it was already a subject of interest to anthropology as an aspect of Chinese popular religion; yet the two are not entirely unrelated. Already, in the 1960s, a new interest in Chinese philosophy and popular religion emerged, and a range of both academics and students slowly began to connect it with cultural self-criticism and a search for ideological alternatives in their own societies (further described in Chapter 7).

In modern anthropology, feng shui was introduced as a worthy research subject by the British structural-functionalist Maurice Freedman, having conducted fieldwork in south China in the early 1960s. He wrote two articles on the subject, of which one was a Presidential Address to the Royal Anthropological Institute in 1968 (Freedman 1969: 5–15). Here he proposed a new functionalist interpretation of feng shui, which he saw as a representation of Chinese religion in general. Opposing common views of feng shui, such as being merely deep-rooted superstition born out of fear and ignorance, he emphasized its social functions. Since rural feng shui was concerned with how well a village fared compared to others, how high and big could people build their houses, where and when deceased family members should be buried and so forth, he saw in feng shui an institution that set the rules for social competition while maintaining village solidarity and harmony – that is, an instrument of competition (Freedman 1979: 329).

Another side of his interpretation became more influential, however. His general work on Chinese popular religion (inspired by C. K. Yang, among others) introduced a new systemic approach emphasizing overarch-ing structures, order and unity of some sort. He expressed it in terms like 'behind the superficial variety there is order of some sort', deriving from what he termed 'a Chinese religious system, both at the level of ideas . . . and at that of practice and organization', in which elite and peasant religion 'rest on a common base, representing two versions of one religion that we may see as idiomatic translations of each other' (Freedman 1974: 352). Follow-ing Freedman, most anthropologists have seen feng shui as a tradition that may have its own features but most certainly belongs to Chinese popular religion in general, with which it shares a number of traits: first, it contains a number of reflections or mirror images of Chinese imperial culture and elite customs, thus bringing the ways of the elite down to villagers; second, it is expressive of a pragmatic and eclectic approach to the world, rejecting any single religion or perspective on life.

According to the premises above, Freedman treated feng shui as simulta-neously being a standard system of metaphysics and a form of divination, the elements of which were 'transposable' into Chinese religion (Freedman 1979: 331). In his first essay, he mostly discussed the connections between the geomancy of tombs and ancestor worship, arguing that together they form a system in which ancestors, on one hand, are worshipped and, on the other hand, are manipulated for the selfish benefit of their descendants. Also prominent among Freedman's conclusions is that feng shui forms a system of amoral explanations of fortune as an alternative to Confucian, Buddhist and other ideas of a moral order in the universe. The second essay, which shall receive some further attention below, played with ideas of feng shui as ecology, shifting its focus towards graves and houses as members of a single class, forming 'one system'.

Freedman considered only a fragment of the rural feng shui tradition, but he embraced a variety of themes with many open ends, all formulated with scholarly shrewdness and made ready to be pursued by other China anthropologists.

A few years after Freedman, the American anthropologist Jack Potter picked up feng shui as an expression of the religious life of Cantonese peasants (Potter 1970). He built on Freedman's approach to Chinese religion as a whole, but carried it further by attempting to show peasant religion as a consistent philosophy of life. At the base of this cosmology, argued Potter, was a belief that 'the universe contains as its essence an impersonal supernatural power' (Potter 1970: 140). To him, 'the occult pseudo-science of feng shui' was built up to handle and regulate this power, and the geomancer mediated between corporeal and supernatural affairs; although feng shui in principle deals with impersonal forces, it will always be merged with considerations of a range of supernatural beings. Potter stressed, however (much in line with Freedman), that an important effect of the system was that it regulated envy and jealousy: 'The magical and impersonal explanation for differential success... softened to some extent the effects of great social differentiation' (Potter 1970: 147). Peculiar to Potter's work was the notion of peasant religion as only one cognitive model out of several, which allowed the villagers to jump from one model to another. Since Potter presented this view as a conclusive statement rather than pursuing it in his analysis, it was inadequately developed (picked up by Bruun 2003).

In fact, a long line of early works on Chinese religion had emphasized the lack of individual commitment (e.g. H. Smith 1968: 172; C. K. Yang 1959: 193). C. K. Yang's description of worship in a southern Chinese village was characteristic of a polytheistic tradition: 'the worshippers had no permanent or exclusive connection with any single temple or priest, but visited temples or priests of different faiths as personal occasions demanded' (C. K. Yang 1959: 193). According to Yang, Chinese religion encompasses all the possibilities of the totality of religious life and experience.

At this point in time, Chinese scholars did not contribute significant studies. Not only was the country engaging in the Cultural Revolution, which branded any aspect of popular religion as feudal superstition and viciously persecuted its practitioners (Bruun 2003: Chapter 3), but there were also long-standing prejudices against popular religion among the Chinese elite. They tended to 'bear the responsibility to lead their civilization away from superstition and towards enlightenment' (Teiser 1999: 110). The attention that the early Chinese sociologists and anthropologists such as Fei Xiaotong, Francis Hsu, C. K. Yang and Godwin Chu paid to feng shui came close to deliberate negligence. These gentlemen, despite being trained at western universities, altogether appeared so deeply immersed in a Chinese elite identity that they could not escape the age-old conviction of Chinese men of learning: the religion of the masses was hardly a worthy subject of study and even less a basis for literary pursuits. Wing-tsit Chan commented in 1953 that: 'When it comes to the religion of the masses, one is appalled at the neglect by Chinese writers' (Chan [1953] 1978: 144). As pointed out by Maurice Freedman, 'the most interesting aspects of Chinese religion and thought were closed off to them by their own ideological resistance to "superstition"' (Freedman 1979: 316). Some prominent examples were Francis Hsu's *Under the Ancestors' Shadow* (1948), referring only sporadically to the subject, and C. K. Yang's *Religion in Chinese Society* ([1961] 1970), which even more blatantly avoids it. To Yang, geomancy, together with other forms of divination, was merely a 'religious aspect of Confucianism', to which he devoted two pages. As pastimes of the Confucian gentleman, forms of divination functioned as 'imparting confidence, offering consolation, and giving guidance during a crisis' (C. K. Yang [1961] 1970: 261–2). As a consequence of these inclinations, Chinese social sciences delivered strong descriptions of rural communities, but both before and a long while after the Communist era it had little to offer in the study of feng shui: the most important general information on popular cosmology remained to be found in western works.

Back in England, a student of Maurice Freedman, Stephan Feuchtwang, finished a dissertation on the subject almost simultaneously with Freedman's lecture (Feuchtwang 1974). In addition to a meticulous translation and examination of the rings of the geomantic compass, Feuchtwang offered a complete interpretation of feng shui. He identified four crucial aspects of feng shui: how its natural classifications are parallels to social classifications; how it contains symbolism and psychological projections of the imagination; the possible functions of feng shui as divination; and its role as a particular perception of reality.

Inspired by Durkheim and Mauss and not least by Levi-Strauss, Feuchtwang investigated feng shui as a means of self-identification of social groups and individuals. To the fundamental question raised by Freedman, however, of whether the supernatural world in Chinese popular religion is a mirror of Chinese society, Feuchtwang pointed out that feng shui is somewhat different. Feng shui is a means of self-identification by choice of location on the ground, but it allows a person or a group (a kinship group) to be identified as an ego-centred universe. By including burials and ancestor worship, this may be extended both into the past and the future: the geomancer's compass is oriented from the centre of the dwelling site, the centre of the defined area of one's self-interest. The site itself is a projection of the compass, a miniature universe, and at its centre is the Heavenly Pool and T'ai Chi. Sites are part of a natural hierarchy, however, with strong emphasis on the political centre:

Centralization is the principle upon which the Chinese empire was organized and it was as its centre but not as its top the emperor was equated with the T'ai Chi. In a classification where the criterion is amount of authority, the structure is, however, definitely a hierarchy and here again the supernatural hierarchy is an equivalent of the social structure with the emperor as top. The structure of the natural universe must be distinguished from both the supernatural and the social, on the two counts that it is not articulated either by authority or by Confucian ethics. As a convenient over-simplification we may say that the natural structure is a conception of the way power is distributed from a central source, as opposed to the way authority is delegated from a source above. (Feuchtwang 1974: 241)

If people, by means of feng shui, express self-identification as individuals or as social groups, and if this self-identification involves the establishment of small ego-centred universes, feng shui may engage in a dialogue with the moralizing political centre. While social hierarchy may grant people an inferior position, feng shui allows the individual a centre position.

The last element of Feuchtwang's interpretations also tends to support this finding. He sees feng shui as a way to conceive reality, but also a way of dealing with this reality – that is, an activist approach to this world. Feng shui operates like a cosmological model, applied to reality to serve specific interests. Having previously accounted for feng shui symbolism, which is a discourse with language as the analytical model, and combining this with the natural cosmological model composition contained in feng shui, Feuchtwang sees these two closely linked in a simple scheme of a model, 'its application or exposition progressively more embodied, first in the physical environment and then in social fortunes' (Feuchtwang 1974: 249–50). Thus, the same model is used to explain two fields of reality: the natural and the social; in the first, it is used as an ideal reconstruction and explanation of the natural environment, and in the second, the physical environment of the site is extended as a model for the analysis of social fortune. But since feng shui metaphysics is a self-defining set of concepts, it is not open to contradiction or to being checked with reality – thus geomancers always have a line of escape. Since it is flexible and lacks strict logic, any one part of the metaphysics may be applied in the analysis of a social situation; in the case of a conflict between its principles, feng shui can be used to express both the conflict and its resolution. Nevertheless, the metaphysics constitute an explanation of natural processes that could be believed explicitly by all Chinese.

Feng shui forms an explanatory device that allows for the widest variety of content and a great scope of interpretation. It offers plausible hypothesis, but never proofs. One of its essential instruments is the metaphor: the physical environment and theories about it are used as metaphors for the fortunes of people. It involves a number of cliché images such as the green dragon and the white tiger, which become something like an archetype: 'an understood field of reference which provides the imagery for describing the original unknown field for investigation' (Feuchtwang 1974: 253). As an archetype, it tends to become a self-certifying myth, as those aspects of the analogy that are rich in implication will last and have a following. In the course of centuries of metaphysical speculation, these aspects, or root metaphors, become 'mythologized'; they become 'clichés in the stock of proverbial knowledge which constitutes the metaphoric system by which life is described' (Feuchtwang 1974: 254).

Other anthropologists from this period accounted for Chinese feng shui in a less thorough manner, mainly as an aspect of fieldwork with other foci (e.g. Baker 1965; Hinton 1966). The prevailing notions of China quickly developing into a modern, socialist society and of religion being an outmoded perspective on life had a significant impact on research topics as well as on the personal stance of the anthropologists: many shared views with the Chinese authorities. Soon, China was virtually sealed off from the outside world during the Cultural Revolution, and even after, it only reluctantly opened up for foreign fieldworkers.

A significant contribution to the understanding of Chinese popular cosmology came from the Chinese anthropologist C. K. Yang, who had immigrated to the USA in 1952 and whose work was a lasting source of inspiration for western anthropologists. In his powerful book, *Religion in Chinese society* ([1961] 1970), he showed the political ramifications of popular religion. First of all, he distinguished between 'institutional religion', including both established religions and those aspects of popular religion forming independent social institutions, and 'diffused religion', meaning the religious aspects of common institutional and community life (C. K. Yang 1959: 192). Diffused religion, of which ancestor worship was the strongest ingredient, represented the structurally stronger and more pervasive force in the lives of the common people (C. K. Yang 1959: 192). He presented a general theory on religion and political rebellion in Chinese society, arguing that religiously motivated uprisings occur in times of severe oppression, for instance as a consequence of political unrest or famine. Where the ruling class depreciated the role of religion, the common people always maintained religious beliefs and amplified them in times of increased oppression. As classical examples, he has the increasing imperial intolerance in the first half of the nineteenth century, which eventually led to the Taiping rebellion, and the communist takeover, which gave rise to an emphasis of popular religion in the 1950s and again as a result of the Red Guards' brutality in the 1960s. Civic strife, economic deterioration and social disintegration were circumstances conducive to the development of popular movements that built on notions of superhuman powers, miracles and a host of supernatural ideas (C. K. Yang [1961] 1970: 354).

Another insight into Chinese feng shui, developed by general anthropology, relates to faith, belief and activism. Throughout the twentieth century, foreign and Chinese modernizers had picked on the Chinese peasant for being hopelessly immersed in supernatural beliefs, thought to control his entire existence. When it came to improving his existence, however, the same modernizers – whether of a Christian, a modern democratic or a Marxist conviction – had to realize that, in terms of agricultural skills, there was very little or nothing they could teach him (C. K. Yang 1959; Bruun 2003). In the 1950s, the Chinese authorities introduced motion pictures in the countryside, disseminating agricultural knowledge on depth ploughing, insect control, sanitation, common literacy for technical literature and so forth, but after initial curiosity, 'fatigue from the monotony of the political propaganda soon set in' (C. K. Yang 1959: 191). The Communist party in particular was faced with this fact: popular religion and beliefs in various 'supernatural' agents did not preclude solid agricultural knowledge.

Taking note of circumstances, a number of anthropologists went instead to Taiwan, of which several did religious studies including aspects of feng shui, notably Emily Ahern, David Jordan and Robert Weller. Emily Ahern's fieldwork in a Taiwanese village in particular (Ahern 1973) revealed another appreciation of feng shui than that exposed by the British anthropologists. The villagers did not in general see it as the workings of cosmological forces. Instead, the crucial consideration was the condition of the ancestor in the grave. The use of feng shui techniques and grave offerings were both directed to that end. And the common perspective was that if these were effective, the ancestor himself, not the feng shui of the gravesite, would bring good fortune to the descendants (Ahern 1973: 185). Thus, contrary to the 'mechanistic' explanation of good feng shui emanating from a good location of a grave in terms of the cosmic breath (*qi*), and with the ancestor in the grave being a passive agent in this process, they saw the ancestor himself as the direct source of good or bad fortune. The grave was likened to a dwelling and if kept well, and the ancestor properly worshipped and offered to, he would bestow fortune to all.

This point is in stark contrast to the functionalist interpretation offered by Maurice Freedman, that feng shui was a means of social competition, seen, for instance, in the competition among brothers for the most lucrative position of their father's grave. Rather, Ahern points out, 'the ancestor cares for all his descendants equally so if the grave is comfortable, the descendants will all prosper' (Ahern 1973: 185). Another consequence was that the surrounding landscape to a grave was less important than the grave itself. A further point worthy of notice here is that while the villagers shared a concern for their ancestors, which they honoured for what they had passed down to them, there was a discrepancy of perspectives between villagers and the feng shui specialist. The latter would concede that the ancestor would be comfortable in a grave with good feng shui, but would not agree that the ancestor was the source of good fortune. Instead he would hold that when the cosmological forces were good and balanced at the site of the grave, such as when the azure dragon and the white tiger were both represented, good fortune would automatically flow to descendants while at the same time the ancestor would be happy.

The differing perspectives are not only of exclusive interest to a few but are as much a question of research methodology. Presumably, and to some degree confirmed by later studies, much research on feng shui has focused on its practitioners – who are often men of some learning and certainly of great ability to explain their cause – rather than on the common rural people whom they serve. The specialist commands a vast repertoire of consideration, with reference to the terminology of the classics and which underpins his authority. The rural people, on the contrary, may be both more sceptical of the specialist's knowledge and be more concerned with the core elements of Chinese popular religion (see Chapter 3).

In the case of Hong Kong, also building on the work of Maurice Freedman, Rubie Watson has shown how residents in the New Territories use feng shui as a framework for expressing local identities, with a number of specified groups struggling over the right to define and maintain such identities (Watson 1995). Here, feng shui has a privileged status as a vocabulary or mode of explanation offering both a critique of and a remedy for environmental woes. Although Watson primarily interprets rural feng shui as a means of harmonizing with the physical environment, she still admits it has mystic, cosmological, asocial, technical and individualistic strands. She concludes that people in the setting of today live multiple lives that defy easy categorizations: 'The anthropologist can only hope to understand let alone represent or translate these complexities by grounding her or his work in the lives of these people' (Watson 1995: 25).

Of the more recent period, several works have brought new perspectives and new debates on feng shui, while at the same time all relating to its rising popularity in the West. The folklorist Juwen Zhang in 2004 published a translation of the *Book of Burial* (*Zang shu*), presenting a classic Chinese work to an English-speaking readership, including commentaries and an introduction explaining the history and development of feng shui. Zhang addresses the shortcomings in the western interest of feng shui – namely the lack of studies in the Chinese classics, the lack of fieldwork on the everyday functions of feng shui and a lack of interdisciplinary perspectives (J. Zhang 2004: 3). Apart from the value of the *Zang shu* itself, Zhang's work contributes a unique scholarly perspective on the long tradition of feng shui, spanning the Chinese classical tradition as well as the modern western and Chinese studies. Zhang concludes that feng shui, in its syncretic nature, is eminently representative of Chinese thought and culture as much as its metaphysical or magical thinking reveals the fundamental nature of human curiosity and creativity (J. Zhang 2004: 31–2). Furthermore, with considerable bearing on the present rise of feng shui in the West and relating to our comments on the rise of feng shui in contemporary society, Zhang notes that: 'The rise and fall of feng shui practice and intellectual interest (in divination as a whole) throughout Chinese history are often indicators of changes in socio-economic conditions and prevailing ethics' (J. Zhang 2004: 32).

Another recent work is that of Hong-key Yoon (2006), one of the key writers in the rising ecological interpretation of feng shui in the 1970s (described further below). Being himself a Korean who grew up in a village community, Yoon's recent work is dedicated to the study of feng shui culture in Korea, closely resembling the Chinese case and drawing on the same classical material. His work also includes several general aspects, such as the origin and evolution of feng shui, its interaction with established religion and its various principles and practices. One aspect may have great significance for the general study of feng shui: Yoon identifies three basic, interacting images of nature in feng shui, which at the same time form the essence of the east Asian conception of nature. They are the Magical Image, implying that nature has magical and mysterious powers that influence humans; the Personified Image, attributing human or animal-like characteristics to individual components of a landscape such as mountains (known from the dragon and tiger concepts); and the Vulnerable Image, implying that animate and inanimate landscapes are vulnerable systems that embody the flow of vital energies and which may be destroyed or remedied by people in their interaction with nature (Yoon 2006: 137–42).

My own previous work (Bruun 2003) attempted a joint historical and fieldwork-based anthropological investigation of feng shui as a broad tradition that both interacted with, and stood in contradiction to, Chinese state rationalism, arguing that feng shui gained momentum as a system of thought and reflection in conjunction with increasing intolerance on the part of the Chinese state, continuing into the modern period. It argued that alternative or co-existing rationalities are at hand in any given society, providing people with important variable means of reflection in everyday life. In retrospect, the distinction between 'life as' and 'subjective life' (Heelas and Woodhead 2005), such as outlined in Chapter 1 of this book, may well have been applied to denote this historical conflict in Chinese religious life. The fieldwork chapters investigated the present role of feng shui in rural China, finding that feng shui thinking is alive and well and making a colossal comeback after the initiation of the economic reforms around 1980. One chapter traced the new western interpretations of feng shui after the 1960s, noting the introduction of a range of new concepts and meanings (this theme will be picked up in Chapter 7).

STUDIES IN ECOLOGY AND NATURE PERCEPTION

The rising science of ecology in the 1960s became pivotal to the introduction of feng shui in the West: it picked feng shui as an example of a radically different approach to nature, while at the same time both contributing to common awareness and laying the foundation of a new radical interpretation. Several writers and academic institutions made their contribution, but much points to the University of California, Berkeley, as one of the early motors. In an elevated spirit of ideological, social and anti-war protest, new lifestyles and life-philosophies were wrought; for many people, Oriental philosophies became leading stars for a breakaway from the man-and-nature-oppressive western culture. Lynn White Jr. wrote his deeply influential article, 'The Historical Roots of Our Ecological Crisis' (1967), arguing that Judaeo-Christian theology was fundamentally exploitative of the natural world. C. G. Jung wrote his famous 'Introduction' to the *Yi jing* (1968), Fritjof Capra wrote *The Tao of Physics* (1977) and Buddhist studies were in the rise. From an early date, ecology was linked to eastern philosophy, particularly Buddhism.

At the University of California at Berkeley, the geographer Clarence Glacken wrote his influential book, *Traces on the Rhodian Shore* (1967), showing the connection between the Greek and Christian view of nature; it is usually interpreted so as nature was there to serve human interest. He strongly inspired an ecological approach in his students, of whom several went to China and later published in his spirit. Clarence Glacken presumably took a great interest in feng shui; former students tell that he had a feng shui compass (*luopan*) on the wall in his office. One of his students, the Korean Hong-key Yoon, in the early 1970s wrote the first dissertation on feng shui as ecology, described further below.

To start from the beginning, however, the great writer on Chinese science and civilization, Joseph Needham, in the late 1950s and early 1960s laid the foundation for a new, sympathetic approach to Chinese traditional sciences. Although he did not pay much attention to feng shui itself, his few remarks on it were highly influential. For instance, in a much cited passage (see Chapter 7) he implied the value of feng shui in ecology and landscape aesthetics.

The geographer Andrew March in 1968 attempted a new interpretation of feng shui, inspired by Needham and Freedman. Being highly critical of de Groot, Eitel and other historical writers, whom he claimed to be Eurocentric and patronizing, he argued that feng shui was addressing both landscape ecology and psychology. Showing great sensitivity in the choice of a site, he argues, feng shui is oriented towards how a landscape 'feels' – that is, the 'psychic properties' of the landscape. With reference to C. G. Jung, he proposed that Chinese science is of a 'synchronistic nature' (March 1968: 265), interpreting meaningful coincidences rather than causality and thus being holistic in essence. In short, they were concerned with 'human experience' and the 'meaning' of the natural world. March's work contributed new concepts to be explored by others in the study of feng shui.

Maurice Freedman in the same year gave his Presidential Address (Freedman 1969), which indirectly inspired an ecological reading of feng shui. In the opening sentence, he addressed it as 'what we may go as far as to call mystical ecology'. Since the Chinese see the universe as being alive with forces, Freedman wrote, 'any building is an intervention in that universe, composed of the physical environment and men . . . every act of construction disturbs a complex balance of forces within a system made up of nature and society' (Freedman 1969: 10). In the final passage, he refers to our own domination of the environment, as contrasted to the mystical relationship that the Chinese have with theirs. The concepts of ecology, landscape, nature, environment and management are attached to feng shui.

The young anthropologists E. N. and Marja Anderson also wrote on feng shui as an aspect of Chinese cultural ecology. Along with other writers of their time, they dismissed all previous work on the subject for approaching it as superstition and thus not doing it justice. Instead, they introduced a series of new concepts inspired by ecology. As an overall term, they called feng shui 'the traditional Chinese science of site planning', containing 'an organized body of knowledge, intensely practiced in application, and of specific intent' (Anderson 1973: 127–8). Another central concept is that of environmental management, according to which feng shui represents a whole complex of planning strategies to preserve their environment in spite of fantastic population densities (Andersons 1973: 143). They further noted that feng shui was an embodiment of the Chinese axiom that man and the rest of the universe are in a constant, dynamic relationship with one another, each able to influence the other's flow. Referring to an influential book, *Design with Nature* (McHarg 1969), they argued that the Chinese already had a science for ensuring that ecologically sound decisions were taken and public interest was preserved. Apart from introducing new concepts in the study of feng shui, however, works like this did little to explore their actual application.

Another of Glacken's students at the University of California at Berkeley, Armando da Silva, wrote a thesis on ecological adaptation in south China. This study showed in great detail how Chinese farmers used astrology, the traditional calendar and feng shui in their agricultural cycle. This complex lore, da Silva wrote, 'is really an attempt to harmonize everything, astrology, astronomy, landforms, and the life-giving seeds planted by man, into a unified cosmic ecosystem' (da Silva 1972: 64).

Much more influential was Hong-key Yoon's dissertation, *Geomantic Relationships between Culture and Nature in Korea* (1976), tutored by Glarence Glacken and Wolfram Eberhard at the University of California at Berkeley, and immensely inspired by the rising environmentalism in the West. Yoon proposed a theory taking its outset in a series of postulates about man's inborn knowledge about his environment, for instance that Chinese geomancy represents an 'instinctive response to the environment'. 'At first, Chinese geomancy may have existed as simple knowledge about the environment . . . This knowledge was probably handed down from generation to generation by elders' (Yoon 1976: 252). Yoon was perhaps more specific than other writers on the subject when he stated that:

Probably few ideas in the world are more closely related to the natural environment than is geomancy . . . geomancy is defined as a unique and comprehensive system of conceptualizing the physical environment which regulates human ecology. (Yoon 1976: 1)

With Yoon's work, feng shui had been definitively transferred from the sphere of superstition to that of ecology, a comprehensive field of studies without definite borders between science and human intuition. By making the concepts of ecology and environmental knowledge the cornerstones of his argument, he simply evaded any question of verification. Being himself a Korean with a rural background, Yoon contributed to a new reading of feng shui as alternative wisdom, created by the instinctive feel for the environment of the ancient Chinese.

E. N. Anderson, in his later book *Ecologies of the Heart* (1996), repeated many of his thoughts on feng shui: it was a system of folk beliefs based on empirical observations and interpretation of experience (Anderson [1980] 1996: 18). It has motivated people to plan good land use and reasonably sound architectural principles, he argued, without it being 'perfectly effective', however. The political overtones in ecology shone through in this statement: 'But compared to the almost total failure of environmental planning in the United States – with its superior scientific establishment and law enforcement capabilities – *feng-shui* was nothing short of miraculous' (Anderson [1980] 1996: 26). Let it be sufficient to comment that in the entire period of Anderson's life and work, China's environment has deteriorated rapidly.

Overall, the contribution of ecological studies remains vague. They have introduced a new set of science-oriented concepts, including ecology, landscape, nature, environment, environmental management, land use planning and so forth, which have opened a new field of enquiry into the total significance of feng shui. But both these concepts and their rationalistic foundation remain difficult to fit in with Chinese cosmology, while at the same time solid studies in real-life Chinese settings have been scarce. The political overtones and ideological criticism contained in ecology are explicit. Chinese studies in ecology began somewhat later than in the West due to the fact that they awaited China's opening in the late 1980s, but they tended to be inspired by the same sources. A few examples are given in Chapter 7.

STUDIES IN ARCHITECTURE

Since the 1980s, feng shui has been a popular topic in architectural studies, first in the West and more recently in China and elsewhere. Literally thousands of essays, master's theses and Ph.D dissertations have been written on the subject. From the outset, architecture naturally borrowed many feng shui interpretations from ecology, dealing with human adaptation to the environment. This implied a view on feng shui as an art of placement according to objective criteria. Obviously, such would be a sanitized version of Chinese popular cosmology, without any reference to graves, ancestors, spirits or astrology. For the purpose of designing and placing buildings in landscape, the Forms School of feng shui has had the greatest attraction, seeming more tangible – or less esoteric – than the Compass School.

Borrowed from ecology was also the Ancient Wisdom hypothesis, the sense of a magical formula lost to modern man. There is no doubt, however, that architecture, to a greater extent than any other branch of academic studies, had broken with the past in the modern-functional breakthrough. Some may have seen feng shui as a means by which architecture could recover from its modernistic fall by reintroducing curves, colour and cultural connotation. Others have seen in feng shui an inspiration for new models of conscious or intentional design, including value-oriented processes that capture the richness and complexity of cultural life.

Putting the arts on precise formulae is a hazardous undertaking, however, and many architectural works in the Ancient Wisdom line of thinking hardly meet common standards of academic enquiry.

A number of studies relate feng shui as theory, such as 'a Chinese traditional theory for selecting a favourable site for dwellings' or 'a theory of building layout and design associated with domestic architecture' (e.g. S. H. Lee 1986). The ecological roots are also commonly visible (often building on works like Yoon 1976 and Anderson 1996), such as seeing feng shui as a traditional means of 'providing an equilibrium amongst nature, building and people' (Mak and Ng 2005).

Several attempts have been made to prove the 'scientific basis' of feng shui in relation to site selection. For instance, Mak and Ng 2005 compares the preferences of Hong Kong and Sydney architects in relation to a set scheme of four different scenarios for a house, each containing the landscape elements hills, trees and lake. Despite one group of architects – those of Hong Kong – being influenced by feng shui and the other not, they find almost total agreement on the scenario where the hills and the high trees are towards the back of the house and the lake and open space are at the sunny front side of the house. This is in accordance with the principles of the Forms School of feng shui. But taking this as proof that feng shui is a science based on 'ancient wisdom' is rather absurd: such would be the choice in practically any culture around the world. A second section of this survey tests the two groups of architects' preferred layout for a main lounge in a domestic building with a fixed outer environment. The architects' sketches are measured against an 'ideal model' of the room according to the Forms School. Again the authors find near complete correspondence – though with the Sydney architects scoring slightly higher. They conclude that the theories of Forms School feng shui correspond to the current work practices and knowledge of eastern and western architects; even that 'the ideal Feng Shui model has been subconsciously adopted by practicing architects despite they may not even know the existence of such a model' (Mak and Ng 2005: 433). What the authors prove is rather that feng shui would not go against sound architectural principles and common sense.

Since the late nineteenth century, a range of both western and Chinese writers have noted that when given freedom of choice for the position of a house in landscape, the preferences of Chinese feng shui men and western architects would often concur. Others have evaluated the ancient tomb sites in China (Xu 1990) and the property locations in Hong Kong (Tam *et al.* 1999) according to scoring systems like the above, and arrive at similar conclusions. It should also be noted, however, that, quite similar to ecology, the role of feng shui in architecture has been ambiguous: it may be used as cultural criticism in the West and simultaneously be used in a nationalistic discourse in China. Nevertheless, it is a matter of fact that feng shui terminology has provided powerful inspiration and distinct identity to a post-modern Chinese architecture, especially in the southern Chinese cities (see Chapter 6).

CHAPTER 5

Cosmological principles, schools of interpretation and the feng shui compass

This chapter will outline the essential concepts, theories and doctrines that are found in feng shui. The most common ingredients such as Heaven, Earth, dragon, tiger, *qi, bagua* and Five Elements were drawn from Chinese natural philosophy through the ages and were given many individual interpretations; some classical and modern uses of the terms will be offered. The most fundamental doctrines of feng shui, at least when seen from the outside, were also shared with other strands of Chinese philosophy and rooted in classical Chinese literature. More than anything else, the *Book of Changes* is the mother of Chinese divination, having fostered both its diversity and persistence; it will be shown how feng shui is anchored in its perception of reality.

Being a broad tradition with both a large philosophical literature and rooted popular uses as well as both classic forms and new interpretations, it may only be depicted in terms of very broad generalizations. Moreover, from at least the time of the Neo-Confucian synthesis, several interpretations of feng shui have competed in China, giving rise to separate 'feng shui schools'. In the Chinese sources, these are known by a range of different terms. This chapter will outline the main concepts and principles of these two schools and indicate their historical significance as well as how and where they are applied. In addition, some of the schools recently developed in the western world will be explained and compared to the original ones.

Chinese feng shui manuals, being produced from an early date but emerging in increasing numbers from the eighteenth century onwards (reproduced in Taiwan and overseas Chinese communities), are less strict in the application of these separate schools but tend to mix them. The most popular uses of feng shui, often with little reliance on literary sources, tend not to distinguish between the two schools or even recognize their existence.

The most cherished device for 'seeing feng shui' is the elaborate feng shui compass, consisting of a wooden disk with a compass needle in the centre and a series of concentric rings with cosmological signs around it. The compass will be depicted and explained, and the most common forms being produced today will be shown.

THE BOOK OF CHANGES

The *Book of Changes*, or *Yi jing* in Chinese, is one of the five ancient classics in Confucian philosophy, the others being the *Book of Songs* (*Shi jing*), the *Book of Rites* (*Li ji*), the *Book of History* (*Shu jing*), and the *Spring and Autumn Annals* (*Chunqiu*). The *Yi jing* by far surpasses the others in importance, and stands out as the single most important book in Chinese civilization, essential to understanding its basic premises and comparable to the sacred scriptures of the other great civilizations, including the Christian bible, the Muslim koran, the Jewish torah, the Buddhist sutras and the Hindu vedas. The literature on the *Yi jing* is as enormous as its impact; like feng shui, the *Yi jing* is now becoming globally known, studied and used (R. Smith 1998, 2003). The term '*Yi jing*' refers to change – the Chinese characters playing on 'ever changing', 'never changing'.

In a Chinese work from around the fifth century, we find a conversation in which Mr Yin once asked a Daoist monk, 'What is really the meaning of the Book of Changes?' The latter answered, 'The fundamental idea of the Book of Changes can be expressed in one single word, Resonance (*kan*)' (J. Needham 1962: 304).

Through the historical era, endless scholars have commented upon the *Yi jing*. In the Imperial edition of the *Yi jing*, published in 1715, a work including 218 commentaries, the list of scholars that have participated in the compilation, provided commentaries or been quoted is so long as to span the bulk of Chinese philosophy. The Chinese commentaries are highly contextual, however, indicating that the meaning of the *Yi jing* was interpreted in accordance with the prevailing attitudes of each era: divination, oracle, wisdom, morality or statecraft.

Several important facts may be read from the primary status of the *Yi jing* in Chinese civilization. First of all, that some form of divination persisted as a mainstream activity and belief system through the ages, used by royal courts as much as by private individuals. Second of all, the significance of the *Yi jing* indicates the primary belief in immanent, creative forces in the universe as opposed to belief in a personal creator. In this thinking, all life is spontaneously created by the same inherent forces that shaped nature itself. The *Yi jing* is essential to a broader understanding of Chinese culture and civilization, although such an approach to the world that *Yi jing* represents never inhibited a rationalistic drive in administration, agriculture, crafts and technology. Rather, it indicates a pragmatic, or complementary, fitting together of several independent perceptions of reality without insisting upon a single truth.

The *Yi jing* is traditionally attributed to Fu Xi, the first of the three mythic rulers of China from the period preceding the Xia dynasty; in some sources, it is placed many thousand years earlier. Traditional Chinese sources attribute important *Yi jing* commentaries to Confucius himself, although this is hardly correct. Historical evidence can neither confirm nor deny the prehistorical origin of the *Yi jing*. It is a fact, however, that during the Han dynasty, a set of commentaries known as the Ten Wings were integrated into the text, after which it received imperial approval as one of the Five Confucian Classics in 136 BC. Modern linguistic and historical scholarship tends to indicate that the *Yi jing* was compiled in the Late Western Zhou era, perhaps during the late ninth century BC, as an accretion of concepts used by the Western Zhou divinatory experts.

During the Qing dynasty (1644–1911), Chinese scholars by means of philology and textual criticism attempted to penetrate through the multiple layers of interpretation to grasp the original meaning of the *Yi jing*. These so-called 'contextual studies' gained a new impetus with the discovery of the Shang dynasty oracle bones in 1899, which led to a better understanding of the pre-classical Chinese language also used in parts of the *Yi jing*. As a consequence, in the early twentieth century the *Yi jing* was stripped of its 'book-of-wisdom' image and instead conceived as a divination manual consisting of omens, popular sayings, prognostications, historical anecdotes, nature wisdom etc. (Kunst 1985: 2; Nielsen 2003: xvi).

An undisturbed version of the *Yi jing* (building on the same cosmological assumptions, but slightly different), written on silk and dating back to ca. 168 BC, was discovered in a grave in Hunan in 1973. This sparked a new wave of interest in the work and led some scholars to suggest a direct relation between the *Yi jing* and the inscriptions on oracle bones, thus attempting to push back the origin of the book.

Traditionally, Chinese studies of the *Yi jing* have been divided into meanings and patterns on one side and imagery and numerology on the other. While the first branch focuses on textual studies, the second branch interprets the trigrams, hexagrams and related charts and diagrams in accordance with Chinese numerology. The majority of western translations, such as the Wilhelm edition, are clearly biased towards the meaning-and-pattern tradition, creating an image of a book-of-wisdom type of work.

When integrated into Confucian tradition, the *Yi jing* became a repository of morality and cosmology as much as a timeless tool of divination. In the following dynasties, an immense range of Chinese scholars added their own commentaries, and each era had its own dominant school of interpretation, infusing it with, for instance, Daoist, Legalist or Neo-Confucian ideas. The Neo-Confucian scholars Cheng Yi (1033–107) and Zhu Xi (1130–1200) in particular produced commentaries that became orthodox readings for the rest of China's imperial history and were adopted in the state examination system. It remains a fact, however, that the *Yi jing* had a deep and profound influence on China's sciences, mathematics, music, military strategy and the arts through her entire history (Needham 1969: 268), only to be discredited as modernization picked up momentum in the early twentieth century. From then on, the *Yi jing* was increasingly associated with the obscurity and stagnation of the old society, in the communist interpretation, the relic of a feudal past. Accordingly, several generations of Chinese have been brought up to ignore such aspects of their tradition, to the effect that *Yi jing* studies have been inconsistent in China (for an overview of some recent works, see Nielsen 2003: xviii). The *Yi jing* is presumably now more popular in the overseas Chinese communities and the West than in China itself. Yet, the type of thinking that the *Yi jing* represents is not without influence in China today – apart from its expression in the widespread use of feng shui; it may also be traced in a belief in a 'magic' inter-connectedness between language and reality.

The *Yi jing* was first translated into European languages in the early nineteenth century, yet better known in English from the James Legge version of 1882, but with an unrivalled translation into German by Richard Wilhelm in 1924 (and from German into English by Cary Baines in 1951). Long before Legge's translation, however, a range of western scholars paid attention to it, including W. G. von Leibniz, from a mathematical viewpoint (Leibniz 1977). It later appeared in a vast range of new translations and re-workings, to the extent that hundreds of versions are now available. It was the Wilhelm translation with the foreword of C. G. Jung from 1951, reprinted several times, that most profoundly positioned the *Book of Changes* as a monument of the new youth culture in the West after 1968 – and in a sense also prepared the way for the introduction of feng shui in the West.

No one was a more obvious author for a foreword than Jung, the psychiatrist exploring beyond the boundaries of western philosophical thought. Committed to remain 'unbiased and curious' in exploring the unconscious, he saw in the *Yi jing* an encouragement to the careful scrutiny of one's own character, attitude and motives (Jung 1968: xxxiv). More significantly, however, in his own work with synchronicity (the fundamental interconnectedness of events across time and space, an idea much encouraged by modern physics), Jung looked around for new sources of inspiration: he sought to establish a picture of the fundamental link between outer events and psychic states. The *Yi jing* was a sort of missing piece in his puzzle, to him a proof of a radically different way of looking at nature, occupied with totality and chance events rather than causality. He saw the hexagram as an indicator of the essential situation prevailing in the unique moment it was cast, a peculiar interdependence of objective events in themselves as well as with the psychic state of the observer. This was a true expression of synchronicity, he found, diametrically opposite to causality. He summed up his encounter with the *Yi jing* in this famous statement:

I know that previously I would not have dared to express myself so explicitly about so uncertain a matter. I can take this risk because I am now in my eighth decade, and the changing opinions of men scarcely impress me anymore; the thoughts of the old masters are of greater value to me than the philosophical prejudices of the Western mind. (Jung 1968: xxxv)

The structure of the Yi jing

The *Yi jing* is structured around sets of three horizontal lines. Each line can be full (*yang*) or broken in the middle (*yin*), creating a total of eight possibilities. These are the so-called trigrams or *bagua* (meaning eight divination symbols). Each trigram has a name and is attributed a nature and a direction (north, northeast, east, etc.) (see Fig. 7.1 on p. 150).

The trigrams are then put together in sets of two, placed as an *upper trigram* and a *lower trigram*. These are called hexagrams, of which there are sixty-four, for mathematical reasons. Each of these combinations are again attributed a name, a sequence, a judgement and a brief written statement for each of the six lines.

The names of the hexagrams may refer to movement, human character, situations, actions or people. The nature and meaning of the hexagram is briefly described, commonly in terms of potentials, opportunities and dangers. The judgement usually points to ways of achieving success. The statement for each line in the hexagram explicates the meaning in relation to the number reached when casting the hexagram (see below). The *Yi jing* is deliberately written in multi-faceted language and has since been given a refined literary style, which translators have attempted to capture in European languages. An example (in the Wilhelm edition), picked by a random selection of the six lines, follows:

46. *Sheng*/Pushing Upward

>   Judgement:
>   Pushing upward has supreme success.
>   One must see the great man.
>   Fear not.
>   Departure toward the south.
>   Brings good fortune.
>
>   The Image:
>   Within the earth, wood grows.
>   The image of pushing upward.
>   Thus the superior man of devoted character.
>   Heaps up small things.
>   In order to achieve something high and great.

The basic philosophy of the *Yi jing* is that all phenomena of Heaven, Earth and Man are correlated and follow the same shifting balance of opposites (as expressed in *yin* and *yang*). Change is the inevitable outcome of this pulsation, but change is bound to process. Due to the inherent correlation of all events in the universe, the processes of change may be captured in the 'random' selection procedure of divination. By tossing coins, sticks, dice, other objects or using other random methods to choose broken or unbroken lines, the hexagram representing this particular situation and this unique moment is built up (from bottom to top). In a Chinese context, the result will need the interpretation of a specialist, while in a western context, most users of the *Yi jing* will see it as a strictly personal matter.

The hexagram itself includes transformation into another hexagram, as determined when it is cast, thus producing almost infinite combinations. When casting the hexagram, each line has four possible outcomes, being unstable *yin*, stable *yin*, stable yang and unstable *yang*. They are attributed the numbers 6, 7, 8 and 9 respectively. Each line may be found by, for instance, tossing three coins at once, the heads and tails of each representing the numbers 2 and 3. By adding the numbers of the three coins, one of the figures above is reached. The unstable, transformative lines of this particular hexagram may change into their reverse, either one by one or together, thus producing new 'opposite' hexagrams.

The *Yi jing* deals with the most essential aspects of human activity, including success, fortune, superiority, character, power, ambition, energy,

discipline, integrity, devotion and refinement, but also with its negative
aspects such as danger, difficulties, disgrace, self-deception, arrogance,
humiliation and failure. It relates to themes such as career, hierarchy, relations between men and women, family affairs, struggle, war and peace. It
does so by interpreting the influence of the cosmological forces of Heaven
and Earth, the Five Elements, dragon and tiger, mountains, thunder and
lightning. It places human strength and character and the will of the mind
alongside these forces of the universe, firmly positioning human life and
intervention in its centre. Its cosmology incorporates the meaning of time
and of moving in space. It is patriarchal in orientation and this-worldly in
ambition, yet curiously devising divinatory means for secular pursuits.

Most feng shui specialists will agree that the principles of the *Yi jing*
are essential to their art, irrespective of their school of interpretation.
Although they may not explicitly use or study the *Yi jing*, its philosophical
ideas are identical to their own: that things eternally change; that the
universe is made by creative forces represented by opposites; that there is
a fundamental correlation between all events; that there is no distinction
between, for instance, social, psychological and natural fields of reality;
that situations on the macro level may be encapsulated in the divination
act on a micro level; and that specialists have a capacity to grasp and
interpret totality by means of divination. As noted, the very outlook of
the *Yi jing* is of great significance (if not peculiar to Chinese civilization):
entirely materialistic and self-centred pursuits may be backed by entirely
insubstantial and intangible means.

THE FIVE ELEMENTS (WU XING)

Chinese philosophy from an early date identified five constitutive elements, five simultaneously being a sacred number in popular religion and
ceremony. They were explained already in the *Huainanzi* (*Huai nan tzu*),
compiled before 122 BC (Bodde 1981: 240). For instance, the historian and
astronomer Sima Qian (Ssu-Ma Chi'en), in the year 90 BC, wrote in his
Astrological Treatise:

Since the beginning, when humankind came into being, rulers in successive eras
have observed the motions of the sun, moon and stars. Through the reign of the
Five Emperors and the Three Kings, as the effort was continued, their knowledge
became clearer . . . Looking up, they contemplated the signs in sky, looking down-
wards, they found analogies to these on the earth. In the sky there were the Five
Planets, on earth the Five Elements. (Yosida 1973: 71)

Building on the analogy between Heaven and Earth, a general orientation of Chinese philosophy in the direction of man–nature–cosmos analogies and the search for unifying principles is further seen in the following explanation from the book *Zuo Zhuan* (*Tso chuan*) in the year AD 25:

> Men follow the laws revealed in the celestial signs, living in accord with the nature of terrestrial things. Heaven and Earth give rise to the six Ch'i [*yin* and *yang*, wind and rain, dark and light], and from these are born the Five Elements [metal, wood, water, fire, earth]. Out of man's use of these come the Five Flavors [sour, salty, acrid, bitter, sweet], the Five Colours [virid, yellow, scarlet, white, black] and the Five Modes [in music]. But when these are indulged to excess, confusion arises and in the end man loses sight of his original nature. (Yosida 1973: 74)

This form of five-fold classifications was developed by the school of naturalists (*yin yang jia*) in the early Qin era and forms part of the *Book of Rites* (*Li ji*). Extended into every thinkable aspect of both nature and human life, it became a common doctrine applied, for instance, in ritual, medicine, alchemy, astrology, astronomy and the arts. It survived the Neo-Confucian reformulation of cosmology, though it became part of a more complex process of creation, representing the level of material substance.

The Five Elements were not considered static substances, but merely stages in the grand, eternal transformation processes of the cosmos. Since the Elements were themselves creations of the shifting *yin* and *yang* and pulsating *qi*, they were subject to alteration. One such series of transformation is called the Mutual Production order (*sheng*), in which wood gives rise to fire, fire yields earth in the form of ash and earth produces metal growing in its ores. Another series is called the Mutual Conquest order (*ke*), in which fire conquers metal by melting it, metal overcomes wood by cutting and wood defeats earth by growing out of it. A wealth of dynamic relationships can thus be accounted for by choosing either the Production or Conquest order of things. Such thinking was also developed in the Qin and Han dynasties, and survived through later ages to be adopted by feng shui manual authors.

A great difference between Chinese and western expositions of the Five Elements is the fact that the original concept rose in a context of competing Chinese factions of thought, in which every participant was aware of the philosophical and ideological alternatives of the other schools. Natural philosophy was one way of addressing fundamental human issues by means of metaphor and analogy, whereas other schools such as Legalists and Mohists, together with a range of Confucian scholars of later eras, opposed this way of addressing society.

There are substantial problems of translating Chinese philosophical terms into western languages, for which reason several terms such as '*yin*', '*yang*', '*qi*' and 'feng shui' have been gradually adopted in their Mandarin Chinese form. The Five Elements are literally 'five movements/goings' (*wu xing*) in Chinese. Joseph Needham, the great writer on Chinese science and civilization, has suggested that a more proper term for the Chinese Five Elements is 'Five Phases' (others have suggested 'Five Agents'), which better captures the idea of cyclical transformation. A related point made by Needham is that Chinese naturalist philosophy gave prominence to a wave type of thinking, in contrast to the predominant particle thinking of European antiquity.

THE CONCEPT OF QI (CH'I)

The concept of *qi*, which may be translated into 'breath' or 'breath of nature', is fundamental to Chinese natural philosophy. It is strongly indicative of an organic predisposition in Chinese thinking in general, as opposed to the mechanistic orientation that became dominant in European natural philosophy after the Middle Ages. It has a certain parallel in the Greek concept of 'ether', one of the Five Elements, but which perhaps is of a more static nature. In the Chinese organic philosophy, the universe is perceived as a self-generating organism pulsating with life-giving forces. It may be said in very general terms, however, that Chinese philosophy is not so much concerned with the origin of the universe as with the origin of man and civilization. To a considerable extent, the history of the world that matters is the history of mankind.

In early Chinese philosophy, *qi* is something that existed prior to the material world. According to the Han-dynasty philosophical treatise (*Huainan tzu*) from ca. 200 BC, the first original *qi* was born of the continua of space and time. This *qi* was heavy and stable, but its lighter parts rose and formed the sky. Its heavier and turbid parts gathered to form the earth. After that, the *qi* of sky and earth met to become *yin* and *yang*. The active *qi* of *yin* and *yang* became the four seasons, and as the seasons' *qi* scattered, it formed the various phenomenal things of the earth. The hot *qi* of *yang* gathered and became fire. The essence of the *qi* of fire gathered and became the sun. The cold *qi* of *yin* gathered and became water. The essence of the *qi* of water became the moon. The encounter of the *qi* of sun and moon gave rise to the stars.

Although such texts contain a considerable feel for physical processes, it is evident that cosmogeny is explained in an impressionistic and poetic tone, intended to satisfy rulers on a heavenly mandate rather than men of science. Accordingly, the central concept of *qi* is elusive, with multiple meanings, possibly swathed in deliberate obscurity. In general cosmology, the *qi* of Man was often represented as equal to that of Heaven and Earth. The philosopher Dong Zhongshu (179–104 BC) formulated it as: 'the qi of Heaven is above, the qi of Earth is below, and the qi of Man is in between' (Yosida 1973: 79).

The idea that *qi* gave rise to material substance is also reflected in Daoism. Laozi (*Lao-tzu*) described Dao as one of the basic manifestations of *qi*: the beginning was undifferentiated chaos, shape without form, form without objects. Dao was the origin and principle of all things, from which the *yin-yang* duality arose. *Yin* and *yang* combined to become plurality, and from that, individual things came into being. The idea of a primordial *qi* was taken further in the Daoist classic *Lizi* (*Lieh-tzu*), compiled around AD 300. An example of its wording follows:

There was a Primal Simplicity, there was a Primal Commencement, there were Primal Beginnings, there was a Primal Material. The Primal Simplicity preceded the appearance of the *ch'i*. The Primal Commencement was the inception of the *ch'i*. The Primal Beginnings were the *ch'i* beginning to assume shape. The Primal Material was the *ch'i* when it had begun to assume substance. *Ch'i*, shape, and substance were complete, but things were not yet separated from each other, hence the name Chaos. Chaos means that the myriad things were confounded and not yet separated from each other. (Yosida 1973: 78–9)

The Neo-Confucian scholars of the Song era returned to and reformulated the cosmology after ages of moral discourse in mainstream Chinese philosophy. Zhu Xi (Chu Hsi) in particular returned to the concept of *qi*, which he merged with the concept of *li* in a new dualism. While *qi* was the basis of all things (and in accordance with ancient philosophy described as the origin of Heaven and Earth, giving rise to *yin* and *yang*, which again formed the Five Elements representing the level of substance), *li* was the principle of organization. In contrast to earlier thought, however, Zhu Xi gave *qi* a rotating, centrifugal force, forming both a stable sediment in the shape of a central Earth as well as a purer and constantly moving part forming Heaven. *Li* was constituted by another dualism, represented by the concept of Grand Polarity (from *Zhou dunyi/Chou tun-i*), or *Taiji* (T'ai Chi). This Grand Polarity was the underlying rhythm of change in the universe and the pattern-principle of Heaven and Earth.

While Zhu Xi's concepts of *qi* and *li* indicated ways of investigating the material world and stressed the pursuit of individual knowledge for self-cultivation, other contemporary thinkers laid stronger emphasis on knowledge through meditation and contemplation. As derived from Buddhism, writers such as Lu Jiuyuan (Lu Chiu-yuan 1139–93) and later Wang Yangming (1472–529) saw *li/qi* as an idealistic unity, primarily giving access to innate knowledge because the natural order was immanent in the mind of Man. To Lu, '[t]he universe is my mind, and my mind is the universe'. This was the foundation of a moral consciousness, since the same pattern-principle was inherent in the world upon which one acted.

In modern works on feng shui, the concept of *qi* likewise has multiple meanings: they tend to vary with each individual writer and feng shui specialist (some examples will be given below). Yet the writings of Zhu Xi are reflected in a vast range of historical interpretations, which again are reused in contemporary Chinese and western works. Zhu Xi's synthesizing approach to natural philosophy as well as his own personal interest in divination for both self-cultivation and practical matters (particularly the *Yi jing*; see, for instance, K. Smith *et al.* 1990) make him a key philosopher in feng shui literature.

SCHOOLS OF FENG SHUI

In China, usually two separate schools of interpretation are recognized: the School of Forms and the School of Directions. These shall be explained below. Several new schools have arisen outside China proper, either in the West, in the Chinese communities of Taiwan, Hong Kong, Singapore, etc. or as globalizing processes of exchange. Some of these currents are accounted for in Chapter 7.

Both of the two Chinese schools of feng shui draw much of their philosophy from the Neo-Confucian learning that arose with Zhu Xi and his contemporaries. Yet the two schools of feng shui developed on top of an existing division between competing factions in Chinese divination: *Hong fan* (Great Plan), Five Phases (Fujian School) and Orthodox Five Phases (Jiangxi School) (Huang 1991: 19).

School of forms

One school, namely the one usually termed the 'School of Forms', shows greater continuity with the earlier divination philosophy. This school is primarily concerned with the 'influence of forms and outlines' (*jing shi*), including mountains, hills and water courses, and recognizes as its founder the famous ninth-century geomancer Yang Yunsong. Yang wrote a number of books, many of which carry titles emphasizing the influence of the dragon (see p. 23). Yang even held the office of Imperial Geomancer during the reign of Ji Zong (874–88). The School of Forms is also termed the 'Jiangxi School' or '*kanzhou*' after the department in Jiangxi Province where Yang Yunsong worked.

The School of Forms is occupied with reading the configuration of the landscape surrounding a site of a grave or a building. It considers all visible aspects of it, including mountains, ridges, slopes, rocks, streams and vegetation, as well as man-made constructions such as towns, villages, houses, graves, temples and pagodas. In addition, it considers the flows of wind, water and *qi* in order to reach a comprehensive judgement of the forces at play in a given site. By means of a series of correlations, such as between landscape forms and dragons and between mountain shapes and the Five Elements, it identifies the best possible site for a given purpose.

As derived from Yang Yunsong, the most basic rules are:

- All constructions should be placed on sloping, well-drained ground, avoiding low-lying wet areas.
- Dwellings for the living, including houses, villages, towns and cities should have to the north a shield of mountains or trees, protecting the site from malicious influence from this direction.
- Dwellings for the dead should be placed on south-facing slopes, preferably protected towards the sides and with vegetation towards the back.
- Entrances of houses and settlements should point towards the south to catch or absorb the beneficial influence from this direction, although specific land forms and local traditions may alter the orientation towards southeast or southwest.
- Landscape formations hide the presence of the azure dragon and the white tiger, representing *yang* and *yin* shapes and *yang* and *yin* currents of *qi*. The dragon must be placed to the east and the tiger to the west of any site, preferably forming soft curves (of which many different variations are identified), altogether comprising a horse-shoe shape of protecting hills.
- If these configurations are not at hand, other manifestations of *yang* and *yin* ground may be used for placement. Sharply rising hills are identified as *yang*, whereas the softer elevations are identified as *yin*. These may be placed on either side or complementing each other, so that areas with strong *yang* features should have local manifestations of *yin*, and the two forces combine in proper proportions, preferably with a slight male dominance.

- Since completely flat land is inappropriate for building, artificial mounds and screens of trees may remedy the site, just as waterways and ponds may be established or changed to help the accumulation of *qi*.

In the Forms School of feng shui, mountains play a vital role as abodes of dragons and tigers; dragon veins in particular are crucial energy lines in the landscape. As an embodiment of the masculine *yang* forces, mountains nearby or visible in the horizon are required for the most auspicious influence of *qi*, whereas flat land is considered powerless and thus unhealthy. Mountain ranges, with the Kunlun range in northwest China as the progenitor and centre of the earth, are everywhere in China swathed in myth and poetry.

After identification of the dragon and tiger, the interpretation of mountain shapes is therefore a central activity for specialists of the Forms School. From the visible mountain silhouette, the specialist must judge the presence of elements and forces. Following Yang Yunsong, endless Chinese feng shui manuals categorize the shape of mountains and correlate them to planets and elements, using the traditional five-fold classification. An example:

If a peak rises up bold and straight, running out into a sharp point, it is identified with Mars and declared to represent the element fire. If the point of a similarly shaped mountain is broken off and flat but comparatively narrow, it is said to be the embodiment of Jupiter and to represent the element of wood. If the top of a mountain forms an extensive plateau, it is representative of Saturn, and the element earth dwells there. If a mountain runs up high but its peak is softly rounded it is called Venus and represents the element metal. A mountain whose top has the shape of a cupola is looked upon as the representative of Mercury, and the element water rules there. (Eitel [1873] 1984: 46)

Certain mountain forms and landscape configurations are further compared to each other to avoid conflicting forms or symbolism: two shapes that are likened to Chinese zodiac animals, which stand in a fighting relationship, must be avoided or altered. Thus, local lore and naming of hills and mountains play a crucial role for interpreting the landscape; for instance, the same mountain may derive different names and associations to villages viewing it from different angles.

The animal sign and corresponding element of the owner of a house or inhabitant of a grave (the Twelve Animal signs are combined with the cycle of Five Elements, creating a total of sixty personality types) is a further factor of utmost importance for establishing the correct site. Using common folk knowledge of the animal signs, as well as the 'Five Phases' creative and destructive cycles, the specialist must determine whether the owner's data is in a harmonious or conflicting relationship with the surroundings. The day of the month according to the traditional lunar calendar may be added to such symbolism and is certainly taken into consideration when deciding on the day to start building.

Yet another categorization that may be employed is that of the Nine Moving Stars, which again are associated with mountain shapes, planets, elements, personality traits and career paths. Many such systems are shared with the Directions School, indicating the lack of practical distinction between them.

The crucial symbolism of the Forms School – the dragon – is ancient in China and contains many elements. First of all, it bears evidence of a pervasive animism, with a vast range of beings inhabiting mountains, rivers and trees. Further, it indicates conceptions of a living earth, which grows and transforms through the interaction of the impersonal forces of *yin* and *yang* and the interference of various beings, including humans. The dragon is also an imperial symbol indicative of social and political power as well as of tradition, for which reason it is an attractive astrological sign.

Dragons are both feng shui-related and everyday metaphors for mountain forms. Endless place names in China refer to dragons, for instance Wolong (lying dragon) Jiulong (nine dragons), Longquan (dragon spring), Longtan (dragon pool), Longtou (dragon head) and Longwan (dragon bend). Since feng shui applies a strictly contextual and visual interpretation of dragon forms, local communities may have specific names referring to the form of a mountain, for instance 'dragon backbone', which for another community seeing it from another angle may be termed 'dragon head'.

School of orientations

Under the influence of Zhu Xi's school of metaphysics, a second school of feng shui came into being. By granting principal importance to the *bagua*, the Heavenly Stems and Earthly Branches, as well as to the Constellations, it became closer attached to the compass and therefore derives its name – the School of Orientations or 'directions and positions' (*fang wei*) – from this. Another name is *liqi*, 'pattern of *qi*' School (Field 1999: 15). This school is also termed the 'Fujian School' after the place of work of its principal representative Wang Ji, to whom several works are ascribed: *Canon of the Core and Centre* and *Disquisitions on the Queries and Answers*. The School of Orientations is to a greater extent occupied with determining directions according to compass points, using the feng shui compass (*luopan*) as its essential instrument.

As opposed to the interest in outlines and breath of nature of the Forms School, the Orientations School is more occupied with cosmological order and cosmological correlations (including numerical proportions) to the compass directions, potentially bringing the entire range of Chinese cosmological speculation into play when investigating a site. While the Forms School is based on subjective interpretation of the landscape (though easy to practice), the Orientations School is based on mechanical application of its principles and is very difficult to practice due to its much larger repertoire of categories and their lack of internal consistency: the feng shui compass is itself a sketch of Chinese agglomerative philosophy.

The key observations of the Orientations School may be summarized as follows (and further explained in the description of the compass, below):

- According to the general laws of nature, Heaven and Earth are reflections of each other, Heaven being the ideal type and Earth its material manifestation. In order to achieve a harmonious and prosperous living, a dwelling site must fit in existing cosmological processes such as the movement of the sun and moon, the changing of *yin* and *yang* and the transformation among the Five Elements, itself becoming a little centre of the cosmos.
- By copying the pattern of the larger cosmos, buildings and their inhabitants may tap into the life-giving cosmological forces and live in harmony and prosperity.
- Taking a primary bearing towards the south, in which direction doors and openings should face, all man-made and natural elements in the surroundings should conform to their symbolic representations on the compass in their specific directions. Similarly, elements out of their correct placement should be avoided or modified.
- The *bagua*, and the symbolism of each trigram, must be considered for a given site, and the site may have hidden numerical aspects.
- The entire range of planets, stars, mountains, elements and so forth, as represented on the feng shui compass, should in principle be considered in relation to a site and conflicting correlations be avoided.

The two schools prevailed ever after without any significant competition from other denominations. Yet a number of texts combine theories supposedly unique to one denomination, just as late classical feng shui literature often attempts to include them all (Bennett 1978: 4; Choy 1999; J. Zhang 2004).

To a certain extent, geography may determine which of these two schools, will dominate in each region, since the School of Forms is better adapted to mountainous landscapes such as in south and west of China, whereas the School of Orientations may fit better into flatter, featureless landscapes. As was shown in the previous chapter, however, this distinction is more academic than practical, since most Chinese specialists have their own distinct ways of practising and may not even be aware of the two separate philosophical schools.

THE FENG SHUI COMPASS

Magnetic devices pointing north–south were apparently used for divination in Chinese antiquity. Historical records of the Warring States Period (475– 221 BC) and the Han dynasty (206 BC – AD 220) show the use a spoon-shaped compass made of lodestone or magnetite ore for divination. The first known, the *Si nan luopan* ('south-pointer'), had a magnetic spoon placed on a bronze plate, a 'heaven-plate', inscribed with the *bagua*, the twenty-four directions based on the constellations, and the twenty-eight lunar mansions based on the constellations dividing the Equator. The luopan of the Han dynasty, called *Shi pan*, had both a square plate, symbolizing Earth, and the circular plate, symbolizing Heaven. In the centre disc, the Big Dipper (Great Bear) was sometimes drawn. These early luopan compasses were used to divine the best location and time for burials and other events. For instance, a story tells that the first Qin emperor used this instrument in court to affirm his right to the throne.

Only much later, presumably around AD 1000, did the compass begin to be used for navigation along with China's increasing maritime activity. Magnetized iron needles were suspended on water, in a thread or on a pointed shaft.

The feng shui compass, however, is a direct descendant of the divination spoon, as these various forms of north–south pointing devices have been used for divination continuously since the Han dynasty: they were believed to respond to the flow of *qi*. Several early geomantic manuals, such as that of Master Guan's Geomantic Instructor, eighth century, describe the workings of compasses, indicating them to be essential instruments for geomancers from an early date. Presumably, the maritime use of the compass generated a technological development that spilled back into its divinatory use: during the Song dynasty, the pivot-suspended magnetic needle began to be commonly used in the luopan, and during the Ming and Qing dynasties the rings became more detailed and complex.

Historically, several different feng shui compasses have been in use. The most commonly known are the *San he*, *San yuan* and *Zong he*, but many more have been designed by individual masters for their own use.

The *San he* (Triple Harmonies) luopan is distinguished by being further divided into Heaven Plate, Earth Plate and Human Plate, thus having three rings showing the twenty-four Mountains. The *San yuan* luopan is distinguished by its sixty-four trigram configurations (hexagrams) based on the *Yi jing*, thus is closer related to personal divination. The *Zong he* (Combination) luopan combines features of both by containing both the three twenty-four-Mountain rings and the sixty-four-Hexagram rings. The most common forms of these compasses have fifteen to eighteen rings.

The feng shui luopan is at once an assembly of the entire range of concepts and ideas upon which feng shui is based and the Chinese specialist's most important means of determining the feng shui situation of a place. The feng shui compass embraces and puts into operation the most common concepts of Chinese cosmology, built up during centuries of agglomeration and competition among the great traditions. By drawing up convention and permanence, and at the same time engraving mysterious characters in beautiful design, the compass grants considerable authority to its user, while being put to use with great ceremonial solemnity. The authority of the compass is presumably one reason why, in China, specialists of both schools are fond of it, although it is more central to the School of Orientations.

The feng shui compass that has been in use for the last several hundred years consists of a circular disk of wood or lacquered wood, usually four to six inches across, flat on the top side and rounded at the bottom. A small compass needle, about an inch across, is placed in the centre and protected by glass. The flat surface around the compass needle is inscribed with characters in concentric rings, showing all the root concepts of feng shui; the *bagua* is often represented in the innermost ring. All rings are in a fixed relationship, permitting the compass to be turned only around the compass needle.

Depending on the degree of refinement, these rings may number from nine up to twenty-four or even thirty. Usually, the wooden compasses used by rural Chinese specialists, and which are still produced today, are only four inches across and inscribed with nine to fifteen rings. They are quite modest in appearance and have been adapted to the political climate in China, where feng shui practices are tolerated but not in any way encouraged. A number of compasses that have belonged to great masters are kept in museums in China and the West: they tend to be bigger, with over twenty rings, and very delicately crafted. Some recent compasses made in Hong Kong and Taiwan are square or round lacquer plates with up to thirty rings, modelled on historical pieces. As noted, the feng shui compass espouses the entire range of philosophical concepts involved in the art of feng shui: the rings with their roots and meanings shall be explained below.

The rings of, for instance, an eighteen-ring *San he* luopan may be laid out as follows:

The centre is the Heavenly Pool.

(1) The *Bagua* in the Former Heaven sequence
(2) The Changing 9 Stars
(3) The 24 Heaven Stars
(4) The Earth Plate 24 Mountains
(5) The 24 Solar Terms
(6) The Earth Plate 72 Mountains/Dragons
(7) The Earth Plate 120 Dragons
(8) The Human Plate 24 Mountains
(9) The Human Plate 120 Dragons
(10) The Earth Plate 60 Dragons
(11) The Earth Plate 240 Dragons
(12) The Jupiter stations
(13) The 12 Provinces
(14) The Heaven Plate 24 Mountains
(15) The Heaven Plate 120 Dragons
(16) The Five Elements
(17) The 28 Lunar Mansions
(18) The 28 Lunar Mansions with Five Elements

Further explanation of the rings of the luopan may be found in a number of both older and more recent works (e.g. de Groot 1897; Eitel 1873; Feuchtwang 1974, 2002; Skinner 2008; Choy 1999; Cheng and Fernandes-Goncalves 1999).

CHAPTER 6

Feng shui in the Chinese cityscape: China proper and overseas

As the historical situation since 1949 has been radically different on the Chinese mainland and in the overseas Chinese lands of Hong Kong, Macau, Taiwan and Singapore, the respective uses of feng shui in these places shall initially be sketched separately. Much has happened in recent years, however: Hong Kong and Macau have been returned to China, and economic co-operation and integration between Taiwan and China tends to even out previous distinctions in lifestyle and culture. The great cities of eastern and southern China in particular increasingly resemble Hong Kong and Taipei in both commercial drive and architecture. Moreover, feng shui is again being integrated in the vibrant and universal Chinese urban culture along with quick business, intensive shopping, conspicuous consumption, going to temples and chatting on mobiles.

CITIES IN CHINA PROPER

Until just one or two decades ago, feng shui was little practised in Chinese cities. Already the modernization drive of the late nineteenth and early twentieth century and the foreign grip on Chinese education did much to repress common feng shui practices in the major Chinese cities, such as Beijing, Shanghai, Chengdu, Xian, Wuhan and Guangzhou. Both foreign and Chinese descriptions from the early twentieth century tend to indicate that feng shui was little used and feng shui masters were marginalized. Feng shui had mostly become a rural phenomenon, associated with backwardness and superstition (*mixin*). The new breed of western-educated Chinese scholars resisted it strongly, even to a point of being ashamed of it on behalf of their culture. Chinese sociologists like Fei Xiaotong, Godwin Chu and Francis Hsu, and philosophers like Feng Yulan, mainly saw feng shui as a rural phenomenon not worthy of much attention. There were exceptions. An interest persisted among those traditionally-minded scholars working in the fields of classical literature and philosophy, and books on the subject were still produced up until the communist revolution. It was also evident that those privileged few who had access to burial in auspicious sites would maintain the tradition. Another exception related to internal geographical and cultural divisions. The south-eastern parts of China in particular (notably the province of Fujian, which is also known for its massive graves) appear to have held on to feng shui practices in both rural and urban areas. The coming of Communism in 1949 and the Cultural Revolution of 1966–76 added a new layer of criminalization and vicious punishments to both religious and folk-religious practices. The communist state cleansed the cities they controlled from all traditional culture and beliefs. Thus, from the 1920s and until the 1980s, feng shui was mainly a historical artefact, shunned as an unnecessary cultural burden in the modernization of the Chinese nation and repeatedly classified by the ruling authorities as a feudal superstition.

The urban feng shui revival of the 1980s to 2000s had dual sources: business and academics. Taking academics first (and leaving business until later), a great number of Chinese intellectuals, many of whom were quite young, reacted to the pursuit of wholesale foreign ideology and culture in the previous decades and thus began to explore their cultural roots. They were to some extent supported by the Chinese government, which attempted a modernization without westernization. Gradually, but persistently, new aspects of native Chinese religion, cosmology and culture were being revived, often in modern interpretations. For instance, Confucianism, *qigong*, clan organizations and clan halls, all kinds of divination, Buddhist and Daoist temples, family altars, ancestor worship, *Yi jing* and *bagua* studies are now part of public life again. China's economic success has certainly also boosted national self-assuredness and inspired new faith in those traditions that were previously associated with backwardness, such as Confucianism.

Today, massive environmental problems in China and a growing public concern in that regard have inspired new interest in ancient Chinese natural philosophy, particularly those thought systems professing harmony and balance (see Chapter 8).

Hence, a number of trends have contributed to a new academic pursuit of feng shui studies, although everyone must work with due caution because the subject remains controversial in the eyes of the state. Many young intellectuals have started dabbling with feng shui in a guise of modern science, drawing parallels to modern geography, human ecology, environmental philosophy, psychology, magnetism and much more. It is also evident that the strict censorship on all media favours these rationalistic interpretations of feng shui over others. For instance, feng shui studies relating to *yang* dwellings (those of the living) may be fairly easily published, while feng shui studies relating to *yin* dwellings (those of the dead), which plays just as large a part of the feng shui specialists' work, are very difficult, if not impossible, to publish.

New debate

Since 1990, a steady flow of new books on feng shui have appeared in the Chinese bookshops (see Chapter 7), although with a temporary setback in the early 2000s when the government's campaign against Falungong spilled over to other parts of the religious book market. With the rapid economic integration with Hong Kong and Taiwan, books from these markets have been republished or copied in China, adding to a growing feng shui literature; today, these books are displayed openly in urban bookshops, in campus bookstalls and in airport kiosks alongside books on medicine, Chinese cooking and the Great Wall. Books on feng shui are also among the best-selling categories of Chinese books abroad, thus serving as a Chinese cultural marker despite decades of denigration.

Along with feng shui gaining a foothold among groups of intellectuals and manifesting itself in architecture and business, a public debate on the issue is currently unfolding, even occupying the central state-controlled media. One opinion poll among several pointed out that 39 per cent of the population now believes in feng shui (China Association for Science and Technology). The most eminent Chinese academics are divided on whether feng shui is 'science' or 'superstition'. Chen Zhihua, a professor of architecture from Qinghua University, stated that feng shui is no science – '[i]t only fills the wallets of some charlatans' – while in rural areas, feng shui gives rise to generation-long feuds: 'these are the tragedies of the Chinese nation' (*China Daily*, 15 September 2005). Another strong critic is Fang Zhouzi (Fang Shimin), China's foremost 'science policeman', who has made it his vocation to reveal pseudo-science, academic plagiarism and academic corruption in China. His point is that the Chinese are too easy to cheat since they lack 'the spirit of scepticism, rationality and empiricism' (*China Daily*, 18 August 2005). In his view, feng shui is simply pseudo-science without any backing in facts and driven by a rising commercialism in Chinese society that enables 'masters' of all kinds to bribe the media and even professionals to bolster their supernatural powers (his website (in Chinese): www.xys.org, last accessed 22 March 2008). On a similar note, a renowned science-fiction writer warned in public that '[f]engshui is coming back in the name of science'.

Positioned on the other side is a growing line of academics seeking new inspiration in Chinese tradition. Yu Xixian, a professor from Beijing University and among the first to study the subject, maintains it is a sound and integrated part of Chinese culture and points to its rising recognition in other parts of the world. Han Zenglu, a specialist on city planning, finds, with reference to Chinese history, that feng shui is the simple philosophy of living in harmony with your environment: 'Feng shui stresses balance and co-ordination in urban planning, ideal space between buildings and comfort of the dwellers – modern constructions often lack these qualities.' Still more academics challenge the official view on 'superstition'; for instance, Xie Jinliang, a renowned *Yi jing* scholar of Fujian University advised that his department at the campus had its gate changed to avoid trouble and improve performance – and the university government carried out the change.

The Chinese government has reacted with a mixture of dismay and pragmatism. Despite relatively easy access to book publishing, explicit reference to feng shui still tends to be discouraged in the public sphere and kept out of state institutions. Universities may be permitted to organize seminars on feng shui, such as when Beijing University in 1992 held a large symposium on feng shui studies (Wang Q. 1992), and professor Yu Xixian offered a lecture series at this university, obviously inspired by the great popularity of feng shui in the West. University professors may also engage in feng shui study tours to China for foreigners, or give lectures on the subject at home and abroad. Yet, when it comes to establishing it as a subject at campuses, the authorities stall.

In a much publicized case from 2005, the famous Nanjing University (Jiangsu province), in co-operation with the China Architectural Culture Centre, announced a feng shui training course (the first of its kind in China) to teach traditional architecture and ancient feng shui practices. Since both architects and property developers are in want of such initiatives, feng shui courses are becoming a lucrative market. Nanjing University immediately came under pressure from both public authorities and local media, however, accusing it of 'promoting superstition', and the university eventually denied its involvement. A range of sources, both public media and private individuals I spoke to in Nanjing, maintained that there was a tremendous interest in the course. In such cases, the will of the government is extended through the university party secretaries, who despite usually giving in to the universities' desire for development still defend key policy issues.

Nanjing universities have been in the forefront of the feng shui revival in China. A young scholar of the Southeastern University, He Xiaoxin, in 1990 published a study, 'Exploring the Source of Feng shui', which received national recognition both because it was the first serious study published after 1949 and because of its novel interpretation and good quality. This small book is, in fact, among the books I have most often seen in the possession of modern feng shui specialists. Over the years, a circle of Nanjing scholars have established themselves in *Yi jing, bagua*, feng shui and other studies, for instance at the Yi jing Research Institute of the Nanjing University. Examples of the range of new feng shui books in China will be given in Chapter 7.

Apart from publishing books and articles, academics are increasingly active in lecturing and consulting on feng shui matters, though mostly for businesses. In want of feng shui masters with formal education and social recognition, many corporate executives turn to the universities for assistance in seeing feng shui, for instance among scholars in the fields of philosophy, ethics and religion. Some may find it tempting to supplement their income, and in the fastest developing cities the market seems insatiable. State units may also turn to university teachers for feng shui assistance, feeling more secure among academics than on the open market. A university professor whom I visited in Nanjing confirmed that he had frequent enquiries about the subject. He musingly expressed the use of feng shui this way: 'It is like prostitution – the government maintains it doesn't exist, but wherever you scratch the surface you will find it.'

Feng shui for business

While feng shui as an academic subject has been troublesomely pursued by a small avantgarde, the interest in it from Chinese business has been explicit and almost universal. In fact, the bigger the business, the bigger the interest. In the beginning, it was driven by overseas Chinese investors and returnees: Taiwanese, Hong Kong and Singaporean investors as a matter of course brought their own conventional feng shui considerations to China. When engaging in any large joint-venture operation (and later entirely foreign-owned operations) such as factories, businesses, shopping centres, hotels and housing complexes, they would demand the advice and approval of feng shui specialists; most often, they would bring in their own. The

Chinese government, denouncing feng shui in public, was put in a squeeze, but reacted pragmatically.

Today, even the official news agency, Xinhua, will quote feng shui specialists for saying that 'at least 70 percent of [Nanjing's] real estate projects are appraised by feng shui masters before the construction starts' (*Xinhua*, 14 September 2005). In the case of the southern cities of Xiamen and Fuzhou, the percentage is presumably much higher, and in Hong Kong it is a *sine qua non* (see below).

Fig 6.1 New office buildings towering above older ones quickly alter the feng shui situation in Chinese cities; here, at the waterfront in Xiamen, China. Photograph by Ole Bruun.

The urban feng shui masters

It is well known from Chinese tradition that everyday people were served by specialists with little bookish learning and for a modest fee, while higher echelons of society went to masters with higher cultural level and literary skills; many such were found in Buddhist and Daoist temples (for an explanation of the geomancer-monk, see Yoon 2006: 182). Today, this pattern is quickly returning, the size of the specialists' fees alone creating sharp distinctions. Several kinds of feng shui specialists offer their services in Chinese cities, at the same time belonging to different stages of a spiritual revival.

First of all, there is the traditional, village-type feng shui specialist practising for mainly the suburban population among which they live. Along with the immense urbanization process set in motion by the economic reforms, the feng shui men came to the city, where they kept practising the only profession they had ever known. Similarly, the urban sprawl constantly gobbles up old villages and neighbourhoods, which had their own conventional specialists. Traditional feng shui specialists are very similar to those described for rural areas, rarely being dependent on books and mainly being trained in apprenticeships. The challenges they face are new, however. Everywhere around them, old houses are demolished and new private houses and towering apartment blocks rise. As their conventional clientele move to new housing, they will still invite them; yet, when a specialist used to working on the ground and interpreting signs and forces at earth level is brought up to the eighteenth floor to see feng shui, he must develop new conceptions. Most of them prefer to regard the ground plan of the block as a common source of feng shui for the whole building, combined with a consideration for the arrangement of doors on the floor level and a comparison of the floor number with the owner's astrological data, primarily his birth date.

An example of this type of specialist and his work: in the outskirts of Xiamen on the Chinese south coast, my assistant and I found Mr Lu, after enquiring in a nearby temple. He is in his mid-fifties and moved in from a rural area twenty years ago. His present house is a small one-storey shop and dwelling in one, a conventional Chinese construction without any refinement. He used to be a rural geomancer, mainly seeing feng shui for graves, which he had learned from his father and grandfather. Today, he still works with urn-burial in rural areas, mainly for recent migrants who want a final resting place in their home villages. But the main part of his work is concerned with new housing, office desk arrangements and solving workplace-related problems. To Mr Lu, urban feng shui is essentially the same as rural. Most important is the main entrance: it must face right – which is south, southeast or southwest – and have the right forms around it, including the dragon and tiger, and the right elements identifiable in the right directions (north is water, south is fire, etc.). He confirms that the ground plan of the building determines feng shui and the upper storeys take it from that. In the city, other buildings in front do not matter, even very tall ones, if only the main entrance faces right. What cannot be, he says, is a sharp corner pointing towards the entrance (*sha* position). Similarly, he depreciates telecom antennas in front of houses. What also cannot be is east overlooking west: if you look down upon the houses at the end of the street to the west, that is very bad – he shows a downward line with his hand and twists his face (this rule is obviously taken from rural feng shui in the Orientations School). According to Mr Lu, architectural style and rooftops (a concern of the higher classes of specialists) do not mean anything, as long as the roofs are not too pointed – this is bad for coming generations.

The other aspects of his work stem from the increasing competition in the job market and the ability of feng shui to adapt to any new circumstance. A growing number of clients want his assistance in placing their desk in the most auspicious position at their workplace for maximum performance and career opportunities. This new trend is presumably inspired by overseas Chinese business executives, who have long used feng shui specialists for choosing the best offices and best position for their desks, and has now trickled down to office staff. In addition, when employees fail to be promoted, suffer defeats at their workplace or are sacked, they may ask him to see feng shui in relevant places: offices, homes or ancestors' tombs.

Mr Lu belongs to the group of traditional feng shui specialists that have profited from the urban economic boom: his clients increase and he has even been invited to the Philippines for a job. Although he only receives new clients by word of mouth, he has had flaming red name cards printed that explicitly refer to his trade. When he goes out, he carries a briefcase with a huge Hong Kong luopan with thirty rings; yet his little house has no signboard. As he says, 'we have more freedom than ever to practise feng shui, as long as we don't get too boisterous'.

Another very common type of specialist in the city is the Buddhist or Daoist monk, having taken up feng shui besides his regular vocation. This tends to be controversial, although it is apparently consistent with Chinese history. Today, they are found in most of the larger temples and monasteries spread across China (see Fig. 6.2). An example, also from Xiamen (but it could have been Beijing, Shanghai, Chengdu or Guangzhou): we visit a large temple complex in the city with the specific purpose of tracing monks who practise. Several enquiries are futile, even met with disapproval; one monk takes us to the visitors' office, where a higher cleric carefully explains why feng shui is not supported by Buddhism. New temples may be oriented by feng shui specialists, but the art itself is not of the Buddhist literature and belongs to a lower level of learning. We are urged to leave.

Fig 6.2 Buddhist monk. Many Daoist and Buddhist monks actively engage in feng shui consultations for temple visitors, tapping into a booming market. Photograph by Ole Bruun.

Again we must scratch the surface; walking along the monks' living quarters, we meet and address an elderly monk. Hearing about our interest he first looks bewildered but indicates some knowledge on the subject. My assistant reacts quickly and asks if we can come inside to talk. Sitting in the monk's private chamber, sparsely but neatly furnished with bed, tea-table and chairs, bookshelf and TV, another layer of reality begins to unfold. He confirms his interest and starts explaining simple rules of feng shui as he has gathered it from classical literature, while writing excerpts from classics for us on a note-block. As common in China, he only reveals his own involvement much further into the conversation: he does actually see feng shui for clients who come here to look him up. The conflict between his Buddhist vocation and practising the art of feng shui is elegantly resolved: he merely serves the community of Buddhist believers! Thus, going out on jobs several times a week, he is deeply involved in the new feng shui boom in Xiamen city, and so are, according to him, a couple of other monks at the temple; seeing feng shui is among the services that the temple can offer and which, in return, contribute to the rising wealth of the temples and their monks. He sees feng shui only according to the Jiangxi (Forms) School and does not use a compass, as he says he practices only according to the books. Clients come to the temple in growing numbers and from all sectors of urban society: private house-builders, people with relatives to bury, real estate agents and factory owners. The conversation goes on for much of the afternoon, and as we get better acquainted while drinking green tea from tiny cups, the monk turns to the subject of plagiarism and cheating: 'Too many Chinese feng shui scholars have a low level. They just copy books from Taiwan or Hong Kong to get famous and start making money. They are not respectable. It is like Falungong, you know, just a confused mixture of everything, and people are too easy to impress.' Before leaving, the kind monk presents me with a gift: two new books on feng shui that were given to him by the Chinese author.

A third type of urban specialist is the academically trained 'feng shui professor', either working independently on the market as a sideline to his university position or full time. These are growing rapidly in numbers but tend to remain in a dubious situation. As noted above, many renowned university professors in architecture, philosophy and the arts receive enquiries from potential clients who prefer them to unconvincing specialists readily available 'on the market'. Some decline, others give in and still others decline formally but accept privately. An example from Shanghai: a history professor having published on Chinese natural philosophy was contacted by several housing developers in the early 1990s in order for him to provide them assistance in 'placing apartment blocks so as to make people feel comfortable'. He did so according to very common rules of feng shui, as he knew from the literature, and the clients were satisfied. With the Shanghai construction boom setting in, he was drawn into new projects, soon working for overseas investors who found it more convenient to use a local feng shui master instead of constantly bringing in their own. Having started early, he has built up his reputation as a scholarly trained feng shui professor, making a far better income that way. He holds on to his professorship, however, both for job security and for the prestige drawn from it.

Many other specialists claiming to be academics have lesser formal education, if any at all. They belong to the budding undergrowth of feng shui specialists with some measure of formal education but rarely higher degrees. They work entirely according to market conditions, providing assistance for anyone willing to pay, and the market is generally good: some specialists are known to charge several thousand yuan per hour, and the most famous much more. The modern feng shui scholar epitomizes the ambiguous position of feng shui between academic learning and popular religion, between official denigration and private use. He is a striking continuation of Maurice Freedman's depiction of the classical geomancer as a dubious figure with some academic training but without formal position, perhaps an exam failure or mid-term dropout, thus occupying a middle ground or mediating between the scholarly elite and the everyday person.

Yet another category consists of the Taiwanese and Hong Kong professional feng shui specialists, who have moved to Shanghai, Beijing and other cities to take part in China's economic success and who are generally believed to be more authentic than many native and more recently trained men. Several originally came with the overseas investors they worked for, and decided to move over permanently to exploit their advantage.

Architecture and construction

The interest in feng shui that developed in many departments of architecture and architectural firms in the Euro-American world since the 1980s quite naturally encouraged Chinese architects and housing developers to take their own cultural heritage more seriously.

Today, construction companies, housing developers and real estate agents all over China pay attention to feng shui as a matter of course – and many have a craving for better knowledge and training courses for their employees. In their line of business, the wishes of customers and clients are decisive: developers must be prepared, in any situation, to account for the feng shui situation of new premises if clients enquire, and make amendments upon demand. To further explore this aspect, we paid a number of visits to real estate agents. An example: in an office tower on the seaside of Xiamen, we entered the spacious hall of a major real estate agent. The great reception hall where they seat clients around low tables has a huge seaside glass wall with a view towards the beautiful Gulangyu Island. All furniture and equipment, it turns out, is laid out by a feng shui master according to the Five Elements. According to Chinese custom, we only gradually receive the information we need, but the senior staff member that we are referred to is very friendly and, in fact, genuinely interested in what we are doing. She explains that the company owner is a firm believer in feng shui and takes all possible measures. Accordingly, the company has long wanted to increase their expertise on the subject because an increasing number of clients express that sort of consideration. As the staff member explains, however, clients are very different: when rural people get rich and move into the city, they naturally want their houses to have right feng shui and therefore employ specialists to check it. The wealthy businesspeople are another group, of which 99 per cent ask for good feng shui for the sake of their business, and most of them also bring their own specialists when investing in property or construction. But it depends very much on people's background and education. People from certain local areas with great feng shui traditions pay greater attention than others. Well-educated people will not refer explicitly to feng shui, but will still want a nice environment with a good view, etc. And nobody will want to live on a former graveyard or where public toilets have been placed. Similarly, temples and gardens are supposed to attract good feng shui, and all want to live around them, whether or not they refer it to feng shui. Being in contact with people from all walks of society, the staff member can tell us of many clients' interpretations of good feng shui. Some come from humble backgrounds and want to live modest lives, for which reason they may not want perfect feng shui: one client thus asked the specialist to lay out his house with one degree variation from the perfect orientation.

TAIWAN AND HONG KONG

While general religion was discouraged and later prohibited in mainland China, it took a different course of development in the overseas Chinese territories.

In Hong Kong in particular, feng shui assumed the role of native Chinese religion as opposed to foreign influence and Christianity: it became an element in a Chinese identity in relation to the European elite. It was seen all over China that local Chinese reacted to the construction of railways and telegraph lines when under foreign domination, in many cases encouraged by the Chinese gentry. Under native Chinese government, these protests were quickly muted in mainland China, however, even in cases with far greater interferences with landscapes associated with the Dragon and Tiger. In Hong Kong, the ruling British authorities at an early date showed sympathy towards native religion, quite in accordance with the imperial policy of respect for ethnic identities and religious beliefs in all parts of the empire. From the correspondence of some early colonial administrators, it appeared like a relief that the true belief of the native Chinese could finally be identified, after a long period when the Chinese pragmatic and eclectic relation to religion had baffled foreigners.

From about the late nineteenth century, the British administration in Hong Kong paid out considerable amounts in compensation to local Chinese who felt their feng shui was being obstructed by new public constructions such as roads, bridges, office blocks and housing.

Taiwan

In early 2000, both Taiwanese and foreign media reported an incident relating to the upcoming presidential election, in which two candidates got entangled in a fierce feng shui dispute. Lien Chan, the official presidential candidate of the Nationalist party, had hired a master of various spiritual arts to check out his feng shui, including that of his family grave in Yangmingshan, the hills outside Taipei. At inspecting the gravesite, this master, who obviously had done some investigation beforehand, detected a 'black miasma, an unwholesome and foreboding atmosphere' emanating from a particular nearby tomb. This tomb happened to belong to the family of James Soong, a breakaway Nationalist candidate who had achieved great popularity among Taiwanese voters, presumably surpassing that of Lien Chan. The master reportedly had placed nine iron nails around the Soong family's tomb, nine being the sacred cosmological number and iron commonly believed to expel evil influences. A public exchange of statements quickly developed into a series of mutual allegations. Mr Soong's camp accused Mr Lien of thinking only about his own good fortune and not that of the whole country. There followed attacks on the financial dealings of the two families, those of Mr Soong relating to property deals in the USA and those of Mr Lien relating to embezzlement of Japanese assets after World War II.

The Democratic Progressive party candidate Chen Shui-bian, who won the election and thus ended fifty years of Nationalist party rule in Taiwan, wisely stayed clear of the row between the Nationalist party candidates. With only 39 per cent of the vote, the rift in the old party facilitated his presidency. Ironically, after winning the presidency, Chen Shui-bian apparently began consulting a famous feng shui master; up to the next election in 2004, he sought advice on his attire and position when addressing the public (*Taipei Times*, 6 June 2004).

The master who performed the inspection, Li Jian-jun, also attracted attention. Being a self-taught ex-mainlander who claims to have magical powers of *qigong* and who soon after the incident published a book in the USA, he himself embodied the clash between traditional beliefs in incomprehensible cosmological forces and modern scepticism towards scores of Taiwanese practitioners with dubious backgrounds. Many are accused of economic opportunism and swindling.

Right up to the election in 2004, a range of feng shui masters and other diviners appeared on TV to comment on the chances of each candidate: Chang Hsu-chu made a prediction in favour of Guomindang with a view to the favourite position of their family graves, but saw signs of a rift between the two candidates in the form of cracks on the paved ground around the Soong family's tomb; furthermore, the putting for sale on the internet of president Chen's family houses in Tainan 'could trigger negative consequences'. Jenny Lin, a physiognomy diviner, saw the birth signs of the Guomindang candidates being out of favour while reading the character of the two candidates by means of their faces, lips, chins and noses; she suggested that both candidates moved the bags under their eyes and treat bad teeth, as 'both features foretell troubles with friends and subordinates'. A *Yi jing* diviner and head of the Chinese Fortune-telling Research Association, Chang Chien-chiu, observed that the *Yi jing* heralded drastic changes for Taiwan that year (*China Post*, 17 March 2004).

The theme of the 2000 incident is itself noteworthy: Chinese history has countless reports on emperors who felt threatened by rebel leaders or extraordinarily successful individuals, and thus moved to demolish their ancestors' graves in order to stamp out opposition; one such case was the demolition of those of the Taiping rebellion leaders (R. Smith 1991: 157). Traditionally in China, destroying people's graves was a privilege of the ruling authorities; among everyday people it was considered a most horrible offence, and according to the Qing dynasty penal code resulted in capital penalty.

As opposed to China proper, where all religion became a political issue after 1949, and Hong Kong, where feng shui in particular became a vital aspect of Chinese identity, in Taiwan a rich and complex religious life has continuously been adapted to modern life in country and city without much state interference. While in China, chairman Mao incriminated all religion (while secretly consulting diviners himself), the Nationalist leader Chiang Kai-shek openly used them and presumably had his own feng shui consultant. When withdrawing to Taiwan, both the Nationalist leaders and a range of practitioners brought their religious perspectives with them.

Today, there are three large religious traditions in Taiwan, namely Buddhism, Daoism and Christianity, but a wealth of other religions and Chinese classical teachings contribute to the diversity. Temples abound, honouring the Buddhist and Daoist pantheon, often in a mixture, as well as local city and neighbourhood gods; on average, there is a temple for every 1,500 people. The Chinese traditional festivals of New Year, Festival of the Dead (Tomb Sweeping), Dragon Boat Festival and Mid-Autumn Festival, as well as a range of local ones relating to specific gods and events, are part of public life. As in China before the communist revolution, popular religion is integrated with family life. There are family altars in most homes, honouring family gods and ancestors, and common ancestor worship includes offerings and the burning of paper money. Charms and mirrors against evil spirits are common, pictures on front doors tend to the good luck of the family, lucky seals help in business and a range of Chinese rituals are upheld. An amazing range of fortune-telling is practiced, inspecting hands, faces and ears or using sticks, cards, horns or various other objects, which are drawn or tossed. Taiwan is the perfect example of complex religious traditions not being thwarted by modernity, but in fact thriving on its wider distribution of wealth (Clart and Jones 2003). An exhibition on Taiwanese folk-cultural artefacts held in Taipei in 2005 encapsulated the religious mood on the island state in the title 'Pursue Good Fortune and Ward Off Evil'.

Feng shui forms a natural part of all this, being practised in rural villages as much as in the modern city environment. To an extent hardly seen elsewhere, it penetrates every aspect of life: people will see to the proper outdoor and indoor feng shui of their homes to secure their lives in all aspects; countless charms, figures, flowers and other items will prop up the *qi* or expel evil inside; offices and workplaces are rearranged for auspicious influence on people's careers; businesses, big and small, will regularly have experts checking and correcting their feng shui; investors demand feng shui considerations in every undertaking; politicians place their offices and headquarters in surroundings that may bring luck to their campaigns; and housing complexes, towns and cities are judged according to their feng shui. The uses are boundless, and practising the art of feng shui has become entirely commercial.

A Taiwanese newspaper recently estimated that there are up to 30,000 feng shui practitioners in Taiwan, which is 1 for every 750 inhabitants, and their business is booming. Merely 3,000 of these are licensed, however, seen as an indication that there are 'a lot of charlatans out there' (*Taipei Times*, 17 October 2004). Chang Hsu-chu, the chairman of the Chinese Geomancy Research Association and among the most successful masters with merits including the famous Taipei 101 tower, deplores the number of self-made experts and economic opportunists counselling people on the basis of reading a few books. There is intense debate on the authenticity of feng shui experts in Taiwan. Some argue that practitioners should have a basic education in classical literature, while others point out that feng shui was always taught with simple means within the master's own family. Similarly, it is argued that practitioners should be a member of one of the authorizing associations. Contrarily, scores of village geomancers practice in traditional ways just like in mainland China. The means of consultation is also debated, as some very successful and highly paid masters will give advice on the basis of telephone calls or ground plans sent by fax, while many traditionally trained masters will emphasize that the totality of the feng shui situation can only be sensed personally. There are Taiwanese who refuse feng shui altogether, and many scholars who consider it a superstition that should be kept out of academia. The huge number of both practitioners and clients testify to the fact, however, that in private homes, workplaces and businesses, feng shui considerations are commonplace.

Chang Hsu-chu, mentioned above, in an interview with *Taipei Times* confirms that the modern feng shui master in Taiwan deals with issues very similar to those of the traditional mainland Chinese master. People come with money problems, health worries and family issues. According to Chang, more and more people turn to feng shui to bring order and stability to their lives: 'We are like doctors. People come to us when they are sick. We don't give out medicine, but instead prescribe better living and working environments for our patients,' he says, and adds: 'The more complicated everyday life becomes the more people will turn to feng shui for their financial, physical and mental well-being' (*Taipei Times*, 6 June 2004). He devises a range of cures including rearranging furniture, moving beds and placing carved stone talismans or crystals at key locations. In contrast to the traditional practitioner, however, corporate clients now make up 65 per cent of his annual caseload: these clients have both the incentive and the financial means to ensure that the flow of *qi* is helping the company to prosperity. According to Chang, these clients may pay as much as NT$ 30,000 for a single reading. The Chinese shortage of high-profiled masters often takes him to Shanghai, where the development of the city's business district keeps him busy. Another aspect of his work deserves comparison: he estimates that 75 per cent of his private clients are women, very similar to what we have noted for Chinese rural areas and also quite in accordance with the experience of practitioners in Euro-American cities.

The role of feng shui in protecting the Taiwanese environment is much disputed. Like on the mainland, a range of younger scholars have interpreted feng shui in terms of ecology and environment, seeing in it an early Chinese contribution to the protection of nature. Those Taiwanese architects who integrate concerns for the environment in their designs have also contributed to a new understanding of feng shui as a Chinese conceptualization of the environment, for instance the famous Pao-teh Han, president of the Tainan National College of the Arts. Environmental organizations tend to think otherwise. Green Formosa Front, for instance, criticize the illegal construction of temples in mountainous regions believed to have auspicious feng shui, because they involve extensive felling of trees and thus cause soil erosion and landslides. Even more serious is the construction of tombs on mountains in order to provide good feng shui for the next generation; as de Groot noted for south China in the nineteenth century, they may leave entire hillsides barren since no grave can have trees right in front. In these cases, feng shui is jeopardizing the preservation of a healthy environment.

Like in the West, students of architecture and design begin to study feng shui to find ways to integrate it into their professional work, if not out of belief then at least to satisfy demands. University departments have begun to organize seminars or offer lectures for their students, of whom an increasing number write theses on the subject. For property developers as well as architect and interior design companies in Taiwan, respect for feng shui is a must. In any assignment, they will ask the client what kind of role feng shui will play and be prepared to have feng shui masters look over designs and blueprints at an early stage in order to accommodate their recommendations.

Taiwanese businesses provide a ready market; in general, the bigger the business the greater the role of feng shui. A high-profiled case occupied the media in February 1998. A China Airlines plane coming in from Bali crashed near Chiang Kai-shek International Airport, killing all of the 196 people on board. Among them was the governor of the Taiwanese Central Bank, Sheu Yuan-dong, and three other high-ranking bank officials. An article in the *Economic Daily News*, Taiwan's largest economic newspaper, reported that the accident was just another in a series of calamities and that the bank had been 'cursed' since it moved to new premises in 1994 (*Economic Daily News*, 17 February 1998). A number of bank employees had long complained about the bad feng shui of the new building, a large square-shaped concrete construction facing right into the corner of the traditional-style National Theatre Hall. This is a taboo, and the employees maintained that this corner directed negative energies onto the bank. They backed their explanation by a range of facts: the construction company putting up the building went bankrupt, a worker fell from the building, a fire had occurred on the roof and, worst of all, the bank's former governor and a director had both died during their tenure. Several feng shui practitioners had been involved, but their recommendations were ignored by the bank.

While Taiwan's English-language media only selectively report on feng shui matters, the Chinese newspapers and magazines overflow with them; this only accentuates the argument made in the previous chapter, that those aspects of Chinese culture that may be branded as superstition by some tend to be ignored by Chinese intellectuals writing for a wider audience. Thus, many of the Taiwanese debates on the possible influence of feng shui on political elections, traffic problems, the fate of the country and so forth are for domestic consumption only. A recent case in point: after a series of bad traffic accidents, including plane crashes and the derailment of a train, the transport minister Lin Lingsan apparently sought the advice of a feng shui man, leading, for instance, to expensive changes to the Taipei Train Station's south gate. A feng shui master also appeared on national television proclaiming that the Transportation Ministry had very bad feng shui and a faulty *bagua* symbol on its premises. Other media commented that 'the more the ministry spends on feng shui the worse it gets' and eventually the transport minister resigned. His successor in 2006, Kuo Yaochi, stated that 'relying on feng shui is not helping us to solve the problem', while a weblogger commented that 'our feng shui is probably messed up because of Taiwan's corrupt officials'.

Everywhere in the Chinese-speaking world, feng shui-thinking has been most candidly applied by entrepreneurial groups. Very few large businesses have not, at one point, invited a feng shui specialist, and most of them do it regularly, either intentionally to improve their business or defensively to ward off bad luck or to oblige their employees. Large corporations and state organizations may even fight each other over feng shui issues, such as when the state-run Chinese Petroleum Company complained over the construction of a new metro-line, which involved the erection of two pillars in front of its headquarter main gate, allegedly because it would violate its feng shui and bring bad luck (*Taiwan Headlines*, 16 August 2005). Foreign companies have followed suit, first to adapt to local culture and later presumably driven by the new spiritual movement among trendsetting international companies ready to experiment with any performance-oriented device, from crystal energy to Buddhism and meditation to astrologers and feng shui specialists. Foreign banks like Standard Chartered and Citibank have openly employed feng shui specialists in the design of their Taiwan offices and bank branches, including waterfalls, bamboo groves and special furniture to generate wealth, but as much to make offices more beautiful and comfortable (*United Daily News*, 21 February 2006).

Taiwan is where traditional Chinese feng shui first adapted to a city environment in new popular forms. While the old Chinese manuals were mostly concerned with the surroundings of the house, the layout of buildings and courtyards and a mostly rather sketchy distribution of rooms, Taiwanese feng shui masters and manual authors began to elaborate on the indoor placement of doors, windows, separating walls, screens, various furniture and flowers as well as on indoor directions and colours. An efficient publishing industry brought out both copies of classical Chinese manuals and new interpretations in endless numbers, supplying Chinese communities elsewhere.

The diversity of the forms of feng shui practised in Taiwan is as great as in the West. Some forms relate to the placement of buildings and objects alone. Other forms, for instance that practised by Chen Hsuan-yi, another famous expert and chairman of the Yi jing Association, focuses on the person and attempts the ideal balance with the natural surroundings in terms of light and colouring, while stressing the importance of keeping things green. Thus, by placing the person in nature, they accommodate the new craving for both better natural environments and the use of natural materials such as expensive hardwoods, polished stone and fine carpets.

A range of Taiwanese popular magazines and TV programmes deal with feng shui matters, either as their specialized topic or as regular features.

Hong Kong

Nowhere in the world is feng shui so intensely integrated into every aspect of social, religious and commercial life as in Hong Kong. This is where big business and globalization entwine with popular religion, fortune-telling and gambling: a living testimony to the endurance of traditional cosmologies throughout the process of modernization and beyond. Hong Kong architecture captures this mode of existence by combining pre-modern ideas with post-modern design.

Three important historical factors have spurred the intensification of feng shui in the former British crown colony as compared to China proper: first of all, the inclination of the British government to take it seriously and accept it in public life; second of all, the predominance of a business-oriented Chinese community as opposed to an educated elite, which tended to distance itself from traditional beliefs in the modernization period; and finally, the continuous presence of foreigners making feng shui a vital aspect of a native Chinese identity. These shall be briefly described below.

It was only after the Opium War and the subsequent opening of Chinese ports to western interests that feng shui became generally known to foreigners. A striking fact is that during the first several decades of Chinese-western interaction in the treaty ports, and increasing inland missionary activity, feng shui was not commonly known among foreigners, and references to the subject are almost nonexistent. It was not until the late 1860s that a number of queries and small articles appeared in missionary journals and popular media, focusing on the possible meaning of feng shui (Bruun 2003: 42). In these years, things happened fast, and in the 1870s, everyone was intensely aware of the importance that the everyday Chinese attributed to feng shui. Much of the debate and controversy that the topic would subsequently cause, however, was centred in Hong Kong. Rising contradiction between colonial powers and the Chinese authorities as well as colonial rivalry among the western powers contributed to strained relations. Western industrialism, commercial vigour and military might was contrasted with Imperial Chinese economic stagnation and political decline. From this period stem the countless stories of Chinese resistance to railways, telegraph lines and building projects on grounds of severed dragons and obstructed feng shui. But as much as it may have expressed sincere concerns on the part of the local population, it became a language of resistance to western expansion and economic enterprise that contradicted native Chinese interests. It is interesting to note that while protests of railway building were at their peak, thousands of south-Chinese migrant workers flocked to the USA to work on its grand railway projects in the 1860s.

Christian missionary activity was the single issue that became a major controversy as much as a symbol of Chinese-western differences. Expanding rapidly into the interior and challenging both the authority and competence of local government, while different missionary denominations competed intensely among themselves, missionary societies were perhaps trying to gain abroad what they were losing at home.

Strong forces in Britain were against missionary activity in the colonies, and the Hong Kong administration pursued policies that avoided contradiction with the Chinese over issues of religion. At the same time, the new social sciences rose in Europe and America, deliberately striving to explore and represent the marginalized in the new industrial society. The social sciences expanded to non-western societies, and many famous studies of Chinese culture and society from this period contributed to a burgeoning anthropology, decisively focusing on the lives and outlooks of the everyday Chinese. For instance, J.J.M. de Groot in the 1890s collected the material for his volumes on Chinese religion.

In terms of feng shui, the total effect of these diverse developments was that it was increasingly identified as the 'true religion' of the every-day Chinese, or at least a system to be respected and reckoned with in everyday interaction. Towards the end of the nineteenth century, when the reform movement gained force inside China, the outcome of the pre-ceding decades' cultural conflict was astonishing: the Chinese imperial government commonly swept aside all obstacles to construction based on feng shui thinking, while the Hong Kong government had initiated a long tradition of paying out monetary compensation for public works interfer-ing with the feng shui of local communities, a tradition that lasted until the very end of British rule in 1997.

The second factor mentioned above, that Hong Kong remained dom-inated by Chinese business families rather than members of the political elite, follows naturally from its location in the south coast. Contradictions between centralized political power in the northern-Chinese heartland and various cultural, ethnic and dialect groups in the south are as old as Chinese civilization itself. It remains a sensitive issue today, as the Chinese state strives to remove all local dialects from schools and public institutions. Today, it is evident that feng shui is much more openly used and frivolously treated by authorities in the south: graves are bigger and more pompous, feng shui specialists practise more liberally and architecture plays with new inspiration from feng shui. The business communities everywhere in the Chinese world inherently have fewer reservations to feng shui ideology than educated elites; it fits well with the aims of business.

The third factor mentioned was that the prolonged interaction between Chinese and foreigners in Hong Kong was strengthening Chinese cultural elements radically different from western culture. That cultural identities are generated in the interface between cultural groups – that is, in awareness of and conscious distinction from other cultural identities – is well known from the social sciences. It is as much accentuated by experience from contemporary world-wide migration, which shows that culture does not simply level out and globalize but remains an active force in creating new identities and new cultural hybrids. Feng shui is an aspect of local identity and the connection between people and land in all Chinese rural areas, but in Hong Kong it has became more explicitly used to represent local communities in relation to a government administration based on an entirely different rationality.

Today, Hong Kong is not least famous for its skyline, each season adding new fabulous constructions, newer towering over older ones and each competing for auspicious feng shui like trees competing for sunlight in the jungle. The architecture is extremely varied and diverse, but with a distinct influence from the feng shui masters, who are involved in virtually every project. Sharp corners are avoided, many buildings have curved rooftops and silhouettes and each building is consciously located with an open view towards the waterfront or open spaces, as circumstances allow. Together with Shanghai, Xiamen and several other south-Chinese cities, Hong Kong has become a centre for post-modern architecture, with Chinese characteristics and older buildings giving way for new constructions at a rapid pace. Several commercial and residential buildings are among the tallest in the world, including Two International Finance Centre, Central Plaza, The Centre, Nina Tower I, One Island East, Highcliff, The Arch, The Harbourside, Bank of China Building and others.

Hong Kong's probably best-known building in relation to feng shui is the Bank of China Tower, which raised controversy when its design was released to the public and continuing many years after its completion in 1990. The building was accused of emitting negative feng shui energy over central Hong Kong due to its straight lines, sharp angles (concept of *sha*) and two aerials on top, resembling the incense sticks burned for the dead. In particular, popular legend had it that the building was deliberately designed in a blade-like shape to reflect bad feng shui to the Government House and its British administration. It is believed that willow trees were planted in the Government House Garden to deflect the 'secret arrows' from the building and thus block the ensuing bad luck. But also the surrounding towers were said to be affected since the Bank of China Tower was a deliberate design without feng shui considerations for its neighbours and was an act of mockery on the part of the Chinese state.

Another building, which became world famous for its feng shui-related architecture, was a large residential building complex in Repulse Bay, designed with a large square hole in the middle to allow *qi* to flow through. It is commonly known as 'the building with the hole'.

Feng shui is an integral part of everyday life in Hong Kong. Thousands of specialists practise freely for all classes and at all prices. Property buyers and estate agents consult specialists as a matter of course. Few building projects do not have their ground plans and blueprints checked by a feng shui man. Everyday people use the specialists for the same purposes as do rural people in south China, while the wealthier tend to have their own personal feng shui advisors, just like the family GP. Book stores display endless Chinese and international volumes on the subject; for instance, a new variety of Hong Kong manuals deal with website and internet feng shui, giving advice on the right placement of your desk, chair, computer and other objects in order to increase the traffic to your own personal website or to have success on the internet. Feng shui specialists regularly appear on Hong Kong channels, from ATV or Phoenix TV, to give daily feng shui advice concerning building, burying, living, working, web-surfing and so forth.

Even Beijing's top executive in Hong Kong, Dong Jianhua (Tung Chee-hwa), who took over from the last British governor, Chris Patten, in 1997, was known as a staunch believer in feng shui. He refused to move into the old Government House on grounds of it having bad feng shui, and had his own expert pick another site for himself as well as for his government buildings – all despite the fact that Chris Patten had the building redecorated and furnished according to the advice of a feng shui specialist.

So great is the power of feng shui thinking in Hong Kong that it has become customary for international corporations to use specialists for all major constructions. Some great banks are even known to make feng shui forecasts for clients and investors on a yearly basis or in relation to big events, such as when China took possession of Hong Kong in 1997.

As an example among thousands, Disney officials in 2005 consulted Chinese feng shui experts before building Hong Kong Disneyland, making several changes to the original plan to accommodate their recommendations. Several such changes were tilting the site of the park several degrees to achieve the correct alignment in relation to the mountains behind and the water in front, setting up 'no fire zones' in kitchens to balance the Five Elements and choosing an auspicious date according to the traditional calendar for the grand opening.

Most, if not all, businesses adhere to the principles of feng shui. Banks, airlines, telephone companies, shopping centres, hotels and so forth will all have regular feng shui checks and spend large sums of money to accommodate recommendations. The Mandarin Oriental Hotel, for instance, one of the most exclusive hotels in Hong Kong, has all rooms furnished according to feng shui principles. In the lobby sits a small statue of a unicorn that chases away bad *qi*. Lion statues have been placed in the offices of many of the hotel's corporate officers to catch money, and the placement of office furniture has been closely supervised. The hotel even boasts its own in-house feng shui master, Joseph Chau, who may assist corporate and individual clients.

Hong Kong has a number of famous feng shui specialists who practise widely across Asia and beyond. They have been trendsetters in a new Chinese post-modern architecture with soft edges, curved lines, waving roofs and other elaborate rooftop designs, such as now seen across Chinese cities from Hong Kong to Xiamen and Shanghai (see Figs. 6.3 to 6.5).

Fig 6.3 Feng shui-inspired, waving rooftop design on new apartment buildings in Xiamen, China. Photograph by Ole Bruun.

Fig 6.4 The postmodern architecture of South Chinese cities borrows considerable inspiration from feng shui doctrines, such as avoiding sharp corners and pointing shapes. Photographs by Ole Bruun.

Fig 6.5 Chinese property buyers viewing a model of a new housing complex. Property developers in most parts of China integrate feng shui considerations in planning and design and take great care to avoid unlucky symbolism (floor numbers with bad connotations are often left out). Photograph by Ole Bruun.

CHAPTER 7

Modern feng shui interpretations and uses

Throughout the modern period, practically all writers on feng shui, Chinese and foreign alike, foresaw its rapid demise. The stance of these writers varied, depending on their belief in modern education, Christian enlightenment, Communism or just the power of progress, but their predictions were very similar. A few examples may suffice.

The missionary Joseph Edkins believed in the power of the light itself when he wrote: 'the shining of true science may pale its ineffectual fire and cause it to disappear as a thing of darkness without special effort to bring about its extinction' (Edkins 1872: 320). The Sinologist Herbert Giles described a system that, 'in the last years [has] been shaken to its centre, and is now destined very shortly to collapse' (Giles [1878] 1974: 71). E. J. Eitel in his famous treatise on feng shui predicted: 'based as it is on human speculation and superstition and not on careful study of nature, it is marked for decay and dissolution' (Eitel 1873, 1984: 69). The sinologist J. J. M. de Groot mocked it as 'a mere web of speculative dreams and idle abstractions, the product of a credulous faith in absurd vagaries' (de Groot 1897: 979), bound for destruction along with the 'petrified' culture that produced it. Although the Korean folklorist Hong-key Yoon wrote much later and from an entirely different perspective, his forecast was little brighter: 'This naive but stable and harmonious culture–nature relationship has been ignored and overcome by so-called "modern civilization" ' (Yoon 1976: 231).

Chinese modernizers of every persuasion were all hostile to the popular traditions like feng shui, and fought them vigorously. For the founder of the new Republic in 1912, Sun Yat-sen, feng shui stood for fear and ignorance, something that needed to be eradicated as a condition for progress for the nation (D'elia 1931: 11). Mao Zedong not only believed in the power of communist modernity but was prepared to take matters into his own hands and aggressively stamp it out along with other aspects of 'feudal superstition', forming vicious policies to that end during the 1950s and 1960s. Most onlookers to the communist revolution tended

144

to agree to the general aim; the new generation of Chinese sociologists described the rapid transformation of the lives and minds of rural people. The Chinese anthropologist Wing-tsit Chan simply noted that feng shui 'is fast becoming a thing of the past' (Chan [1953] 1978: 145). Chinese writers of the 1960s to 1980s echoed those of earlier decades, though wrapped in Maoist propaganda.

These Chinese and foreign observers, who either did not see a place for feng shui in the 'modern' world or saw it as an outright obstacle to progress, all shared a range of visions for their societies. Whether Marxist or liberal in orientation, men of religion or laity, professionals or common sojourners, they all took part in the great modernizing project up until, and some time after, World War II. With a consensus of the disappearance of feng shui in the Chinese heartland, who would have imagined its rise on the global arena, let alone its transfer to the West? What these observers ignored was the prospect of radical change within modernity itself, such as outlined in the Introduction (Chapter 1).

The recent growth of feng shui thinking is the story of an astonishing transfer of ideas from a pre-modern to a post-modern cultural setting, their reinterpretation in the process and, in a sense, their return to their native lands with new inspiration. It is a story that is still unwinding under the impact of globalization.

A NEW PERSPECTIVE ON AN OLD SUBJECT

In the decades following the northern-European rediscovery of feng shui (they were presumably unaware of the work of the Jesuits) and into the early twentieth century, China was finally modernizing from within and popular religion was under fire from a new western-educated elite. The first half of the twentieth century became a turbulent time in China: a new Republic was established in 1912 but gradually slipped into civil war, a cultural renaissance movement (from 1917) ravaged old conventions, two world wars left their marks and Japanese invasion (1931–45) eroded the integrity of the nation. A new breed of Chinese sociologists (several mentioned in Chapter 4 and further below) only had a short interval to practise before the civil war and the revolution in 1949.

In the West, there were indications that a new interpretation of feng shui was underway. In addition to the works of sinologists, books by ordinary travellers and sojourners became more numerous. Many were written with a poetic strain. These writers commonly expressed admiration for the beauty of the Chinese landscape, described feng shui pagodas and, perhaps implicitly, linked landscape properties to feng shui. Similarly, the role of feng shui in architecture and the arrangement of villages and towns in the landscape were intimated. Well into the new century, feng shui had become a standard topic for anyone wanting to show deep acquaintance with Chinese culture (Myron 1915; Willoughby-Meade 1928). A whole new set of keywords had been introduced, including landscape, beauty, architecture, aesthetics and culture.

After World War II, a number of writers from various disciplines laid the foundations for new readings of Chinese history, society, culture and cosmology. Now, several decades later, it seems evident that this was linked to cultural self-criticism in the West and a search for spiritual and ideological alternatives in the outer world. An interesting figure in this respect was Joseph Needham, who unfolded his tremendous amalgam of Marxism, Christianity and modern science in the progression of his monumental work, *Science and Civilization in China* (1962). While himself an example of how the Chinese sources were read through glasses tinted by his own personal convictions, Needham sought to raise the standing of Chinese science and civilization in the West: his perspective was that modern science was 'world-science', built on contributions from Chinese civilization as much as others. He paid limited attention to feng shui, however, but nevertheless examined it as superstition (pseudo-science) rather than early Chinese science (still he credited it with the discovery of the magnetic compass for divination). A small passage he wrote on the subject is quoted widely and probably gained significance far beyond its intention:

In many ways fêng shui was an advantage to the Chinese people, as when, for example, it advised planting trees and bamboos as windbreaks, and emphasized the value of flowing water adjacent to a house site. In other ways it developed into a grossly superstitious system. But all through, it embodied, I believe, a marked aesthetic component, which accounts for the great beauty of the siting of so many farms, houses and villages throughout China. (Needham 1962: 361)

More specifically relating feng shui to awareness of the environment, and suggestions of feng shui being a regulating agent between man and nature, was the famous article by Andrew March (1968, already mentioned in Chapter 4). He criticized early sinologists like De Groot, Hubrig, Dyer Ball and Eitel for their scorn and patronizing tone against the Chinese beliefs in feng shui, while introducing a new radical interpretation. At the University of California at Berkeley particularly, two professors made their contribution to a rising awareness of Oriental nature perceptions. They were Clarence Glacken and Wolfram Eberhard (both 1909–89), both outstanding scholars with long experience of the Far East. Clarence Glacken had a background as an American army specialist in Japanese language and culture, had served in Korea and had later done ethnographic studies in Okinawa before eventually taking a Ph.D. in geography. In the 1960s, while at Berkeley, he wrote his monumental work on nature and culture in western thought, *Traces on the Rhodian Shore* (Glacken 1967), which became one of the intellectual pillars for the new environment movement in the following decades. Several of his former students noticed that he kept a geomantic compass (luopan) in his office.

Wolfram Eberhard was born in Germany and trained as a sinologist and ethnologist there before political circumstances and war drove him to Turkey and later to the USA, where he was offered a position at the Department of Sociology at Berkeley. Through his immense scholarship on Chinese history and folklore (e.g. 1962, 1967, 1970, 1988), countless travels to Asia and famous lectures, his influence spread into Oriental languages, anthropology and history.

One manifestation of the intellectual weight of these two men was the doctoral dissertation of Hong-key Yoon, a young Korean student who came to Berkeley in 1972. Yoon's dissertation was published as one of the first western language academic books on feng shui after de Groot's general work on Chinese religion. This book offered a new ecological interpretation of feng shui, while being very critical of western nature perceptions, thus kick-starting the popularization of feng shui (see Chapter 4). Popular writers here found proof of the superiority of Oriental understandings of nature as well as backing of the use of feng shui as a harmonizing agent between man and environment. Interestingly, Yoon's work later became influential for a new avant-garde interpretation of feng shui in China, where scholars needed hard-science arguments for the subject in order to stay clear of censorship.

It is a matter of great historical implication, however, that the propagation of feng shui to a wider audience was not the work of particular scholars and study centres alone – it was blowing in the wind, so to speak. It merged with criticism of environmental degradation, the role of Christianity and western imperialism as much as it was propped up by the student movement, anti-war sentiments and the new socialist groupings.

In the discipline of anthropology, there had been some awareness of the subject for some time, not least owing to de Groot. Emile Durkheim and Marcel Mauss used it as an example of social and natural classifications running parallel (Durkheim and Mauss [1903] 1963), Max Weber pointed to popular cosmology as evidence of a lacking rationalization in Chinese religion (Weber 1920) and a new generation of western-educated Chinese anthropologists doing village studies in China had scattered references to popular feng shui (e.g. Fei Xiaotong, Francis Hsu and C. K. Yang). As noted at the beginning of this chapter, however, they all assumed the rapid dissolution of popular cosmology. It was the work of British anthropologist Maurice Freedman, already described, that brought back feng shui as a separate topic of study; curiously, it happened in 1968, right when student movements across the West went up against conservatism and denigrated old authorities.

Stephan Feuchtwang, a student of Freedman's, finished his doctoral dissertation on feng shui and embarked on a long career as an anthropologist specializing in Chinese cosmology and religion. His dissertation, published as a book in 1974, was among the first to introduce feng shui to a western audience, and still stands as a widely read and genuine piece of scholarship (referred to in Chapter 4).

Also in England, Stephen Skinner, a young Australian graduate of English literature and geography, started writing on Chinese feng shui and published his first book, *The Living Earth Manual of Feng-Shui*, in 1976. His interest in the subject sprang from comparison with European magic of the Middle Ages, and his authorship has since included a range of books on occult philosophy, prophecy and magic. His main interest has remained feng shui, however, resulting in an impressive list of books including *Feng Shui for Modern Living* (2000), *Flying Star Feng Shui* (2003) and *Feng Shui Style* (2004). Most recently, he has published a series of translations of manuals written by Chinese feng shui masters of the eighteenth century (e.g. Skinner 2006). Skinner was certainly among the key actors introducing feng shui to a wider audience, with an enormous range of activities in addition to his authorship, spanning lectures, seminars and the publication of his own journal in English and Chinese (1998–2000).

In the 1980s, the popular book market began to embrace feng shui introductions and simple manuals, with an accelerating rate of new authors and publications. Among the early ones were Stephen Skinner (1976), Evelyn Lip (1979) and Sarah Rossbach (1983).

Presumably, however, the western market for feng shui books peaked around 2000, subsequently finding a stable level. Today, over a thousand titles are available in various European languages, with those in English being by far the largest group. Many hundreds of titles are found in classical Chinese (Taiwan, Hong Kong, etc.) and an estimate of 150 titles in simplified Chinese (China) (Yu and Yu 2005: 568), but which are rapidly increasing in these years. A substantial scholarly literature, easily comparable to that of the West, is available in Japan along with popular manuals (and to a lesser extent in Korea, both countries having their own independent traditions). As feng shui is going global, new markets open up in countries like the Philippines, Indonesia, Malaysia and Thailand, all having significant Chinese population segments serving as success models.

NEW SCHOOLS OF FENG SHUI

In the course of its introduction to the West, several new schools or interpretations of feng shui have emerged, of which some of the most common shall be described below.

Bagua school

A now common, modern school of interpretation is centred on the *bagua*, primarily drawing on correlations between the eight trigrams and directions, elements, colours, functions, people, situations, emotions and more, as explained below. It is mainly applied to the design of homes, offices and other indoor spaces (for its application, see, for instance, Walters 1991: Chapter 5).

It is necessary here to add some comments on the nature of the *bagua*. Although the eight trigrams appear as the basic elements of the *Yi jing*, they are a concept in its own right and perhaps developed independently out of the *yin-yang* dichotomy. Similar to the *yin-yang*, Five Elements, *Yi jing* and so forth, the *bagua* enjoys some autonomy of interpretation – the individual concepts of Chinese natural philosophy tend to be pragmatically constructed and eclectically applied. During the course of Chinese history, the *bagua* has found countless uses, for instance as a fundamental Daoist conception, in Chinese proto-science, in martial arts, in various forms of divination, on talismans and as an art element such as on mirrors or in gardens; the Korean flag also uses it as its symbol.

Each trigram has its own name, which is fixed from classical literature (see Fig. 7.1). It also has a huge set of symbolisms and correlations, which are subject to interpretation between various schools and philosophers. The application of the trigrams to living spaces draws on Chinese classics such as the *Book of Rites*, which indicates which room in the palace may be used by the emperor at each season of the year, which activities should be placed in which segments and the placement of dwellings for types of lesser ranking persons. The *bagua* signifies change – or changing transitional stages – as each trigram is based on the changing between *yin* and *yang*. The sequence

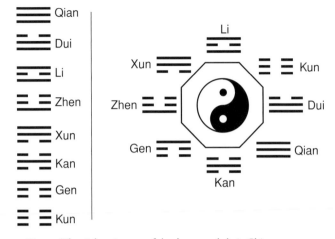

Fig 7.1 The eight trigrams of the *bagua* and their Chinese names.

of their placement in a circle indicates how they change into one another. However, for mathematical reasons, there are numerous (40,320) ways of placing them in the circle, and in Chinese philosophy several different systems apply: for instance, the Former Heaven sequence with three *yin* lines (*kun*) to the north and three *yang* lines (*qian*) to the south, the Later Heaven sequence deriving from the *Yi jing* with *kun* to the northwest and *qian* to the southwest (Walters 1991: 93).

Thus, in the feng shui application, each trigram has a series of correlations that the specialist must interpret. However, their placement, their succession in a circle and their opposites (which are the converse trigrams in the Former Heaven sequence but not in the Later Heaven sequence) also indicate factors that the specialist may interpret for the full exposition of the *bagua* correlations of a given site.

The essential task of *bagua* feng shui is to plan living spaces according to the meaning of the trigram belonging to each section. In the division of the house, for instance, the spaces for mother, father, son and daughter may be drawn from the trigrams. Similarly, activities such as sleeping, working, studying, cooking, eating and worshipping may be placed according to the qualities of each trigram. For business spaces, too, particular segments may be given specific functions according to the *bagua*, such as receiving visitors, concentrating, designing, manufacturing, storing, etc.

Taken by itself, *bagua* feng shui is a fairly straightforward and neutral way of performing feng shui inspections and recommendations for a site. It is far removed from the popular religious roots of Chinese feng shui and is thus more acceptable to both westerners and modern-minded Chinese. A great number of feng shui teaching centres use the *bagua* as their most fundamental conception, just as the *bagua* has been adopted by many practitioners of architecture and design.

Many writers and practitioners of *bagua* feng shui go much further than this, of course, either combining it with other philosophical conceptions or retaining part of the original folk-religious ideology and symbolism. Some examples will be provided below.

Flying star school of feng shui

Flying Star feng shui is based on the traditional nine-digit diagram known as the *Luo Shu* (*Lo shu*) magic square (*Luo Shu* meaning the 'Luo River Document'). It is also referred to as the *Jiu Gong Tu*, meaning the 'Nine Halls Diagram', referring to the layout of a palace and use of its individual sections in accordance with the *Luo Shu* diagram. Basically, it is a form of numerology. The diagram is constructed of the numbers one to nine so that number five is in the centre and the remaining numbers are distributed with equal numerical intervals on either side of it, horizontally, vertically or diagonally (even numbers in the corners). The result is that any possible line of three numbers will add up to fifteen. The diagram may be represented with dots (even numbers black and odd numbers white) or with digits. For *Luo Shu* studies, see, for instance, Berglund (1990) and Swetz (2001).

Chinese legend relates the *Luo Shu* to the pre-historic Emperor Yu (Da Yu, a cultural hero credited with controlling the rivers). It is told that during a flooding of the Luo River in ancient times, offerings were made to the river god to appease him in his anger. A turtle emerged from the water, carrying the magical *Luo Shu* design represented by dots on the back of its shell. However, as with many other aspects of Chinese cosmology, the age and origin of the *Luo Shu* remains undecided. Several different philosophical documents and traditions refer to the *Luo Shu* or to Nine Halls laid out in such pattern. The *Luo Shu* is mentioned in the *Huainanzi*, a philosophical work from the second century BC, and mentioned together with the *He Tu* ('Yellow River Diagram', a system of numbers associated with the Five Elements) by Sima Qian (ca. 154–86 BC). Yet no graphic representation is known prior to the Song dynasty, during which Zhu Xi incorporated it into a synthesis with the *Yi jing*, the *bagua* and compass points. Since magic squares are found in most of the ancient civilizations, it is equally possible that the *Luo Shu* derived from a different intellectual milieu, engaged in mathematics and numerology rather than general philosophy and later being accommodated in cosmological speculation (Nielsen 2003: 170).

The system of Flying Star feng shui makes use of the same basic elements and correlations as the *bagua* system: the eight trigrams of the *bagua* may be placed in the eight outer chambers of the *Luo Shu*, while the remaining centre chamber (containing the number five) is termed 'Earth' or 'Centre'. The main difference is that while the *bagua* form uses a static interpretation, the Flying Star form uses a dynamic interpretation, so that meanings change over time. The figures in the *Luo Shu* move around in the square to form different permutations.

Flying Star feng shui takes its name from the stars of the Northern Laddle (part of the Great Bear), of which there are seven, and two imaginary 'assistant stars', by means of which the number nine is reached. The Flying Stars are seen to move around the North Pole star by the daily rotation of the earth, as well as to appear at different hours due to the earth's yearly rotation around the sun, thus forming a giant clock. Each of the nine stars are associated with a trigram as well as with a range of good or bad meanings, very similar to those that make up the bulk of feng shui cosmology. Four stars are lucky, signifying health, wealth, offspring, longevity, honesty, intelligence and so forth, while the other four stars signify mishaps, disease, death, dishonesty, gambling and the like (the two assistant stars here count as one). The exercise of Flying Star feng shui is to make a chart in the shape of a *Luo Shu* diagram, insert a number of stars in each chamber (or 'Palace') of the diagram. These may be termed, for instance, the 'Period Star', the 'Water Star' and the 'Mountain Star', corresponding to the time that the house was built (each twenty-year period in the Chinese calendar has a leading star), the direction that the house faces and the sitting direction (counted as opposite to the facing direction). When placing a star in a given chamber, it is represented by a number one to nine, and the remaining chambers will then have their numbers altered along the sequence of the standard *Luo shu* diagram (with number five in the centre).

The final chart, consisting of nine chambers each with a trigram and a number of stars inside, will then be placed over the ground plan of the house – or possibly of the house and garden – and each section is evaluated according to lucky and unlucky influences. For instance, a section that contains three lucky stars may be especially good for a bedroom, an office or a lounge, while sections with bad combinations may be reserved for less important functions such as bathrooms and kitchens. There are as many variations of the Flying Star method as there are additional influences that may be reckoned with, such as annual, monthly, visiting or personal stars as well as the standard aspects of the feng shui as found in the common schools. As a consequence, any feng shui situation may be remedied by means of the Five Elements, altered flows of *qi*, use of colours and other symbolism. For detailed expositions of the Flying Star methods, see, for instance, Skinner 2003.

Black hat sect school of feng shui

The Black Hat, or Black Hat Buddhist School of feng shui is associated with its founder, Master Lin Yun. His story is deeply entwined with the introduction of feng shui in the USA and is worthwhile portraying in some detail. Lin Yun was born in Beijing in 1932 by Taiwanese parents working for the Taiwan Cultural Association. At the age of six, he was enrolled at the Yonghegong Lamasery of Yellow Hat Sect of Lamaist Buddhism in Beijing, allegedly because his spiritual gifts were discovered by Tibetan lamas. At the lamasery, he was taught the Black Hat Sect Tantric Buddhism, however, as well as was introduced to feng shui (in present-day China, Buddhist temples also offer feng shui services; see Chapter 6). At the age of seventeen, he left for Taiwan, where he continued his studies with Buddhist scholars. From an early date, he sought to combine elements of Buddhism, Daoism, *Yin-yang* theory, fortune-telling, psychology, medicine, colour theory and construction into his own brand of feng shui, for which reason he (according to himself) was 'ostracized' in Taiwan (*Chinese Daily News*, 8 July 1997).

In 1977, while practising his own brand of feng shui in Hong Kong as well working as a language instructor, he made an acquaintance that changed the course of his life. He taught Chinese to a young American journalist, Sarah Rossbach, who strove to become a foreign correspondent in Beijing. During their sessions, when Lin Yun was constantly interrupted by clients seeking feng shui advice, Rossbach gradually became involved in his activities, to the extent that she started taking a serious interest in the matter. After returning to the USA, she wrote an article on feng shui for the *New York Times*, immediately after which she was approached to write a book on the subject (Rossbach and Lin 1998: 8). Rossbach's book, *Feng Shui: The Chinese Art of Placement*, which was published in 1983 at a time when several academic works had been published (see Chapters 4 and 7), became instrumental for introducing feng shui to the general public in the USA.

Upon the great success of her book and the exploding interest in feng shui among average Americans, Sarah Rossbach invited Lin Yun to the

USA to teach and practice. In 1986, he was able to set up the Lin Yun Black Sect Tantric Buddhist Temple in Berkeley, California, the very centre of feng shui's reinterpretation in the West. Later, in 1993, a Cultural Centre was opened in the same place and, in 1994, the Lin Yun Monastery in Long Island, New York was opened. Lin Yun's fame in the USA has certainly also been reflected back on Asian societies. He has repeatedly been involved in high-end feng shui matters in Taiwan, including advice and predictions in the presidential elections. In 1998, a delegation of Tibetan lamas of the Black Sect presented Lin Yun with the title of 'His Holiness' of the Black Sect Tantric Buddhism Fourth Stage. Accordingly, Lin Yun may now be addressed as 'His Holiness Grandmaster Lin Yun Rinpoche'. In his personal style, Lin Yun swopped the Hawaii shirts of his Hong Kong days with Chinese silk Mandarin jackets (Rossbach and Lin 1987: 4). While in the USA, Lin Yun has co-authored a number of influential books propagating his version of feng shui (e.g. Rossbach and Lin 1987, 1994, 1998).

The school of feng shui as developed by Lin Yun with the assistance of Sarah Rossbach expounds a number of traits compatible with the interest of a western audience. First of all, it has a pragmatic approach to Buddhism, emphasizing the convergence with the realities of everyday life, including career and marriage, while keeping an open mind and respect for all religions: rather than forcing certain beliefs on other people, Lin Yun states that everything should follow its karma. Second, while claiming to venerate Chinese tradition, it has shunned all of feng shui's cultural baggage relating to ancestor worship, the influence of spirits and ghosts, the use of feng shui for grave positioning, the competition between people and a vast range of symbolism relating specifically to Chinese history, culture and language. Instead, it has constructed a new version, at once pragmatic and purified, which is focused on buildings, landscape, gardens, colours, interior design, harmonious living and the flow of *qi*.

As noted above, Lin Yun pragmatically integrates a number of traits from Asian traditions. He understands feng shui as 'what occurs when people, using the knowledge they have available to them at any point in time, choose, create, or build the safest and most suitable living and working environment for their needs'. From Black Sect Tantric Buddhism he also draws the distinction between visible forms and invisible, intuitive aspects; thus the aim of feng shui is to devise both physical and transcendental solutions. From Daoism he draws the *Yin-yang* theory and its concepts of balance and harmony between Heaven and Earth, sun and moon, mountains and plains, people and buildings and so forth.

In addition to the common aspects of feng shui, Lin Yun operates with a range of different *qi*, stemming from Heaven, Earth and various personal forms. Personal *qi* may be divided into a range of personality traits, to the effect that different people have predominance of specific forms of *qi*, which are manifested in their non-verbal communication with others.

Developing theories of colours has had a tremendous market in view of the black-and-whiteness of western modernist architecture. Drawing on the classical Chinese correlation between the Five Elements and the Five Colours, and augmented into the *bagua* structure including the eight directions, Lin Yun and Sarah Rossbach have developed a comprehensive scheme of colour application. Their basic theory is that colours naturally affect our human *qi*: they affect our mood and behaviour and make us, for instance, happy, gloomy, distracted or energized. Understanding and controlling that relationship can work for the benefit of human lives (Rossbach and Lin 1994: 16–18). Lin Yun identifies six areas of human lives that are affected by colour: transportation, shelter, clothes, leisure, food and personal cultivation. For each area and activity, certain colours may enhance our potential, improve your luck or restore harmony. As combined with the Five Elements' creative and destructive cycles of Chinese philosophy, Lin and Rossbach devise colours for individual rooms, stores, gardens, situations, personalities, moods, foods and more.

Lin Yun is consciously seeking to 'unite Eastern ideologies and Western concepts' (Rossbach and Lin 1998: 15), in the sense of blending 'wisdom, theories and practicality'. In particular, he has adopted a western concept of knowledge to the Chinese veneration for the classics, at once emphasizing that the fundamental principles of feng shui have never changed, and that feng shui is a knowledge that never ceases to evolve (as inspired by the *Yi jing*). This sensitivity to culture is consciously applied to any aspect of seeing feng shui for clients: arranging homes and gardens for wealthy Americans requires a different catalogue of cures than seeing feng shui for the restaurants of Taiwanese expatriates or predicting the success of a Taiwanese presidential candidate in the radiance of his ancestor's graves (see Chapter 6). Lin Yun's blend of elements from various traditions may strike the observer as odd or even opportunist, but reviewing the history of feng shui in China provides a better perspective: feng shui always was an agglomerative tradition, ready to adopt new popular currents and merge them with perceived tradition.

Although Sarah Rossbach does not belong to the Black Sect, her work may be placed there since her main source of inspiration has been drawn from Lin Yun. Rossbach's books were instrumental in the popularization of feng shui in the USA and to some extent also in Europe. Rossbach's first book, *Feng Shui: The Chinese Art of Placement* (1983), followed the path already projected by the Berkeley scholars of the 1970s, but made feng shui comprehensible for a lay audience. It expressed an unwavering confidence in feng shui as Oriental wisdom, relevant to modern westerners as much as to ancient Chinese. Written in a clear and matter-of-fact style, exposing a strong sense for which aspects of feng shui were marketable in the West and which were not, and serving an insatiable market for quick improvements in personal lives, her books have been sure hits. Rossbach devises a comprehensive range of cures for design problems including house siting, placement of doors and windows, interior decoration, placement of furniture for individual rooms, arrangement of offices and so forth. Sarah Rossbach herself abandoned the journalist career to become a full-time writer and feng shui consultant; scores of new consultants followed her example, using her books as manuals.

Her later works interpret feng shui for design and colour application. Rossbach and Lin's *Interior Design with Feng Shui* (1987) more explicitly plays with the mysticism derived from Tantric Buddhism, again exclusively derived from Lin Yun's teachings. As Rossbach argues, 'mysticism has been inherent in feng shui for centuries and seems to add strength to the practical aspects of its cures... Feng shui without mysticism is like a body without a soul' (Rossbach and Lin 1987: 5). With specific reference to design, Rossbach sees feng shui as a cross between art and science, its goal being 'to arrange buildings, rooms, and furniture in the most beneficial way to achieve maximum harmony with nature'. However, using the terms 'nature', 'landscape' and 'environment' as universal categories uniting China and the West across time and space, as well as uncritically linking feng shui to an inherent Chinese drive towards 'harmony with nature', she unmistakably places herself in the sphere of new religion: feng shui is true knowledge about the man–nature relationship. Some examples from her works will be given further below.

RENEWED EXPOSURE IN CHINA

Along with a booming economy and increasing role in world politics, China wants to be seen and heard and to expose her culture. Yet the advancing popularity of feng shui abroad was met with mixed feelings back in China. On the one hand, many Chinese writers take it as an indication of the originality, or even superiority, of Chinese philosophy, echoing popular statements like: 'Chinese philosophy will rule the world in the next millennium'. On the other hand, they deplore the vulgarization of feng shui for western consumption.

Under these circumstances, the rise of feng shui in the West was used by Chinese writers in support of their cause against accusations of 'disseminating feudal superstition'. He Xiaoxin, for instance, author of the pioneering book *Exploring the Source of Fengshui* (1990), lamented: 'Now the West sets a fashion of studying and imitating it while in China it is almost neglected' (He 1990: 158). At the same time, he declared that the central content of feng shui was the 'learning' (*xuewen*) about people's selection and handling of the environment of their dwellings, thus opposing government policy.

In the following years, however, a steady flow of feng shui books appeared in China, riding on a new wave of interest in spiritual and religious matters. In 1992, a large compendium of feng shui studies was published, including translations of Needham, Eitel and others as well as Chinese historical and philological studies (Wang Q. 1992). Through the 1990s, a number of books were published, many of which either referred to western 'modern' works or to the book by He Xiaoxin mentioned above (e.g. Wang Y. 1991; Gao 1992; Hong 1993; Zhou *et al.* 1993; Zhang H. 1993; Yi *et al.* 1996).

These first books paved the way for more general academic studies (e.g. Kang *et al.* 1998; Yu and Yu 2005; Gao 2005; Chen and Zhang 2005) as well as a wave of popular manuals for interior design, applying colours, garden design, buying property, etc. (e.g. Ou 2004; Hua 2004; Cheng 2005; Du 2005), to the effect that there are now scores of new titles every year (although still having to pass through heavy censorship and publishers risking severe punishment, even closure). Unlike most other Chinese books, Chen J. 2005 contains a long list of references, including many on feng shui.

Many young Chinese intellectuals reacted to westernization and at the same time dabbled with aspects of Chinese classical tradition, either in search of alternative outlooks or to find Chinese contributions to modern philosophy and science. They were particularly inspired by those writers of the 1960s to 1970s, such as Yoon, March, Needham, that were sympathetic to Chinese culture while conveying simple messages and absolute truths about Oriental wisdom. Obviously, many were thrilled with the prospect of feng shui becoming a source of inspiration for modern ecology. Their conclusions were enthusiastic; an example was: 'feng shui no doubt has helped restrain Chinese villages from unwise ecological decisions, nurturing reasonably sound ecological practices and leading to "planned" settlements far ahead of their time' (Fan 1990: 45). Another saw feng shui as 'compatible and compensative to modern technique' and expressive of a unique culture with an orientation towards preserving and ameliorating the living earth (Pan and Zhao 1997: 34–5). The landscape architect Yu Kongjian noted that 'one may find that the ways modern ecologists deal with the relationship between man and nature have been progressing increasingly closer towards what had been stated in the theory and practice of Feng-shui' (Yu K. 1992: 2). Yu goes on to argue that the concept of *qi* may be likened to 'the flow of the total human ecosystem', asking: 'Can qi bring enlightenment to modern human ecology?' (Yu K. 1992: 8).

There are strong cultural codes at work in Chinese publishing, however, particularly when going against the official line. Any alternative thinking, be it in politics, philosophy or science, must be dressed up in patriotism, and there tends to be a general demand that writers on history and culture adopt the leading notion that Chinese civilization is unique. The aforementioned Yu Kongjian, for instance, finds feng shui and indigenous ecology 'expressive of a deep layer of the Chinese mind in the form of a biologically inherited environmental consciousness' (Yu K. 1990: 90). It must rightfully be pointed out, however, that a great scepticism of Chinese natural philosophy, including feng shui, has prevailed among the active Chinese environmentalists, as shown in the next chapter.

Many Chinese authors of the more recent books vent their frustration over the powerful feng shui movement in the West; some claim that westerners can never achieve a deep understanding of feng shui or grasp its true meaning (e.g. Yu and Yu 2005: 566) Yu and Yu further call feng shui 'the art of Eastern living', while seeing a need to develop new Asian theories on the basis of the original form and make it fit for modern Asian societies (Yu and Yu 2005: 30). Juwen Zhang (translator of the *Book of Burial* (2004)) calls feng shui 'eminently representative of Chinese thought and culture' by way of its syncretic nature (J. Zhang 2004: 31). That it has become fashionable, however, and used as a solution to a variety of ills, he sees not as positive: 'It can be extremely misleading to take such culture-specific practice out of its cultural context and practice and study it as an isolated form' (J. Zhang 2004: 5).

NEW FENG SHUI USES: WESTERN, CHINESE OR GLOBAL?

As is obvious from feng shui's short history in the West, the actual number of academic works on the subject is very limited and has tended to be based on historical material rather than fieldwork in China. Much of the popular matter builds on the same few works or employs creative new interpretations. Below, some of these novel uses and adaptations of feng shui to the western 'post-modern' setting are portrayed.

As noted previously, however, feng shui was modified in several dimensions when adopted into the West. First of all, it was *amputated* by excluding everything relating to graves (*yin* dwellings), while focusing entirely on houses and homes (*yang* dwellings). Second, it was *de-spirited* in the sense that the workings of gods, ghosts and ancestors tended to be excluded, while focusing only on impersonal forces. Third, it was to a large extent *taken indoors*, concentrating on interior design and decoration more than the external, physical surroundings. Last, but not least, it was *infused with new concepts*, including ecology, environment, nature and design. Taken together, these modifications have in a significant fashion adapted feng shui to a western mindset (it should rightfully be pointed out, however, that some of these modifications may also be found in Chinese communities, but rarely in such a way as to change its basic premises). Very typical of Western popular manuals, despite maintaining feng shui to be several thousand years old, its basic concepts are interpreted according to a western perception of nature. For instance, *qi* is interpreted as fine electromagnetic currents, *yin* and *yang* as vibrating forces, Five Elements as Five Energy transformations and *bagua* as eight compass directions (Brown 1996), all very tangible concepts. Some associate feng shui with the new concept of nature's 'intelligent design'. By associating feng shui with flows of physical energy, modern feng shui proponents avoid questions of faith and accusations of reviving old 'superstition'. Feng shui's effectiveness is associated with the electromagnetic energies of microwaves, CD-players, radios and TV sets (Too 2004: 7). Similarly, *qi* is often described as an 'energy field', which may be detected with your hands or by means of dowsing rods, while the *bagua* becomes a 'map of energy flows' (Stasney 2004a: 8, 147). All these entities have absolute existence and a mechanistic nature, being independent of human interference, and thus tend to be very different from the original Chinese resonance thinking, intimately linking the natural, social and psychological domains.

Home and interior design

The most common and popular application of feng shui is to the interior arrangement of the home. Initially, many popular authors stressed the distinction between a fast moving world outside – characterized by stress, insecurity and disorder – and the home as a source of relaxation and recovery: the home should be a safe haven, a retreat from chaos.

We are becoming disconnected from the natural world, others argue, exposing ourselves to polluted and toxic environments, resulting in the drainage of our natural energies. Accordingly, we need greater awareness about what we have done to our natural environment and take steps to compensate.

The basic thinking is that all elements of our environment have an effect on our physical, emotional and spiritual wellbeing. Crucial are the natural light in our rooms, the colour of the walls, the style and shape of furniture and ornaments and the presence of living plants. Thus, different arrangements of the home and its decoration will affect the movement of energy or *qi* and ultimately affect our personal *qi* or wellbeing: 'feng shui is the art of arranging your home in a way that stimulates success, health, wealth and happiness' (Brown 1997: 5).

The goal of feng shui is to arrange the home in a way that allows *qi*, or 'energy' in the western version, to flow harmoniously, creating a sense of a balanced environment. As in the Chinese version, *qi* is believed to flow in waves or spirals, and the home must admit its natural flow by emulating nature and avoiding sharp corners and straight lines. The feng shui manuals pay extreme attention to interior design and the conscious choice of every piece of furniture and decorative item. They encourage an orderly environment in which every element of colour, shape and style is consciously selected with regard to its effect on the inhabitants.

Common to much popular feng shui is the application of the *bagua* or magic square to the individual parts of the home. This is derived from ancient imperial uses of the *bagua* such as given in the *Book of Rites*, indicating the emperor's proper ritual use of the individual sections of the palace according to the corresponding trigrams and their meanings. The scheme of the eight trigrams (see p. 150 for their sequence) is laid out, either in the eight compass directions or in relation to the entrance, to indicate the symbolic significance of each section of the home. Accordingly, the auspicious placement of living room, bedrooms and various facilities may be recommended, although adapted to the desires of the individual person.

Much attention is devoted to colours in popular feng shui, either by means of common colour charts and colour associations or by means of a colour scheme built on the *bagua*, as described above. It is commonly assumed that colours should be adapted to the light-intake, the orientation and the function of the room and the personality of the inhabitant. Many different interpretations are at hand, however, usually deriving some clas-sifications from Chinese philosophy but developing colour schemes to fit a western understanding. The ancient Chinese classification of colours fits in with the Five Elements, thus only comprising white, black, red, yellow and blue/green (*qing*) and differing fundamentally from the modern conception of primary colours and combinations. For instance, colours may be interpreted as influencing our lives in various aspects: they define what is and what is not; they disclose the status of our health, such as when used as diagnosis in traditional Chinese medicine; they inspire a wide range of emotions such as vitality, pureness, awe and danger; and they structure behaviour by being used by certain professions or associated with specific occasions (Rossbach and Lin 1994: 11). Colours are seen to influence the flow of *qi*, according to which the auspicious use of colours for homes, clothing, cars, food, health, relationships and so forth may be devised. In line with the western preference for tangible forces, the electromagnetic properties of the colour spectrum is often referred to and colours interpreted according to their energy intensiveness. Most commonly, however, the use of colours is guided by simple colour symbolism – Chinese, western or a combination – indicating the property of each colour, such as green for vitality and growth, red for intensity and love, white for purity and so forth. Other common uses of colours are inspired by the maxim of 'taking nature inside', thus using primarily earth colours and 'natural' colours in balanced combinations, arguing that *qi* flows most harmoniously in a natural setting without too many strong colours.

The use of flowers and green plants also fit in with the above, as they are believed to bring positive energy and new life to a room, for instance by soothing tense areas. One explanation is that plants activate the *bagua* field corresponding to the placement of that room, while at the same time having symbolic meaning (Spear 1995). Manual authors admit, however, that the use of plants is partly determined by cultural and personal habits, which should be respected: some controversy prevails over plants with pointed leaves, often believed to spur a piercing energy into the psyche of a person sitting next to it. A separate use of feng shui is for gardens, based on the principle that gardens offer the opportunity to connect to the natural world and tap into its beneficial energies to achieve balance and harmony (e.g. Hale 2000).

Yet another aspect of popular feng shui, especially speaking to those interested in astrology, is the matching of home and horoscope. This is also common in Chinese feng shui, however, making use of the year of birth and the symbolism of the given animal sign, independent data such as day and month and their prophecy in the lunar calendar or a calculation of all birth data to arrive at a sacred number according to the *Luo Shu*. Except for use of lunar-calendar prophecies, these other methods are also found in western renditions; another difference is that in Chinese culture, only the horoscope of the male head of household would be used. For instance, the full calculation of birth data is recommended by some authors in order to decide if a house facing a certain direction is favourable for a particular person, or which parts of a building are most suited for a particular person and which ones ought to be avoided (e.g. Walters 1991: 107; 121). The methods consists of reducing all birth data (year, month, day, hour) into a single digit by means of the sum of the digits, and correlating it to the trigrams, elements, directions more associated to this number in the *Luo Shu*. This may be developed into highly elaborate schemes of comparing the elements associated with rooms facing in different directions with the element of the house occupant, thus indicating which rooms may be used for which activities (lounge, bedroom, storage, office, etc.).

A whole range of books confront the chaos of things and objects that people tend to be surrounded with in their homes, and provide advice on how to 'clean up your clutter' (Kingston 1998) or 'de-clutter' your home with feng shui. Thus it is argued, presumably with accuracy, that much of our home spaces are occupied by useless stuff and dead objects to which we have no relation. In order for feng shui to be effective, useless, abandoned and broken objects must be removed. Some authors see our connections to these objects in terms of fine energy threads, which can have a positive or negative impact and which may clutter up into an impenetrable cobweb. The basic thinking is that by bringing order to your home you bring order to your life: when clutter accumulates, energy stalls and effects constraints on people's lives. Some specialize in 'space-clearing' and the creation of 'sacred spaces', thought to improve health, wealth and happiness (Linn 1995; Kingston 2003). Practically all photographs in feng shui manuals show impeccably clean and orderly homes, devoid of traces of everyday routines. As compared to the common practices of much of their audience, they articulate order and control.

When western popular feng shui manuals promise changes in people's health, happiness, relationships, love life, wealth, career and opportunities, they address the same essential desires in our lives as the Chinese version. It is also noteworthy that these desires are materialistic in nature as much as spiritual or emotional, putting the individual in the centre and making no distinctions between our aspirations in various aspects of our lives. Yet it is an application of feng shui in which the western concept of personality figures prominently. The home is commonly described as 'a mirror of who we are' or 'a mirror of our personality' as much as a powerful physical force in our lives: 'By becoming aware of how your home mirrors you, and how to shift its energy, you can turn your home into a force that heals, restores balances, and encourages growth' (Stasney 2004a: 6).

Another application of feng shui to the home, particularly adapted to a modern lifestyle, is the association of *qi* energy with moving. It is argued that the local-area *qi* energy influences the personal *qi* in such a way that moving the home is like pulling up a tree with roots. The tree needs to be moved and replanted in a way that does not hurt it, and this should be done at the right time of year. When we move, the direction in which we move and the time of the year determines how our personal *qi* energy will adapt to the *qi* energy of the new place. These factors are laid out by means of the Chinese magic square (*Luo Shu*), in which a year is designated a number one to nine. The year of birth and the year of moving is thus given a direction in the *Luo Shu*, and the numbers are associated with the animal zodiac, the eight compass directions and the Five Elements to create a range of association, good or bad (Brown 1996, Chapter 9).

From a critical perspective, however, many popular applications of feng shui to home design seem to be made up of haphazard associations and inconsistent principles, mixing feng shui with western psychology, medicine, simple animism, new shamanism or a reviving belief in magic. Further, it appears that innumerable pictures of auspicious feng shui designs in popular manuals have this in common: you take a spacious home with favourable light intake, fill it with expensive furniture and design objects, balance the colours, employ a professional photographer and call it feng shui! Any furniture catalogue maker would nod agreeably.

Personal problems

Much western feng shui literature either explicitly or implicitly attend to personal problems, such as depression, anger and lack of success. Typical of a large section of popular feng shui manuals is the promise of instant changes to people's lives. Manuals address a large audience that does not seek to preserve the state of harmony in their homes or protect their own personal status quo; this audience wants change. The manuals capture such desire in their opening chapters with wording like: 'This book . . . will change your life forever . . . you will learn how changes to the interior design of your home will be echoed by changes that are made to your life' (Lazenby 1998a: 7–8); or, 'You can change your life situation by moving furniture, painting or tidying up' (Dittmer 2005: 106). Another book has a chapter title, 'Move the couch – and you get a new life', while arguing that 'feng shui brings hope by re-establishing the connection with the sacred' and 'feng shui brings magic changes to your life' (Kingston 2003).

The manuals state a range of reasons for a personal life not going well. Bad design, old things, collections of objects, photographs from the past, useless clothes, fatigued relationships, annoying people, etc. are all impediments to personal success. They restrain the flow of vital energies around us and must be removed mercilessly in order to gain new vitality.

Some interpret personal problems as deriving from natural personality flaws, which may be addressed and improved by means of adjusting the personal *qi*, such as by the conscious use of colours and their associations (Rossbach and Lin 1994: 130). In a similar fashion, psychological ailments may be addressed with colours, such as alleviating depression by use of the colours green and red, signifying hope/spring and happiness/activity respectively.

The general message contained in western feng shui is straightforward and, in line with Chinese uses, activist or anti-fatalist in orientation, but with post-modern elements of individualism and fragmentation: remove all obstacles, take matters in your own hands and create your own life.

Love and relationship

A long list of feng shui publications speak to those wanting guidance on love and relationships. They promise quick results, such as how moving your stuff and carefully arranging items in the home can lead to remarkable results in love (Carter 2000), how easy tips on the secret workings of feng shui can improve your romance (Too 2000), or how harmonious and successful relationships reached through feng shui can empower every person: 'Attract love, romance and successful relationships immediately into your life with these hundreds of tips' (Wong 2002: back matter). As an example, this book tells of a female banker who experienced males constantly passing in and out of her life and was thus asking for advice:

'Tell you what', I said, 'I'll give you two. Your bedroom door in your marriage area represents the men in your life coming in and out. Keep your bedroom door closed all the time, except when you're using it, and tie two red ribbons on the inside doorknob'.

Two years later, I bumped into the banker again. 'I've been meaning to contact you all this time!' she said. 'Within a month of doing what you suggested, I met the man I married, and we have a baby girl'. (Wong 2002: 4)

Such stories of want for love and romance as well as of successful remedies abound in the feng shui literature and on the websites of manual authors;

for many consultants around the world, it is in fact among the largest portions of their business. Here is another story from the website of an Indian feng shui master, Mohan Deep. A woman complained about a loveless life after having left a marriage with a drunken and violent man. She had been on her own for six years, being disillusioned with marriage:

I suggested the Feng Shui method to destroy the negative energy. A part of her wardrobe, consisting of certain dresses she once wore, had to go as a part of letting go of the past. Only after that, I suggested a better placement for her bed and suggested Feng Shui remedies for the Marriage & Relationship corner. The painting of the Phoenix & Dragon along with the Double Happiness symbol in the right place and a couple of red candles proved to be just right for her.

Her account of what happened soon afterwards is amazing. 'Love bloomed in my life again while organizing the college annual day. The students consulted me about the play. I'd read a play of a Mumbai based writer and suggested that. We required his permission so I met him. It was my destiny. Something immediately clicked between us . . . It was as if we were made for each other . . . We are very much in love and have decided to spend the rest of life together'. (www.fengshuimiracle.com, last accessed 28 March 2008)

In the schools of feng shui using the *bagua* to show the associations of the individual parts of the home, the upper right section is most commonly associated with love and close relationships (trigram of *kun*). To attract or recapture passion, some argue that you should bring touches of red into the *kun* area of your home, red being the strongest and most stimulating of the colours. Or if you want to bring more friends of both sexes into your life, you should place some green plants or candles in the *chien* (friendship) area (Webster 1999). The same popular book associates people with one of the five Chinese elements (wood, fire, earth, metal, and water) in order to indicate the personal element with the birth date. It is claimed that people of certain elements are good matches while others require extra work; 'but don't worry, simple cures for complex relationships are included' (Webster 1999: back matter).

Another recent book teaches readers how to transform their homes to attract, enhance and enrich romantic love in their lives. Based on 'ancient Daoist secrets that join feng shui and Chinese astrology', the author's method is personalized through questionnaires and individualized charts. Readers will learn how to use their own personal styles and areas of special interest to arrange their homes in 'a personally meaningful and effectual way' (Simons 2007).

Yet another book among the hundreds addressing love combines feng shui with Daoist philosophy. According to its author, the principles of *yin* and *yang* represent the polarity, balance, and equilibrium found in nature; thus love is a process of dynamic balance of *yin* and *yang* energies. *Yin* and *yang* are at the same time the experience of love in all its forms. The author says: 'many people have discovered that working with these ancient techniques manifests love and abundance in their lives'; Daoist and feng shui principles can be used in all areas of life to attract lasting love and happiness (Hsu 2003). The introduction says: 'Once you attune yourself and your space to the flow of universal energies, you make room in your home and in your heart for the loving relationship you've been waiting for'.

Business and workplace

A rapidly growing application of feng shui is for business, comprising anything from small single-person businesses to multinational corporations. Starting at a personal level, where leading business executives have employed feng shui specialists to design their offices either for general wellbeing or for optimizing their personal power and success, uses of feng shui have developed along the same lines as in Hong Kong, Taipei or Shanghai to include general outlines for all staff and even the design and placement of entire office buildings. For large corporations already making use of human resource developers, psychologists and astrologers, using a feng shui specialist may be seen as nothing out of the ordinary, and the cost involved is easily incorporated into general expenses for advertising, marketing and branding. It may form part of an employee-friendly branding exercise of showing good working conditions, a pleasant climate and care for the individual.

The general understanding of how feng shui applies to business is this: by simple application of feng shui principles, a business may achieve success, better profit, better terms of competition, satisfied and returning customers as well as employees that feel good and work harder out of free will. Feng shui is applied to business in much the same way as to homes, making use of entities such as the *bagua*, use of colours, *Yin-yang* theory, Five Elements, interpretation of forms and shapes and position in relation to surroundings, but with a number of modifications.

As in Chinese culture, the basic presumption is that the flow of *qi* may be likened to the flow of money in or out of the business. Thus businesses should be placed where the flow of *qi* is dynamic, far more so than for homes, being places of relaxation. Busy streets and plazas are associated with the type of energy suited for shops, while office buildings require calmer locations (Choy 1998: 110). Feng shui for business has as a main goal the abundance of money, associated with flows of *qi* that are strong but easy to seize without flowing right through the business. Flowing water, fountains or aquariums with goldfish are often included to stimulate the flow of *qi*. Open spaces in front and solid backing behind buildings in land- or cityscapes are also among common key recommendations, expressed as such as: 'a strong backing is the key to business success' (Lim 2003: 69). Another concern is the attention to signs and symbols such as business logos, as well as the business' visibility, which may be improved with colours, lighting and signs. Feng shui for business is the application that borrows most directly from Chinese feng shui (many feng shui-for-business manual authors are in fact Chinese). Many rules are identical, such as the avoidance of long straight corridors, which are seen to make *qi* flow speedily through, and directly opposed doors, which may cause clashing energies (Lam 1995: 142).

Some interpret it as a universal law that positive energy is attracted by positive energy, negative by negative; money is attracted by money, bills by bills. By using simple feng shui advice, the business is provided with life energy, and success and surplus come easily: 'Money rolls into the account, almost by itself' (Petersen 2005: 12).

An open space in front of a business is usually associated with good conditions for growth and gain, thus the bigger space the bigger the opportunities. Similarly, businesses must be particularly aware of blocking, pointing or sharp objects in front, likened to obstacles to or attacks on the business. A highly creative application of feng shui for business roofs is inspired by a Hong Kong and south-Chinese trend in elaborative feng shui rooftop designs. Drawing on the old Chinese classification of mountain shapes according to the Five Elements (water, wood, fire, metal and earth), different roof shapes are similarly classified, and the individual elements are given different capacities to 'preserve energy' and thus to hold on to money (Lim 2003).

Feng shui is commonly applied to the individual office or workspace as well. The placement of the desk in relation to windows and entrance is a main concern, interpreted as crucial to success and promotion. The desk should not be placed diagonally opposite to the door, while the user should still have visibility towards the door and solid backing behind. With special reference to executive offices, whose inhabitants may have the freedom of choice, is the position of the office in the floor or building as a whole, for which the *bagua*, Five Elements and a rich symbolism of up–down, north–south and open–closed may be activated. More recent publications may depart more from the Chinese feng shui business recommendations, for instance by including conscious design and personality deliberations. As an example, one such book states that feng shui focuses your awareness on how the arrangement of your space defines and affects your personal development, as well as your work: 'The shape and size of your desk, the comfort factor of your chair, and the colors on your walls all influence your mental and emotional states of being. By carefully selecting decor and placements that support your desired results, your office becomes a physical manifestation of your life's direction' (Stasney 2004b: 5).

Other authors, influenced by Buddhism (see Chapter 5), deliberately play with mysticism, arguing that it adds strength to the practical aspects of feng shui cures: 'feng shui without mysticism is like a body without a soul', Sarah Rossbach argues. An example of advice for good business:

Another mystical means to safeguard a business is to place near the cash register a vase – symbolizing peace – with a red ribbon wrapped around it, and to hang a bamboo flute tied with a red ribbon above it. The flute acts as a symbolic sword protecting profits and patrons and as a funnel conducting ch'i upward through the sections of the flute to help improve business. (Rossbach and Lin 1987: 124)

Feng shui for institutions

As developed for homes in order to make people thrive and feel comfortable, an increasing number of feng shui specialists work for institutions where people spend long periods of time, including old people's homes, kindergartens, schools and hospitals. It goes for large institutions as for businesses, that hiring a feng shui consultant is just a small item in a large budget, and seldom more than one approach out of many to serve the users; it may also support reputation. An increasing number of studies show that conscious design, greenery, improved diet and other initiatives aimed at the general welfare of patients have significant effects on their restoration to health (a title on the use of feng shui for hospitals is Schumm 2004).

MANUAL AUTHORS

Western feng shui practitioners, many of them at the same time being popular manual authors, are often characterized by practising a whole range of therapies and cures, of which feng shui is merely one.

Accordingly, feng shui is frequently offered along with shiatsu, astrology, macrobiotics, crystal energy, chakra therapy, shamanism and a whole range of other trends usually associated with new age. Such examples: one manual author offers feng shui consultations along with Jungian psychology and shadow therapy; another combines feng shui with Chinese medicine, *taiqi* and *qigong*; a third combines it with shamanism and earth radiation; a fourth with astrology; and a fifth with penduling (examples from popular manuals). They are themselves expressive of the general 'pick and mix' approach to Asian traditions that prevails among their clients. At the same time, their manuals work as advertisements for their businesses, offering inspections, courses and products, while providing contact addresses and websites.

Like their fellow Chinese practitioners, few of them have much formal education, having chosen the alternative therapeutic path fairly early or in early mature life. What they also have in common with their Chinese counterparts is that they often write in a self-glorifying style, characterizing their own skills and merits in terms that would be as seen highly inappropriate in other writing genres such as fiction, cookbooks, children's books, popular science, auto-repair and so forth. Many introduce themselves in terms like 'the foremost expert', 'the leading Master', the person 'who introduced feng shui to a western audience', the 'first Chinese Master to write for Westerners', as an author of a book of 'philosophical importance like few others', etc. The manual authors embody the 'self-spirituality' that characterizes much new religion (Heelas 1996: 2). The feng shui manuals are most often made for easy reading and quick consumption ('in the MacFengshui business', as one anonymous commentator had it!). The closest equivalent would probably be commercial advertising, also promising magical quick changes from consumption of a given product, although usually maintaining an ironical distance. We shall return to this new, somewhat outlandish writing style in the concluding chapter.

A major difference, however, is that while Chinese feng shui masters and manual authors are almost exclusively men, the majority of western manual authors, and presumably also a great majority of practitioners, are women. Since the majority of clients and potential manual buyers are women, and given the tendency for many women to prefer other women as doctors, advisors and sources of inspiration, female author manuals have better publishing potentials. There are also a fair number of male authors, however, who tend to deal with the more technical or mathematical aspects, as there are a number of author teams consisting of Chinese males and western women. .

GLOBAL EXCHANGE

It has already been noted in several chapters that feng shui rose in the West under very different intellectual circumstances than in China, and that many features have developed along separate lines. What was also noted, however, was that the new interpretations that arose under influence from western academia were a powerful source of motivation and inspiration for a new generation of Chinese writers, brought up when the Marxist view of religion held sway. The mutual inspiration and transfer of knowledge and ideas between East and West are indeed centuries old. Considering the great inspiration from Chinese philosophy from the seventeenth century onwards, and the Chinese fascination with writers like Marx, Engels, Nietzsche and others in the last century, in a philosophical sense it may be false to pit East against West (Paton 2007). Urban development and new lifestyles in China further blur old distinctions, and at the same time global flows of people, goods, cultural stuffs, information and capital reduce the historical impact of distance. Today, the rate of cultural exchange is accelerating.

Particularly from the mid 1990s, the interaction between people study-ing, practising or taking an interest in feng shui across the continents has risen fast. International conferences and workshops are held, study tours to China are organized, national associations are formed to share knowledge, new training courses are constantly set up, journals and websites abound, new books are written, old classics are made available and renowned experts practise across the globe.

Since 2004, the International Feng Shui Association (IFSA) has orga-nized a yearly event in Singapore called The International Feng Shui Con-vention. This is a high-profile event, with conference sessions and panel discussions among a range of renowned feng shui practitioners and manual authors from several continents. Consisting of practising professionals, the aim of the IFSA and the Convention is to promote knowledge and under-standing of feng shui and to show how it can achieve a harmonious living. They are established 'to encourage and assist in the development of the Feng Shui practitioners' profession globally, in a manner which enhances the image of the Feng Shui profession and fosters the highest standards of Feng Shui competence and practice' (see the IFSA website).

A number of European and American university departments (partic-ularly of architecture, design, Chinese studies and philosophy) have orga-nized seminars, panels and talks, where Chinese and Westerners blend freely and exchange knowledge and ideas. My own experience from such occasions in both Europe and the USA, however, is a sense of great divide, if not insurmountable difficulties in reconciling attitudes and expectations. This is hardly a strife between East and West, but between, for instance, grandiose Chinese masters and their admirers on the one side and academics and students on the other. Chinese universities, too, organize feng shui seminars as well as training programmes, for which there is a huge demand. Universities in Beijing, Nanjing, Shanghai, Wuhan and other cities have engaged in such, but as seen from a recent case in Nanjing (see Chapter 6), they easily encounter opposition, even obstruction, from higher places.

Chinese professors and university departments also increasingly engage in study tours for foreigners to the 'country where feng shui began'. Participants are taken to auspicious sites and presented with classical Chinese architecture encapsulating the principles of feng shui. Michael Paton relates an amusing episode from such a tour, when a Taiwanese expert feng shui practitioner and tour instructor, He Jinzong, was told by a number of participants that they did not wish to discuss burial since 'this was not feng shui' (Paton 2007: 427). Obviously, such tour arrangements must operate according to the market and fit in with the prevalent understanding of the subject, at the same time compromising on the Chinese tradition.

National or local feng shui associations spring up at a rapid pace, often active in organizing feng shui training programs, guest teachers and travel. In addition to countries in western Europe and North America, they include a range of countries in southeast Asia, eastern Europe and Latin America.

Another group of actors in the global exchange certainly worthy of mention is multinational corporations. Having perhaps started consulting feng shui masters in their Chinese-speaking branches to follow custom and please local employees, many bring novel concepts of intentional design and meaningful decór back to their home offices in Euro-American cities. These include, in particular, banks, airlines, hotel chains, telephone and IT companies, but many more follow in their footsteps.

CORPORATE FENG SHUI?

Is feng shui increasingly becoming big business in the hands of successful manual authors and various corporate interests? If so, it apparently shares this fate with other strands of popular spirituality. There are two significant trends pointing in this direction. First, as drawn from a range of sociologists in the Introduction (Chapter 1), people in the present stage of modernity are being freed from traditional bonds and institutions at a rapid pace, while being subject to a new form of individuality that makes them at the same time more searching and potentially more vulnerable. People look for overarching perspectives to create a meaningful whole, or a connecting thread in their lives. Second, those who compete in the marketplace, primarily the media and the corporate world, increasingly tap into this desire by providing meaning and order. According to some writing (e.g. Grant 2000; Carrette and King 2005), while marketing was previously in an 'age of aspiration' by reflecting the buyers' social ideals and values, it has now entered a more aggressive age of 'providing people ideas to live by'; in this new age, brands create the traditions.

The loss of religion in many western societies is a fair target for the market, and provides constant new opportunities for branding. It is symptomatic for the privatization and commercialization of religion that new 'spirituality' in a wealth of forms arises. New marketing practices challenge religious values in society, and they may – in a radical interpretation – be seen as plundering the cultural resources of humanity for the sake of corporate profit. Such challenge to culture necessitates a critical perspective upon the modern phenomenon of 'spirituality' (Carrette and King 2005: 140).

As new popular spirituality is spreading to health care, public institutions, education, management theory and marketing, the Asian traditions in particular are subject to a cultural translation into something that fits the categories of the individual as consumer and the society as market. Feng shui is perhaps faster than other strands in becoming a valuable means to market and sell a product, and still more actors engage in its appropriation for their own gain. Practitioners with three-day course diplomas, manual authors that promise to revolutionize people's lives and corporate businesses luring their customers with new spirituality all contribute to the steady commercialization of religion – or commodification of life itself. A critical stance is needed towards those who, on a corporate or individual basis, tap into human needs to make money without much ethical concern.

CHAPTER 8

Environmental concerns

In the western world, feng shui was often associated with a concern for the environment: when introduced in the 1960s, feng shui was accompanied by a range of new concepts, such as landscape, environment, nature and ecology, and was infused with western ideology; it was even used as an explicit criticism of a 'conventional' European perception of nature. When evaluating such concern, however, several distinctions must be made. First of all, as shown in previous chapters, feng shui was given a new guise when transferred to Euro-American societies, being stripped of much of its original folk-religious content. We should distinguish between what it was and still is in Chinese rural communities and what is has become in the western city and suburban areas, where it mostly has moved indoors and primarily relates to private life, including homes and gardens, or to various other purposes such as running businesses and institutions.

Then there is a distinction in time. During the long haul of Chinese history, feng shui was addressing individual human desires, sometimes extending to entire communities or cities, while nature and environment as such hardly were independent categories of thought and concern. The modern Chinese version looks increasingly similar to its western counterpart, but with the modification that feng shui uses still tend to be broader, including, for instance, burial, ancestor worship, business and links to Chinese religion. Thus the two most radically different versions of feng shui are found in Chinese rural areas and in western cities, being worlds apart, while in the Chinese city it has been adapted to Chinese modernity.

In the current era of global ecological challenges, most attention is directed towards factors from economic, political and social life. However, religions may regain their importance too. All forms of religion provide basic interpretations of who we are, where we came from and where we are going. They provide worldviews and suggest how we should treat other humans. The ethics generated by religion also underlie fundamental attitudes and values of a society in relation to nature, in both conscious and

173

unconscious ways (Tucker and Berthrong 1998: xvi). The vast environmental problems in China, probably surpassing those experienced by any western country, make both higher and lower echelons of society look for new means of changing practices, raising awareness or representing local communities; feng shui may be among those means. This chapter will explore old and new meanings of Chinese feng shui in relation to the environment.

HISTORY AND ENVIRONMENT IN CHINA

The term 'environment' is of a relatively recent date in the West, while the corresponding Chinese term (*'huanjing'*) was only introduced in the republican period. In China, several concepts for 'nature' were instead commonly used (*tian, dao, siran*), drawing from different philosophical traditions and denoting either 'heaven's will', the 'way of things' or transformation. Another common trend may see it simply as a resource base that could be brought under control in the service of man. The modern concept for nature (*siran*) originally referred to the spontaneously generated existence according to the principles of Heaven and Earth, particularly being used in Daoist philosophy. Only in the early twentieth century, under influence from Japanese modernizers, did it gain the western meaning of something separate from culture and society.

Arguments that feng shui has historically contributed to the protection of the environment in China, such as shown in Chapters 4 and 7, lack substantiation. It is true, though, that feng shui thinking, along with other strands of Chinese philosophy, is holistic, making use of analogies between Heaven, Earth and Man. It shares with Confucianism the dynamic and organismic worldview, seeing the universe as a vast integrated unit with inherent correspondence, and vibrating with energy and cosmic resonance.

Accordingly, a sick natural environment should alarm the native people – which it probably does. But instead of changing practices to the better, it may inspire exploitation of new land and other resources. Natural philosophy should not be mistaken for environmental practices (Bruun and Kalland 1995); one belongs to the written tradition and the other to the social and economic life of ordinary people. Undeniably, the Chinese have a long literary tradition of venerating nature, but we cannot simply assume that cultural traits belonging to the elite were applied in practice by ordinary people.

Seen to the western eye, a profound discrepancy has prevailed between word and practice, by philosophy being a moralizing agency stressing

ideal culture rather than observed reality. The contrast between philosophical prescription and popular practice remained strong throughout
Chinese history: the expansion of Chinese civilization invariably implied
geographic transformation, including the levelling of farmland, water control, deforestation, soil erosion and the suppression or extinction of species
not useful to mankind. Developments in the intellectual and philosophical
tradition over time, such as from early naturalism to Confucianism to Neo-
Confucianism, were hardly accompanied by changes in popular practices,
which followed their own independent course (Weller and Bol 1998: 327).

Since Chinese feng shui is essentially anthropocentric and oriented
towards maximizing the benefit of cosmic forces for human satisfaction,
the natural environment as such, including species of flora and fauna,
appears to raise no special concern apart from its material, spiritual or
decorative uses. Dramatic transformation of the land, providing wealth
and subsistence for a rising population, was never seen as an offence to the
principles of feng shui, and if it were, remedies could be found within the
same tradition.

We must appreciate that the roots to China's present environmental
crises go far back in time. Both traditional family ideals and the rulers of
successive dynasties have emphasized the value of many offspring and a large
Chinese population. Thus, since at least the seventh century, population
increase has taken a heavy toll on the environment. Elizabeth Economy,
the great commentator on China's environment, puts it bluntly: 'Through
the centuries . . . exploitation of the environment contributed to the cycles
of war, famine, and natural disaster that plagued China and hastened
the disintegration of one dynasty after the next' (Economy 2004: 27).
Environmental destruction has taken place for centuries, albeit intensified
during the last half century (Banister 2000: 262). The aggressive policy
adopted during the reign of Mao Zedong has been termed the 'war against
nature', as any obstacle to political goals – human or natural – was removed
in a military fashion (Shapiro 2001).

A continuous range of historians have noted that Chinese natural philosophy has not in any way prevented deforestation and destruction of the
environment through Chinese history (e.g. Cobb 1972; Elvin 2004). In fact,
the Chinese have never restrained themselves in changing their environment, even in very drastic and profound ways, e.g. by levelling mountains,
changing the course of rivers or building dams and canals. Mark Elvin has
noted that during the Qing dynasty, there were 'enthusiasts for gigantic
engineering projects, even more demented than Li Peng's Sanxia (Three
Gorges) Dam' (Elvin 2004: 31). Chinese writers on the subject are little

more appreciating. A historian, Li Bozhong, writes about the general role of environmental care in Chinese history:

As a historian of China, however, I must reluctantly conclude that the force of material gain has been persistent, pervasive and pernicious in its effect on the Chinese environment for many centuries. Chinese peasants have long sought to improve their livelihoods by clearing the next wetland, cutting down the neighbouring forest for fuel and arable fields, or tearing up the grasslands for wheat and millet. Noble cultural ideals of Taoism or *fengshui* have had little restraining effect, especially since the population boom of the eighteenth century. (Li B. 1994: 6)

Some of China's most respected ecologists have noted that Chinese history saw the unheeded exploitation of natural resources taking a heavy toll (e.g. Li and Zhao 1989: 1–2). In the modern era, they note, China was very late in forming a conservation strategy. The Chinese veteran fighter for environmental protection and first director of China's State Bureau of Environmental Protection, Qu Geping, notes that while China's environmental problems are rooted in history, her environmental policies only began to develop in the 1970s, when many unique ecosystems had already been badly damaged (Qu and Li 1994: 3–4). Apparently, China has been distressed with an environment overburdened by population since the Spring and Autumn period, from which time it has been a constant concern (Qu and Li 1994: 9). Today, China must bear the brunt of militaristic policies of the 1950s to 1970s, which saw population increase as improving the socialist economy. At the establishment of the People's Republic of China in 1949, its population was 540 million; today it is 1,330 million.

Altogether, both Chinese and western historical sources of the serious kind seem to agree that protection of the natural environment was not a primary concern neither in feng shui thinking nor in other strands of Chinese philosophy and religion. Again, quoting Economy, 'China's history suggests a long, deeply entrenched tradition of exploiting the environment for man's needs, with relatively little sense of the limits of nature's or man's capacity to replenish the earth's resources' (Economy 2004: 55).

SOME FIELDWORK EXPERIENCES

After many decades of socialist experimentation, the Chinese state had penetrated all local affairs, though not necessarily being able to exercise control at all times. The state, represented by local government, regulated production, supervised markets and provided a number of inputs such as energy, chemical fertilizers and pesticides. Today, China is a liberal market society, yet with strong state institutions. In agriculture, the contract system is still in place, which implies that farmers do not own the land they cultivate. They depend on long-term contracts with the state on joint-village basis, which means that the land may still be reallocated within the village according to the number of people who depend on farming in each household. It also implies that state institutions may rather easily take possession of the land for industrial development, housing development or other purposes, with very low levels of compensation to the farmers.

The same applies to the environment. China is an ancient hydraulic society, and a number of crucial functions in agriculture have always been communal tasks. The decades of communist leadership and continued public ownership of land have perhaps moved responsibility for support functions further away from the individual. This includes the management of most of those factors we usually associate with the 'environment': inputs of chemicals, emissions of toxicants, management of waterways, control of drinking water and care for the wild flora and fauna.

Over the last several decades, the primary caretaker of the environment has been state institutions with half-hearted local presence (meaning that their employees are rarely present in local stations). Only they have had any measure of precise knowledge on pollutants in air, soil and water. Short-term economic goals combined with a lack of political transparency and accountability of local leadership until recently prevented any attention being given to the environment.

Part of my own fieldwork in rural areas has concerned rural people's views of their natural environment, including their possible linking of feng shui to their own environmental practices or to the general state of the natural environment. Fieldwork took place in areas where feng shui was strong and used for a large variety of purposes. Due to many centuries of heavy population pressure in the Chinese interior, rural communities have mostly done away with all uncertainty factors in agriculture. The visible organic habitat consists almost entirely of items that are deliberately grown and raised for the sake of humans. Fields are intensively grown with as many yearly crops as the climate permits, all waste products from agriculture and cooking are fed to pigs and chickens, small ponds are used for breeding fish, paddy fields feed ducks and any growth on small slopes is cut for hay or firewood. These are the essentials of Chinese farming and the foundation for its historical success. With the introduction of pesticides, insects are mostly under control and birds have become rare.

This was not quite so in some of my former anthropological field-work areas, however, which included hilly stretches unsuitable for intensive agriculture and instead giving the inhabitants access to other resources. But even in the hills, nothing is left untouched if it has just the slightest value. The green cover of grasses and herbs between the rocks are cut for hay at regular intervals, and occasional small trees are likewise cut for firewood or building materials when grown to a proper size. Practically all wildlife that previously inhabited the hills are now gone, including snakes and reptiles, having all served as a supplement to the overtly monotonous rural kitchen. Any creature that may venture a comeback will be sure to suffer this fate again. Only in an area in Jiangsu bordering on forest farms owned by the Forestry University in Nanjing, as well as some stretches of forest surrounding the Longchang Buddhist temple, could the villagers make occasional hunting expeditions and, if lucky, bring back a rabbit. Otherwise, wildlife simply does not exist after an entire century of civil war, repetitive periods of starvation following disastrous political campaigns and, on top of that, inadequate interest in preserving whatever species that may be left. To make it absolutely clear, present Chinese beliefs in feng shui do not entail making the earth a suitable living space for other creatures than humans and their domesticated animals.

Some rural areas near Yaan in southwest Sichuan were included in the fieldwork. Within memory, these areas had been surrounded by dense forest, even as late as the 1950s. The older generation would recall a time when hunting for deer, fox, wolf and even tiger was good in the forest, and hungry tigers were known to scramble around villages. As elsewhere, all wildlife succumbed along with the forest being felled during the Great Leap Forward, when villages were demanded to set up small wood-burning furnaces. At the time, it took but a year-and-a-half of centrally guided mass campaigns to wipe out both the forest and its animal inhabitants. These days, one does not expect to see tigers or other large game in heavily populated areas anywhere in the world, but the Chinese countryside nevertheless distinguishes itself from that of many other countries.

There has been a general failure of linking control of the use of pesticides to public health. In most Chinese rural areas, the use of pesticides exploded along with the introduction of contract farming in the 1980s. The effect on the environment had been dramatic everywhere. Bees and butterflies, supposedly good indicators of the state of the environment, have become rare indeed in some areas and are totally wiped out in others. When viewing the landscape from a hilltop in any of my fieldwork areas, I always felt that something was missing. Particularly in Sichuan, the lush green vegetation with clusters of trees and bamboos around farmhouses was a pretty sight, but the landscape was silent. Within the reach of the eye, there were fewer birds than in my average-sized garden at home. When enquiring among the locals, they would confirm that there had once been more birds, but it was a very long time ago. Birds were already scarce due to hunting campaigns in the 1960s, net-catching and continued hunting for fun, but they are now also exposed to an environment overloaded with pesticides such as DDT and DDVP, which for many years were sprayed directly on fruit and vegetables.

Furthermore, what pesticides could not finish off would be taken out by humans. In some Sichuan villages, people related that where birds could be found, young men from the city would come out and shoot them for fun. So the birds were gone too, and nobody seemed to miss them much. A routine commentary seemed to be: 'If you want a bird that sings, you can buy one in a cage.' As in city areas, some families had small singing birds in tiny cages suspended from the roof outside the door or in the courtyard.

There has been no general farm-level monitoring of pesticide application whatsoever. The agricultural extension service rarely descend to the villages, and judging the quality of soil and water is generally left to the villagers. During fieldwork in the 1990s, the township government received centrally devised radio programmes that it broadcast locally through the propaganda system, including loudspeakers in all hamlets. Such broadcasts had information on the correct application of chemical fertilizers and pesticides. The villagers, however, only shrugged their shoulders and said: 'We never listen.' After years and years of political campaigning, trying to reach the villagers has backfired; people would automatically shut off their minds when the loudspeakers roared.

Chinese villagers tend to have little interest in other aspects of their environment than what relates to their own production. For instance, when talking to a woman spraying the vines in her orchard, I asked about insects. She told us about a dramatic decline: 'All the butterflies and most of the insects disappeared when we started using pesticides; that was in the late 1980s. But they were such a nuisance anyway.' And indeed, some enormous Sichuanese species of wasps and biting flies are not only terrifying sights but are even highly dangerous. But with these also disappeared a wealth of beautiful butterflies.

So much for the fauna – or one should say the missing fauna. In the classical literature on feng shui, vegetation plays an important part. For centuries, and certainly since Chinese landscape painting came into being, the presence of vegetation in the form of trees, bamboos, bushes and groves is clearly indicative of the auspicious feng shui qualities of a landscape.

Many villages in addition had sacred old 'feng shui trees' or 'feng shui groves'. So to what extent are they present today?

Trees around houses are still associated with good feng shui, but in the inner provinces, the material circumstances of life forbids most villagers to plant more than a few trees or a cluster of bamboos. Variations are mostly related to climate. Villages in the north and central parts are mostly grey, dusty and messy, without any vegetation in excess of the most vital. Villages are generally much prettier in China's subtropical areas. In the villages of the south, southwest and southeast, where small houses are placed close together, the lush greenery may provide shelter and cooling in the hot summer season. However, feng shui is not seen to inspire more vegetation than quite practical considerations will anyhow produce.

For graves, similar deliberations apply. Anything that obstructs the prospect in front of a grave is considered a bad influence and, whenever possible, is removed or levelled out. Trees growing behind or at the flanks of graves are considered beneficial, pertaining to the ideal layout of a grave as an 'armchair'. As a consequence, feng shui theory will advise the planting of trees in some positions and warn against them in others. Therefore, again in theory, if a grave is placed in solitude on a hillside, it will contribute to the preservation of trees and greenery at least in some positions. But in real life, favourable burial grounds are scarce, and almost any serviceable hillside will be sprinkled with graves, old and new in concoction. As noted by Maurice Freedman, in order to obtain the best feng shui, people scatter their graves (Freedman 1979: 197), and since the trees that are beneficial to the grave in front will be intolerable to the grave behind, the compromise is usually no large trees at all but only shrubs and bushes. In some regions, for instance in Fujian, all vegetation is removed in front of graves, the large numbers of which frequently turn hillsides into dreary wastes; this was also noted by J. J. M. de Groot in the late nineteenth century (de Groot 1901: 945).

In very general terms, few people show concern for environmental factors such as outlined above. For villagers, a care for the natural environment outside those factors on which humans immediately depend is a predominantly intellectual pursuit – and why should Chinese villagers be different from other farmers who are mostly under severe economic pressure? Moreover, the vast number of inhabitants in the villages would not recognize any possible connection between the disappearance of bees, butterflies and birds and increasing local health hazards. Neither did anyone suspect that health problems could arise from polluted drinking water or contaminated foodstuffs, let alone interpret such issues in feng shui terminology. Still, there were exceptions. A few individuals in the villages showed a genuine interest in the natural environment outside the culti-vated domain. One such was an elderly barefoot doctor, who deplored the disappearance of butterflies, which he had once collected. Another was a feng shui specialist, who had developed a 'professional' interest in veg-etation around houses. Otherwise, the common view was unaffected by the rising environmental concerns among the higher echelons of Chinese society. When revisiting some of my former fieldwork areas in 2006, the environment had further deteriorated – some places to an extent making them unsuitable for any living species. The villages north of Nanjing in the Jiangsu province in particular, where former farmland had been built on by Chinese, Japanese and Korean petrochemical factories, were heavily pol-luted. As soon as we got off the little motorcycle cab that had taken us from the nearby town, both my two Chinese companions and I immediately felt that this was a hazardous place. The air was thick with yellowish smog and a noxious chemical stink filled our throats. We discussed returning at once, but decided to persevere by staying indoors in people's homes as much as possible. While we worried considerably for our health during the couple of hours we spent in the villages, however, the local people lived and worked there year-round. Visiting farmers only confirmed our antici-pations. The crops in the field looked nasty. The vegetables stood small and frail in a yellowish colour, and some plants had dropped to the ground. Much of it was immediately discarded. Even though people soaked the rest of the vegetables in water before eating them, they were 'not quite sure' if they were edible. The entire area reportedly suffered from many untimely deaths, but no one knew the exact state of affairs. The ground water was heavily polluted and people were ordered not to drink from wells; instead, piped water had been installed from a nearby town.

Some farmers had complained of pollution to the management of nearby factories, and some had received a small monetary compensation. Other-wise, no state institutions seemed involved in environmental management or control, and factories emitted pollutants as they pleased. In the whole area, agriculture was gradually giving way to industry as land was being continually expropriated.

Let me return to the subject of the role of feng shui in addressing the envi-ronment. As I knew from previous fieldwork, feng shui was commonly used and practised in this area and remained a vital aspect of people's perception of the world. It is a common topic of conversation that the noxious smoke is damaging to feng shui. Several farmers had in fact specifically accused the chemical factory managers of destroying the feng shui around their farms – and likewise received a small monetary compensation for the damage. This is an aspect of the feng shui tradition that may be detrimental to environmental protection. As far back as we may trace stories of feng shui accusations, monetary compensation for blocked, stolen or destroyed feng shui has been a common solution; since feng shui is the holistic approach to one's fortune, without any strict distinction between natural, social and psychical domains, loss of value in one domain may be compensated for by gains in another. One may say that, in this respect, the farmers themselves are not much different from the new factory owners. In practice, this is really like putting a price on the environment or on people's health. Frequently, it entails harvesting available resources for wealth and good luck in the present, and when they are depleted turning to resources in other areas in the future. Or, according to a Chinese agricultural expert quoted by Vaclav Smil, the villagers' management style is that of a plunderer, without enthusiasm in long-term planning (Smil 1993: 161).

There have been incidents of local communities jointly addressing environmental problems in terms of destroyed feng shui, but they are few and far between – rural people know that when speaking to factory owners, local authorities and state representatives (most often co-operating if not being a single category), they should speak the language of the modern society. Such a case in Jiangsu was of a group of farmers who went to the management of a cement factory to complain about the emission of black smoke from its chimneys, which was spreading a thick layer of soot on fields, crops and houses in the nearby villages. Since the farmers were not sure of the effect of the soot, and many in addition to the possible harm on their crops, they complained about soot on their washing, and bad feng shui was used as an overall term for their grievances. In this case, the farmers successfully made the factory install soot filters.

Although environmental protests are now commonplace in China, it is not easy to get detailed information about their background and approach to the environment. Some studies indicate that culture plays a significant role, for instance with clan and temple organizations forming the core of protest movements, and that popular religion may be among the means of expression, for instance by activating gods and goddesses against pollution, (i.e. a goddess of purity against water pollution) (Jun Jing 2003). Similarly, Chinese media from time to time report on environmental protests based on traditional cosmology, but rarely with empathy.

If rural people only inconsistently address environmental problems in terms of feng shui, then should not the local feng shui specialists be concerned with the harmful effect of pollutants? Well, many of them are in fact genuinely concerned. They commonly say that pollution is bad for the feng shui, for instance when industrial smog blocks out the sunlight: 'it is like blocking the flow of *qi*', several of them remarked. Similarly, when vegetables cannot grow, fish die in ponds and creeks and poultry can no longer be raised, they will see it as a sign of 'bad feng shui'. For instance, a feng shui specialist in Jiangsu, who had taken over from his father whom I knew well from previous fieldwork, complained about the heavy pollution in his village: 'How to say... it is like a public toilet. Nobody would ever build a house on such a place; it is considered bad feng shui – you cannot build there'. The malicious feng shui influence from black smoke or toilets is often noted (e.g. Ahern 1973: 187–8).

Since the feng shui specialists stand outside the economic life and do not have direct interest in new industrial development and job creation in rural areas, they could potentially organize protests or promote new visions of a cleaner environment. This is not the case, however, and when addressing the new challenges from pollution they do not seem have adequate concepts other than the holistic terms of '*qi*' and 'feng shui'. It must be remembered, however, that the specialists themselves operate at the margins of society, and, until recently, were persecuted. Any public action on their part would alert the public security. Thus, rural Chinese feng shui thinking or feng shui professionals do not encourage action in the way of cleaning up their environment, not even where local people themselves could actually improve things by removing garbage from village ponds and waterways, being more careful in administering pesticides or by joining forces against careless polluters.

NEW CHINESE ENVIRONMENTALISM

In the entire communist era and until the 1990s, political and economic goals were of far higher priority than anything relating to nature and the environment. Forests were felled all over China and in Tibet and Inner Mongolia, while new industries were set up without the least concern for their polluting effects on people and the environment. Information on the pollution of air, land and water was to a large extent suppressed. It took many years for the effects of unsustainable development to become publicly known and for the fundamental problems to be recognized. In the 1980s, pollution began to seriously affect the lives of the ordinary Chinese, partic-ularly in rural areas. Gradually, new earth-observation satellites provided more detailed coverage of environmental phenomena. When the results of China's pollution monitoring became publicly available in the 1990s, there could be no doubt that the country had few rivals in the extent and intensity of its air and water pollution and its chronic water shortages (Smil 1993, 2005). In the early 2000s, it became obvious to the world how critical a state the environment in China was really in.

The pollution of rivers and lakes is now disastrous, with two thirds of all surface water being affected by pollution and several hundred million people not having access to clean drinking water. A severe water shortage is felt in both rural and urban areas, and major rivers have began to dry up annually. Waste water from homes and industry tends not to be treated, and protection measures are grossly inadequate, such as when a petrochemical explosion spilled 100 tons of a cancer-causing chemical (benzene) into the Songhua river in the Jilin province, northeast China, in 2005, threatening the health of millions of people. This was only one of a long line of environmental accidents, which the vice-minister of the State Environmental Protection Administration, Zhu Guangyao, called the result of 'a reckless pursuit of economic growth and a lack of emergency response mechanisms'.

The greater part of China's agricultural land is affected by acid rain from polluted air as well as from chemical waste, such as in the case mentioned above. Crumbling, colourless vegetables and unhealthy crops are now a threat in all rural areas, where little control and a state monopoly on information serve to cloak the actual risks. Soil erosion, salinization, desertification and dust storms are encroaching upon the arable land – which is already scarce – particularly in northern China.

Air pollution had years ago reached alarming levels as a result of a reliance on coal as the main energy source, entirely inadequate smoke filtering and the boundless emission of toxics from rural and urban factories with outdated technology and no incentive to improve. The World Health Organization (WHO) in 2006 listed sixteen of the world's twenty most polluted cities as being in China. These cities are now so smog-ridden that people tend to stay indoors and wear masks when going out. Currently, when flying across China, one mostly sees a hazy-brown horizon over the east. Chinese air pollution is even drifting over seas and continents, to be registered worldwide (*New York Times*, 11 June 2006).

Foreign commentators now typically see China's economic development leading to environmental disaster, a growth-fixated nation heading for ecological suicide (Becker 2004). It has certainly made an impression on the Chinese government that China is still more often portrayed as a major environmental threat to the world's future, first of all in terms of climate change from greenhouse gases. In 2006, the government warned that continued growth will take a heavy toll on the environment and that tougher measures must be taken. Accordingly, the State Environmental Protection Administration (SEPA) has started playing a more active role in halting environmentally unsound development projects such as coal-fired power plants, of which countless were previously pushed forward without approval from central government.

However, struggling with problems of energy supply for a booming industry, poverty in the interior, increasing economic disparity between people and regions, rampant corruption and increasing social unrest, the central government has other priorities. Continued economic growth is still of top priority to solve inequality by 'making a bigger cake', and in the communiques from the Central Committee, references to the environment usually come last.

Thus, to briefly review the western literature on Chinese natural philosophy, the better part has seriously overestimated how general perceptions of the universe, most often merely represented in classical literature, may bring about concrete measures of protection of the natural environment; or it has overestimated how the 'way in which Asian peoples live in their worlds ... provides Westerners with the opportunity to draw inspiration from them in defining a new ecological world view' (Callicott and Ames 1989: 21). To put it bluntly, much of the western literature has been produced as a critique of ideology in the West, without much concern for China's own reality: it is made for domestic consumption, so to speak. It builds on belief and emotion rather than social and natural facts. When, for instance, E. N. Anderson (*Ecologies of the Heart* (1996)) uses Chinese feng shui as a model for a system of environmental protection that includes ethics and a moral code, it is pure fiction. Altogether, China's environmental practices hardly serve as a model for the world: despite the common association of Oriental philosophy with a harmonious relation between man and environment, traditions like feng shui in their original Chinese setting have had little significance for environmental protection. Neither historically nor today have such systems served anything other than narrow human pursuits of wealth and happiness – and most often on an individual basis. Both historical and present experience plainly show that the vague and elusive concepts of Chinese natural philosophy are a weaker foundation for a struggle against techno-economic pressure than the European strands of thinking that created the scientific revolution itself: modern scientific rationalism created new ways of exploiting nature, but at the same time provided the means for its protection. The great achievement of Chinese civilization in relation to nature was rather to support a huge population on a limited space by means of highly advanced systems of agricultural production – the natural domain outside immediate human interest was of minor importance. The implication is that the protection of species just because they exist – because they have proven their worth through the earth's long evolution and thus being inherently important – is very far from conventional Chinese thinking. Rights, all kinds, tend to be socially rather than naturally ascribed.

Since the mid 1990s, environmentalism has grown rapidly in China, inspired by the globalizing discourse of sustainable development and focusing on China's acute environmental problems. A range of new terms have entered the Chinese language, including 'biodiversity', 'GM foodstuffs', 'green consumption' and 'animal rights', while public debates on all aspects of environmentalism have sprung up. The enormous Three Gorges dam-building project on the Yangtze River in particular, necessitating the movement of hundreds of thousands of people and causing massive environmental change, directed the attention of the environmentally conscious towards uncontrolled development. The protests that followed kicked off a new era in Chinese politics, where the state had to take new civil society actors into account when forcing development at the expense of the environment. After the first Chinese environmental non-government organization (NGO), Friends of Nature, received legal status in 1994, new organizations have been established at a rapid pace. Many native NGOs have received considerable media attention in addition to Friends of Nature, including Green Earth Volunteers, Centre for Legal Aid to Pollution Victims, Green Camp, Global Village and those people and organizations addressing the Three Gorges project. Several of them have operated at the margins of public tolerance. Environmentalism has stimulated massive NGO-led citizen action, such as independent environmental monitoring, community recycling campaigns, rural educational projects and a range of protest actions against polluting industries, dam building and corruption in responsible state agencies.

International NGOs, including WWF, Friends of the Earth, World Watch and Greenpeace, have set up offices in China and have sponsored projects in all parts of the country. Greenpeace's aggressive style in particular has made headlines in the Chinese media: the organization accuses China of heading for a global ecological disaster by its economic practice of 'getting rich first and cleaning up later'; it addresses China's status as the greatest importer of illegally logged hardwood; it addresses harmful practices of international companies producing in China; it urges China to control illegal GM rice and foodstuffs; it claims that China is becoming the world's electronic waste bin by importing and depositing old computers, etc.

At the same time, a hundred or more new Chinese NGOs have been formed, and several hundred university campuses have environmental associations, indicating this to be a true grassroots movement (Yang G. 2004, 2005). The state has responded actively, however, by forming and sponsoring thousands of its own 'NGOs', which are connected to local state agencies. During the same period, a large body of environmental laws and policies has been promulgated, paving the way for a future 'greening' of China. Altogether, there are now over 2,000 registered environmental NGOs and several thousand other associations and groups working for a greener China.

Some regional environmental groups have been remarkably successful, building large organizations and expertise from scratch. One such group is the Sichuan-based Green River, founded by the young writer Yang Xin out of his passion for the environment and wildlife. He used the proceeds from his first book, *Soul of the Yangtze*, to found the group, which is mostly concerned with sustainable development in the Yangtze and Yellow River headwater areas. Recently, the group became the environmental advisor to the Chinese government on the Qinghai–Tibet high-altitude railway construction.

Environmentalism in China has primarily grown out of a rising civil society (Ho 2005) and has, as elsewhere, been urban-based. It has been the testing ground for civil and democratic participation in relation to an authoritarian state. Thus, environmentalism has hardly been driven forward by groups or ideologies connected with traditional philosophy and religion – rather the opposite; its participants are modern-educated and the majority of its leaders are intellectuals. As exemplified by Liang Congjie and Liao Xiaoyi (Sheri Liao), the front-figures of Friends of Nature and Global Village respectively, their main source of inspiration has been the international movement and powerful international NGOs. They tend to be moderate ecologists and do not generally question economic growth and modernization. Apart from particular campaigns against unsustainable production, species extinction, pollution, waste, private cars and consumerism, they tend to see their general role as one of educating the general public in new environmental ethics. According to local surveys and confirmed by many NGOs, Chinese citizens have not been particularly concerned with the environment, and tend to think that man should have power over nature. Paradoxically, the Chinese tend to be even less concerned with the environment than populations in countries with a much better environment.

Previously, the environmental movement rarely made use of references to Chinese philosophy. At an early stage, people like Liao and Liang, mentioned above, expressed interest in classical thought, but in the course of building the movement they found it unsuitable as the foundation for a new environmental consciousness. Liang Congjie in 1999 expressed in an interview: 'I am sorry to say that the idea of environmental protection is a Western concept. The more I learn, the more I see traditional Chinese culture is so unfriendly to nature' (McCarthy and Florcruz 1999: 3).

Wholesale westernization always caused scepticism in China, however, both with the party-state and among academics. Thus, with the rapidly increasing environmental awareness, both academics and activists may seek support for their cause in Chinese tradition – it seems fair to say, however, that it has been a question of connecting an external influence with Chinese tradition rather than building on own roots. Recently, many academics have begun to revive and apply concepts from Chinese tradition to modern environmental problems, including those of Daoism, Buddhism and feng shui. But there is everywhere a sensitive distinction between Buddhist or Daoist *philosophy* on the one side (*foxue, daoxue*) and *religion* on the other (*fojiao, daojiao*). After decades of campaigning against religion, and accentuated with the persecution of the Falungong sect in the early 2000s, the latter interpretations are dangerous ground and certainly not saluted in state institutions. This is quite similar in the case of feng shui: many intellectuals tend to think that it has some scientific content, and the real issue is how to sort out superstition (*mixin*) from science (*kexue*). Many comment that feng shui has bad associations and is against modernization, and therefore should have a new name.

Along these lines, there has been a careful and conscious return to use of concepts from traditional Chinese natural philosophy, often engulfed in patriotic language to justify its cause and steer clear of criticism. For instance, my friends at the Department of Ethics at the Forestry University in Nanjing believe that feng shui once included a concept of sacredness, such as sacred trees, groves and places, which is relevant today. All environmental ethics disappeared with the Cultural Revolution, which left rural areas coarse and unrefined. Today, they say, Chinese villagers do not have the concepts for – or interest in – preserving nature, and there is a serious need for building a new ethic for appreciating nature in rural China. Accordingly, some argue for a new environmental policy with concepts of emotional value.

Previously, Chinese NGOs building on, or even referring to, concepts from traditional nature philosophy were rare. The environmental movement is maturing, however, as it achieves many victories and starts organizing nationwide. Its organizers are learning to adapt more skilfully to China's unique political and cultural context, and not just uncritically copying movements in the West. Greenpeace China, for instance, has begun to use Chinese philosophical concepts, such as harmony, in order to define a Chinese understanding of the foreign concepts of ecology and sustainability (*Worldwatch*, 6 January 2006). On a similar note, China Green Student Forum has employed concepts from the Chinese zodiac to forecast the movement's opportunities for the year to come.

This appears perfectly in line with the Chinese government's own trying out of traditional moral concepts, particularly since 2006. As President Hu Jintao formulated his eight new moral values for the Chinese people (*ba rong ba qi*), Confucius was restored and the state began to sponsor Buddhist and Daoist religious conferences; official China has taken a step towards rediscovering religion. Environmental activist Sheri Liao commented that this was a good thing: 'it's been 20 years since we threw our morality out the window... The Chinese government is starting to take an interest in and adopt a friendly attitude to traditional culture and values' (*Associated Press*, 16 March 2006). But beware: one of the eight new moral values is the obligation to distinguish keenly between science and superstition; a wholesale revival of Chinese natural philosophy is hardly welcomed. It is also worth noticing that nature and the environment are mentioned among the eight values; yet the eighth value proposes to live plainly, work hard and avoid luxury. Again, Chinese philosophy takes the form of a moralizing agent – stressing ideal culture rather than observed reality – and aims at social regulation.

To sum up, feng shui has been put to multiple uses by individuals and local communities in their interaction with the natural environment, the results of which are diverse and inconclusive. This only underscores the point that sound environmental practices are something people of all cultures have to *learn*, irrespective of their original perceptions. Perceptions of nature are not equivalent to practices towards nature, as philosophy and economic needs belong to different domains. Concepts from traditional philosophy and religion are not in themselves determining action but are resources that may be mobilized for the environmental cause. Experience from around the world tells us that technological advances such as guns, trucks and chainsaws in the hands of local people will alter any environment, no matter how harmony-oriented a philosophy the people may possess – and there is little room for romanticism in the harsh reality of managing China's scarce resources. With the coming of industrial society, economic practices are further removed from the everyday perceptions of the people, now recruited as workers and clerks without any immediate interaction with the natural environment, while responsibility for sustainable economic practices shifts to new centralized institutions. This is where China presently stands. The industrial revolution is well under way in city and country, while the environmental learning process has only begun. The prospects are clear-cut, however: environmentalism is no longer a matter of philosophy – it has become a matter of existence.

CHAPTER 9

Feng shui as cultural globalization?

Just half a century ago, no one would have envisioned a place for feng shui in modern western societies. The tradition of feng shui, among those relatively few who knew of its existence, was perceived as a most peculiar aspect of Chinese culture, brought down through China's long history because of inherent conservatism and general stagnation. It was seen as superstitious and obsolete, bound for destruction in the quest for modernity. Western observers, whether of missionary, social science or political background, would at least share this faith in progress. Among the Chinese themselves, both revolutionaries and liberals would agree to this. Few saw any purpose of sorting out useful and less useful aspects of traditional cosmology.

At this time, ideologies were moving across continents at a rapid pace. The main currents of thought in the Chinese modernization process – Christianity, Marxism and liberalism – were all western constructs. It is of great importance, however, that such currents inevitably will be adapted to the local culture in the process of their transfer. Christianity was most often mixed with Chinese ancestor worship, and Marxism was adapted in the form of Maoism, a new radical form with a personality cult around Mao himself. Ideologies develop new hybrids when moved across cultures, often to the point of becoming unrecognizable.

In the transfer of ideas between cultures, it is probably less the power of the ideas themselves than the receptivity of the receiving culture that counts. For instance, Christian missions in China during the nineteenth century had very modest success despite its powerful backing, while today, with much less missionary activity, Christianity has become a massive force in Chinese spiritual life.

My point in stating these facts should be obvious. We are in the midst of a globalization process of colossal dimensions, economically, socially and politically. Yet it would be naive to think that globalization merely gives rise to sameness. Globalization will facilitate exchange, but at the same time gives rise to counter-currents: it also creates difference and new cultural forms. This is where the interest in Chinese feng shui comes in.

First of all, Chinese traditional cosmology and divination has been known in the West for several centuries; yet it has only taken off as a popular pursuit after deep and profound changes have occurred within western culture and religion. Second, the feng shui that is seen to rise in western societies is radically different from the original Chinese forms, however varied they may be. Thus, over time, we have both created a spiritual void and have begun installing new spiritual alternatives that fit in with the conditions of our time.

The changes in our own societies have provided endless new opportunities for lifestyles and careers, but have also brought new anxieties, risks, increasing individualism, break-up of ideologies, pressure on the individual, fragmentation of families and communities and, perhaps worst of all, a sense of a loss of overall perspective. Different views on these changes were presented in the Introduction (Chapter 1). It is evident that the ongoing restructuring of our social spaces not only affects our relations with other people and our working lives; they hit deep into the core of our identities and sense of personality.

The popular forms of feng shui address these anxieties, sometimes described in terms of a threatening world outside from which we must turn the home into a safe haven, created and designed to fit the innermost cores of our personality. Or they address a sense of lost opportunities, the feeling that more could have been achieved, that things could have been better, for which, on the other hand, popular feng shui manual authors and practitioners promise quick changes by simple advice. They offer to improve important aspects of daily life or, in many cases, essentially promise people a new life. In this undertaking, popular feng shui proponents are comparable to evangelists, who promise miracles when only faith – and perhaps payment – are unconditional. 'Move your couch and get a new life' – this is like telling a lame person to get up and walk. It may work, but we surely want to know more about what, if anything, really happened.

Feng shui in the western world is, of course, far more than that. Its introduction was effected by a search for the intimate connection between our general human being, the physical aspects of our existence and the living-giving earth we all depend upon. It conveys an intensified awareness of our immediate surroundings, natural and man-made, as well as of the meanings we attach to them: it aspires to attach meaning to things and to turn the home into the centre of a meaningful whole. It advises how to use light, colour, air and greenery, and promotes a return to simplicity, a sense of harmony with what we are and what we need. It may be seen to contain the love and respect for our human predicament that connects all religion. By looking back towards the most ancient perceptions of the universe, it embodies a search for timeless wisdom in the middle of a space-time implosion, where the individual is constantly bombarded with information, images and pressing issues from across the globe. It is holistic in a double sense, bringing together both eastern and western approaches to the totality of existence. Perhaps for the reasons mentioned above, it appeals to women more than men.

Chinese feng shui gives people a grasp of what we all left behind in the cultural evolution of mankind, what had occupied human thought and experience for millennia before the tide of industrial revolution and modernization set in. It is a living piece of history that has gained renewed power and prominence from the counter-surge to universality of modern science and rationality, once believed to eradicate or supersede all pre-existing thinking. It is something we lost in our own culture and re-found in another, giving it a spell of magic; it is the pre-modern uniting with the post-modern.

But it is a construction. Not to say that this construction will not survive or even become the dominant version of feng shui worldwide, but to indicate that it retains a set of fundamental assumptions that derive from strands of our own philosophy and religion. In China, on the one hand, it merges with ancestor worship, burial customs and belief in ghosts and spirits. In the West, on the other hand, it grew in an ambience of ecology, environmentalism, new age religion, psychology and design. Similarly, in the West, it mostly builds on a mechanistic perception of nature, including tangible forces working between discrete entities and simple causality such as expressed in electromagnetic currents impacting our bodies and minds. This is very different from the resonance type of thinking that was characteristic of the *Yi jing* and much of Chinese natural philosophy, particularly of Daoism. The better parallels in our own world are, in fact, extrasensory perception studies, the concept of synchronicity such as formulated by C. G. Jung and a great many discoveries in post-relativity-theory physics. Such forms of knowledge find better parallels in present *Yi jing* and Buddhist studies than in feng shui; it was noted in the Introduction that feng shui tended to be the most popularized version of the Asian philosophical traditions.

It is nevertheless a common characteristic of much new spirituality and religion that it relates directly to 'subjective life experiences', thus bypassing the level of established churches, trained preachers, powerful community organizations and canonical literature. Instead of keeping a close connection between religion, community and life style – that is, 'life as' a Christian, a Buddhist or a Muslim – it intends to link the individual directly to the cosmos by means of immediate and subjective experience.

It is perhaps also this gradual, but nevertheless quite radical, break with conventional religion, outlook and morality that created a new spiritual platform for the self-deification of the practitioner, such as seen in a range of new-age movements. New feng shui practitioners proliferate across the globe, many having just completed a week's training course and presenting themselves as qualified masters and degree holders. Many of the more experienced masters pose in such a pompous manner that it inevitably brings to mind the depictions of Chinese feng shui masters as mere charlatans in the early missionary literature.

In as much as feng shui may be at odds with conventional religion and morality, it also challenges our concept of knowledge. Scientific enquiry is usually premised on an all-absorbing, life-long process, in which any new knowledge opens up new horizons of the unknown; it is anything but mastery. It is for these reasons that many devoted students and scholars – in China as well as in the West – are presently contemplating a new name for feng shui in order draw a dividing line between popular pursuits and fruitful enquiry. Several suggestions have been put forward, with no success other than continuing a long debate on the correct categorization of feng shui.

A range of prominent writers of the past decades – several were mentioned in the Introduction – have called for new overarching perspectives that can bring meaning to a world of increasing complexity. Other late- or post-modern writers such as Bauman have pointed out how, in the face of cultural and social fragmentation deriving from modernity and a general ambivalence of morality, there is a common striving for new and coherent but entirely individualistic outlooks. This resonates with the recent debate on the returning significance of religion and the possible de-secularization of the world in the creation of new regional, national or local identities. Yet this issue is still engulfed in much controversy, in fact as much as is the related issue of globalization. It goes for all these comments on the predicament of contemporary society, however, that traditions like feng shui fit well into the equation – they embody the present stage of modernity.

A last question is whether feng shui is establishing itself as a new popular philosophy, even a religion, uniting East and West. Do we even see the possible emergence of feng shui as a global system of thought? The possible emergence of a global art of feng shui, which strives to connect the social world with the natural surroundings, would add new food for thought to an old debate on fragmentation and wholeness bridging philosophy, natural science and social science. And yet, despite the common use of feng shui terminology, there are still critical differences in the application of feng shui from Chinese villages to modern Chinese cities to European or American societies: philosophical and ideological traditions arise out of specific social and political contexts, which are not immediately comparable across time and space. A nominal sameness interpreted as cultural globalization may conceal very different motives and orientations at the level of individuals and communities.

We should not in the short term, if ever, expect that Chinese feng shui adherents would give up the worship of their ancestor or the application of feng shui to their graves – as little as we should expect western feng shui users to start worrying about the evil influence stemming from ancestors being unhappy with their graves. There are still dramatic differences in the theory and practice of feng shui between China and the West. Chinese villages continue ancient practices and may be encouraged to do so by knowledge of the introduction of feng shui in other parts of the world. The new western forms are themselves sprawling, seen to include a wealth of combinations with old and new thinking. Even if feng shui is returning to the Chinese city in a modernized form, there is at the same time a strong cultural movement at work in re-appropriating and nativizing traditional Chinese cosmology: this is shared by state institutions and intellectuals. In very general terms, too, there are important differences in perceptions of nature between East and West, as well as in values of the good life.

Interaction through books, conferences, travels, famous practitioners moving all over the globe and so forth is increasing, and so is the knowledge of our cultural differences. Despite the obvious differences that persist, the global feng shui movement may be said to be no less connected than the global quest for democracy, the latter obviously also appearing in a variety of forms and shades. The most intriguing aspect of the modern feng shui development is its ping-pong trajectory back and forth between continents: it began as Chinese popular religion, although at an early stage influenced by Hinduist and Buddhist cosmology; it was reinterpreted in the West, both as ecology in the USA and in terms of its social contents in British anthropology; it became a popular practice for home improvement across the West; and not least, the new interpretations in the West have become a powerful source of inspiration for new Chinese writers on the subject. Seen in this light, at least, feng shui is truly global.

Bibliography

Ahern, Emily 1973. *The Cult of the Dead in a Chinese Village*. Stanford University Press

Anagnost, Ann 1987. 'Politics and Magic in Contemporary China', *Modern China* 13(1): 40–61

Anderson, E. N. 1973. 'Feng-shui: Ideology and Ecology', in Anderson, E. N. and Marja, *Mountains and Water: Essays on the Cultural Ecology of South Coastal China*. Taipei: The Chinese Association for Folklore

1996. *Ecologies of the Heart: Emotion, Belief, and the Environment*. New York, NY: Oxford University Press

Baker, Hugh 1965. 'Burial, Geomancy and Ancestor Worship', in Topley, Marjorie (ed.), *Aspects of Social Organization in the New Territories*. Hong Kong: Royal Asiatic Society

Ball, J. Dyer 1893. *Things Chinese, being Notes on Various Subjects Connected with China*. Shanghai: Kelly and Walsh

Banister, Judith 2000. 'Population, Public Health and the Environment in China', in Edmonds, Richard L. (ed.), *Managing the Chinese Environment*. Oxford University Press

Bauman, Zygmunt 1995. *Life in Fragments: Essays in Postmodern Morality*. Oxford: Blackwell

2003a. *The Individualized Society*. Oxford: Blackwell

2003b. *Wasted Lives: Modernity and its Outcasts*. Oxford: Blackwell

Beck, Ulrich and Beck-Gernsheim, Elisabeth 2002. *Individualization: Institution-alized Individualism and its Social and Political Consequences*. London: Sage Publications

Becker, Jasper 2004. 'Wrenching Environmental Problems are Plaguing the World's Newest Industrial Powerhouse. Can China Clean Up its Act?', *National Geographic Magazine* (March): 68–95

Bell, Catherine 1989. 'Review Article. Religion and Chinese Culture: Toward an Assessment of "Popular Religion"', *History of Religion* 29(1): 35–57

Bennett, Steven J. 1978. 'Patterns of the Sky and Earth: A Chinese Science of Applied Cosmology', *Chinese Science* 3: 21

Berger, Peter L. 1999. *The Desecularization of the World: Resurgent Religion and World Politics*. Washington, DC: Ethics and Public Policy Center

Berglund, Lars 1990. *The Secret of Luo Shu. Numerology in Chinese Art and Architecture*. Department of Art History, Lund University
Bernard, Henri 1935. *Matteo Ricci's Scientific Contribution to China*, trans. Edward Chalmers Werner. Beijing: Henri Vetch
Biot, Edouard 1851. *Le Tcheou-Li ou Rites des Tcheou*. Paris: Limprimerie Nationale
Bloomfield, Frena 1985. *The Book of Chinese Beliefs*. London: Arrow Books
Bodde, Derk 1981. *Essays on Chinese Civilization*. Princeton University Press
Bohm, David 1980. *Wholeness and the Implicate Order*. New York, NY: Routledge
Bourdieu, Pierre 1999. *The Weight of the World: Social Suffering in Contemporary Society*. Stanford University Press
Brown, Simon 1996. *Principles of Feng Shui*. London: Thorson
  1997. *Practical Feng Shui*. London: Carroll & Bown
Bruce, Steve 2003. 'The Demise of Christianity in Britain', in Davie *et al.* (eds.)
Bruun, Ole 2003. *Fengshui in China: Geomantic Divination between State Orthodoxy and Popular Religion*. Honolulu, HI: University of Hawai'i Press
Bruun, Ole and Kalland, Arne 1995. 'Introduction: Images of Nature', in Bruun, Ole and Kalland, Arne (eds.), *Asian Perceptions of Nature – A Critical Approach*. London: Curzon Press
Burden, J. S. 1872. 'Causes of Hostility to Missionaries', *The Chinese Recorder and Missionary Journal* (March)
Bush, Richard C. 1970. *Religion in Communist China*. New York, NY: Abingdon Press
Callicott, J. Baird and Ames, Roger T. 1989. *Nature in Asian Traditions of Thought: Essays in Environmental Philosophy*. Albany, NY: State University of New York Press
Capra, Fritjof 1977. *The Tao of Physics*. New York, NY: Bantam Books
Carlson, Ellsworth C. 1974. *The Foochow Missionaries, 1847–1880*. Cambridge, Mass.: Harvard University Press
Carrette, Jeremy and King, Richard 2005. *Selling Sprituality: The Silent Takeover of Religion*. London: Routledge
Carter, Karen Rauch 2000. *Move Your Stuff, Change Your Life: How to Use Feng Shui to get Love, Money, Respect and Happiness*. New York, NY: Fireside
Casanova, José 1994. *Public Religions in the Modern World*. University of Chicago Press
  2003. 'Beyond European and American Exceptionalisms: Towards a Global Perspective', in Davie *et al.* (eds.)
Chan, Wing-tsit 1978 [1953]. *Religious Trends in Modern China*. New York, NY: Octagon Books
Chang Kia-Ngau 1943. *China's Struggle for Railroad Development*. New York, NY: John Day
Chen Changheng 1922. *Zhongguo renkou lun* [Discussing Chinese Population Issues]. Shanghai: Shangwu yinshuguan
Chen Jinguo 2005. *Xinyang, yishi yu xiangtu shehui: feng shui de lishi renleixue tansuo* [Belief, Ritual and Rural Society: The Historical Anthropology of Feng shui in Fujian, China], 2 vols. Beijing: Zhongguo shehui kexue

Chen, Nancy N. 1995. 'Urban Spaces and Experiences of Qigong', in Davis, Deborah S. *et al.* (eds.), *Urban Spaces in Contemporary China. The Potential for Autonomy and Community in Post-Mao China.* New York, NY: Cambridge University Press

Chen Yikui and Zhang Mingyang 2005. Shengcun feng shui xue [Subsisting Feng shui Studies]. Shanghai: Xue lin chubanshe

Cheng Jian and Fernandes-Goncalves, Adriana Jun 1998. *Chinese Feng Shui Compass Step by Step Guide.* Nachang: Jianxi Science and Technology Publishing

Cheng Jianjun 2005. *Cang feng de shui: feng shui yu jian zhu* [Hidden Feng shui and Construction]. Beijing: Zhongguo dianying chubanshe

Choy, Howard 1998. *Feng Shui – The Key to Health, Wealth and Harmony.* Sydney: Pan Macmillan

 1999. 'The San He Luopan', paper for the London International Fengshui Conference, 21–23 May

Clart, Philip and Jones, Charles B. (eds.) 2003. *Religion in Modern Taiwan: Tradition and Innovation in a Changing Society.* Honolulu, HI: University of Hawai'i Press

Cobb, John B. 1972. *Is it too late?: A Theology of Ecology.* Beverley Hills, Calif.: Bruce

Cohen, Paul A. 1978. 'Christian Missions and their Impact to 1900', in Fairbank, John K. (ed.), *The Cambridge History of China*, Vol 10: Late Ch'ing. 1800–1911. Cambridge University Press: 543–90

Davis, John Francis 1836. *The Chinese: A General Description of the Empire of China and its Inhabitants.* London: Charles Knight

da Silva, Armando 1972. *Tai YuShan: Traditional Eocological Adaptation in a South Chinese Island.* Taipei: The Orient Cultural Service

Davie, Grace *et al.* (eds.) 2003. *Predicting Religion: Christian, Secular and Alternative Futures.* Aldershot: Ashgate

de Groot, J. J. M. 1892–1910. *The Religious System of China*, 6 vols. Leiden: E. J. Brill. vol. I (1892), vols. II–III (1894/1897), vol. IV (1901), vol. V (1907), vol. VI (1910).

 1903–4 *Sectarianism and Religious Persecution in China*, 2 vols. Amsterdam: Johannes Muller

Dean, Kenneth 1998. *Lord of the Three in One: The Spread of a Cult in Southeast China.* Princeton University Press

D'elia, Pashal M. 1931. *The Triple Demism of Sun Yat-Sen.* Wuchang: The Franciscan Press

Dittmer, Lone 2005. *Feng Shui: Forstå Fundamentet.* Copenhagen: Klitrose

Doolittle, Justus 1865. *The Social Life of the Chinese: With Some Account of their Religious, Governmental, Educational, and Business Customs and Opinions.* New York, NY: Harper and Brothers

Doré, Henry 1914. *Researches into Chinese Superstitions*, vol. II. Shanghai: T'usewei Printing House

Du Daning 2005. *Fengshui de changshi yu yingyong* [Fengshui Knowledge and Use]. Beijing: Zhongguo Lüyou chubanshe du Halde, J. B. 1736. *Description géographique, historique, chronologique, politique, et physique de l'empire de la Chine et de la Tartarie Chinoise*. La Hare: Henri Scheurleer

Durkheim, Emile and Marcel Mauss 1963 [1903]. *Primitive Classifications*, trans. Rodney Needham. London: Cohen and West

Eberhard, Wolfram 1962. *Social Mobility in Traditional China*. Leiden: E. J. Brill

1967. *Guilt and Sin in Traditional China*. Berkeley, Calif.: University of California Press

1970. *Studies in Chinese Folklore and Related Essays*. Bloomington, Ind.: Indiana University Research Center

1988. *A Dictionary of Chinese Symbols*. London: Routledge

Ebrey, Patricia B. 1986. 'The Early Stages in the Development of Descent Group Organization', in Ebrey, Patricia B. and Watson, James L. (eds.), *Kinship Organization in Late Imperial China* 1000–1940. Berkeley, Calif.: University of California Press

(ed.) 1993. *Chinese Civilization – A Sourcebook*. New York, NY: The Free Press

Economy, Elizabeth 2004. *The River Runs Black: Environmental Challenges to China's Future*. Ithaca, NY: Cornell University Press

Edkins, Joseph 1872. 'Feng Shui: The Wind and Water Superstition of the Chinese' (part 1), *Chinese Recorder and Missionary Journal* (March): 274–7; 'On the Chinese Geomancy Known as Feng-Shui' (part 2), *Chinese Recorder and Missionary Journal* (April): 291–8; 'Feng Shui', *Chinese Recorder and Missionary Journal* (May): 316–20

1880. *Chinese Buddhism: A Volume of Sketches, Historical, Descriptive and Critical*. London: Trübner and Co.

Eitel, Ernest. J. 1984 [1873]. *Feng-shui, or, The Rudiments of Natural Science in China*. Singapore: Graham Brash

Eliade, Mircea (ed.) 1987. *The Encyclopedia of Religion*. New York, NY: Macmillan

Elvin, Mark 1999. 'The Environmental Legacy of Imperial China', *China Quarterly* 156: 733–56

2004. *The Retreat of the Elephants: An Environmental History of China*. New Haven, Conn.: Yale University Press

Fairbank, John K. 1969. *Trade and Diplomacy on the China Coast*. Cambridge, Mass.: Harvard University Press

1992. *China: A New History*. Cambridge, Mass.: The Belknap Press of Harvard University Press

Fan Wei 1990. 'Village Feng shui Principles', in Knapp, Ronald G., *Chinese Landscapes, The Village as Place*. Honolulu, HI: University of Hawai'i Press

Fevour, Edward Le 1970. *Western Enterprise in Late Ch'ing China: A Selective Survey of Jardine, Matheson and Company's Operations* 1842–1895. Cambridge, Mass.: Harvard University Press

Feuchtwang, Stephan 1974. *An Anthropological Analysis of Chinese Geomancy*. Vientiane: Vitagna

1992. *The Imperial Metaphor*. London: Routledge

2001. *Popular Religion in China: The Imperial Metaphor.* Richmond: Curzon Press

2002. *An Anthropological Analysis of Chinese Geomancy*, revised edition. Bangkok: White Lotus

Field, Stephen L. 1999. 'The Numerology of Nine Star Fengshui', *Journal of Chinese Religions* 27: 13–33

Fortune, Robert 1979 [1847]. *Three Years' Wanderings in Northern China.* New York, NY: Garland Publishing

Freedman, Maurice 1966. *Chinese Lineage and Society: Fukien and Kwangtung.* London: Athlone

1969. 'Geomancy', Presidential Address in 1968 to the Proceedings of the Royal Anthropological Institute of Great Britain and Ireland, 1968–70. London: 5–15

1974. 'On the Sociological Study of Chinese Religion', in Wolf, Arthur P., *Religion and Ritual in Chinese Society.* Stanford University Press

1979. *The Study of Chinese Society.* Stanford University Press

Gao Youqian 1992. *Zhongguo feng shui* [Chinese Feng shui]. Beijing: Zhongguo huaqiao chuban gongsi

2005. *Zhongguo feng shui wenhua* [Chinese Feng shui Culture]. Beijing: Tuanjie chubanshe

Gates, Hill 1996. *China's Motor: A Thousand Years of Petty Capitalism.* Ithaca, NY: Cornell University Press

Gates, Hill and Weller, Robert P. 1987. 'Hegemony and Chinese Folk Ideologies. An Introduction', *Modern China* 13 (1): 3–16

Gärtner, Brigitte 1998. *Wenn Räume erwachen.* Aitrang: Windpferd

Giles, Herbert A. 1974 [1874]. *A Glossary of References on Subjects Connected with the Far East.* London: Curzon Press

Glacken, Clarence 1967. *Traces on the Rhodian Shore: Nature and Culture in Western Thought from Ancient Times to the End of the Eighteenth Century.* Berkeley, Calif.: University of California Press

Goosseart, Vincent 2005. 'State and Religion in China: Religious Policies and Scholarly Paradigms', paper for the Rethinking Modern Chinese History Conference, Academia Sinica, Taipei

Graham, David Crockett 1961. *Folk Religion in Southwest China.* Washington, DC: Smithsonian Press

Grant, John 2000. *The New Marketing Manifesto: The 12 Rules for Building Successful Brands in the 21st Century.* Mason, OH: Texere

Gray, John Henry 1878. *China – History of the Laws, Manners and Customs of the People.* London: Macmillan

Gutzlaff, Charles 1833. *The Journal of Two Voyages along the Coast of China.* New York, NY: John P. Haven

1972 [1852]. *The Life of Taou-Kwang, Late Emperor of China.* Wilmington, Del.: Scholarly Resources Inc.

Hale, Gill 2000. *The Complete Guide to the Feng Shui Garden.* London: Southwater

Hall, Stuart 2004. *Questions of Cultural Identity.* London: Sage Publications

Hamilton, Gary 1985. 'Why No Capitalism in China? Negative Questions in Comparative Historical Sociology', *Journal of Developing Societies* 2: 187–211

Harrell, Steven 1987. 'The Concept of Fate in Chinese Folk Ideology', *Modern China* 13(1): 99–109

He Bochuan 1991. *China on the Edge: The Crisis of Ecology and Development.* China Books and Periodicals

He Xiaoxin 1990. *Fengshui tan yuan* [Exploring the Source of Feng shui]. Nanjing: Dongnan daxue chubanshe

Heelas, Paul 1996. *The New Age Movement: Religion, Culture and Society in the Age of Post Modernity.* London: Blackwell

Heelas, Paul and Woodhead, Linda 2005. *The Spiritual Revolution: Why Religion is Giving Way to Christianity.* Oxford: Blackwell

Hinton, William 1966. *Fanshen: A Documentary of Revolution in a Chinese Village.* London: Monthly Review Press

Ho, Peter 2005. *Developmental Dilemmas: Land Reform and Institutional Change in China.* London: RoutledgeCurzon

Hong Peimo 1993. *Zhongguo feng shui yanjiu* [Chinese Feng shui Research]. Wuhan: Hubei kexue jishu chubanshe

Hsu, Francis 1948. *Under the Ancestors' Shadow.* New York, NY: Columbia University Press

Hsu, Shan-Tung 2003. *Yin & Yang Of Love: Feng Shui for Relationships.* St. Paul, Minn.: Llewellyn

Hu, Chang-tu 1960. *China: Its People, its Society, its Culture.* New Haven, Conn.: HRAF Press

Hua Yibo 2004. *Jiaju youdao* [Ways for the Home]. Beijing: Jinghua chubanshe

Huang Dideng 1993. *Dili zhengzong* [Orthodox Geography]. Nanning: Guangxi minzu chubanshe

Huang Liu-hung 1984. *A Complete Book Concerning Happiness and Benevolence: A Manual for Local Magistrates in Seventeenth-Century China.* Tucson, Ariz.: The University of Arizona Press

Huang Yi-long 1991. 'Court Divination and Christianity in the K'ang-Hsi Era', *Chinese Science* 10: 1–20

Hubrig, Herr Missonär 1879. 'Fung Schui oder chinesische Geomantie', *Zeitschrift für Ethnologie*, Elfter Band (vol. XI): 34–43

Huntington, Samuel P. 1993. 'The Clash of Civilizations?', *Foreign Affairs*, 72(Summer): 22–49

Jacobsen, Michael and Bruun, Ole (eds.) 2000. *Human Rights and Asian Values: Contesting National Identities and Cultural Representations in Asia.* London: Curzon Press

Jensen, Tinamaria 2004. *Dansk Feng Shui i Praksis.* Roskilde, Denmark: Vinding

Jordan, David K. 1972. *Gods, Ghosts and Ancestors: Folk Religion in a Taiwanese Village.* Berkeley, Calif.: University of California Press

Jun Jing 2003. 'Environmental Protests in Rural China', in Perry, Elizabeth and Selden, Mark, *Chinese Society: Change, Conflict and Resistance*, 2nd edition: New York, NY: Routledge

Jung, C. G. 1968. 'Introduction', in *I Ching or Book of Changes*, tr. Richard Wilhelm. London: Routledge and Kegan Paul

Kang Liang *et al.* 1998. *Fengshui yu chengshi* [Fengshui and Cities]. Sanhe: Baihua wenyi chubanshe

Kingston, Karen 1998. *Clear your Clutter with Feng Shui*. London: Judy Piatkus 2003. *Creating Sacred Space with Feng Shui*. London: Judy Piatkus

Knapp, Ronald G. 1999. *China's Living Houses. Folk Beliefs, Symbols, and Household Ornamentation*. Honolulu, HI: University of Hawai'i Press

Kuhn, Philip A. 1970. *Rebellion and its Enemies in Late Imperial China. Militarization and Social Structure*, 1796–1864. Cambridge, Mass.: Harvard University Press

Kunst, Richard 1985. 'The Original Yi jing: A Text, Phonetic Transcription, Translation, and Indexes'. Ph.D dissertation, University Microfilm, International

Kwok, Man-Ho and O'Brien, Joanne 1991. *The Elements of Feng Shui*. Shaftesbury: Element Books

Lam Kam Chuen, Master 1995. *The Feng Shui Handbook*. London: Gaia Books

Lazenby, Gina 1998a. *The Feng Shui Handbook*. London: Conran Octopus 1998b. *The Feng Shui House Book*. London: Conran Octopus

Lee, Hui-chen Wang 1959. 'Chinese Clan Rules', in Nivison, David S. and Wright, Arthur F. (eds.), *Confucianism in Action*. Stanford University Press

Lee, S. H. 1986. 'Feng Shui: Its Meaning and Context'. Ph.D dissertation, Cornell University

Leibniz, Gottfried Wilhelm 1977. *Discourse on the Natural Theology of the Chinese*. Honolulu, HI: University of Hawai'i Press

Levi-Strauss, Claude 1967a. *Structural Anthropology*. New York, NY: Doubleday 1967b. *Totemism*, A. S. A. Monographs. London: Tavistock Publications

Li Bozhong 1994. 'The Problem of Timber Supply in Jiangnan in the Ming and Qing Periods', trans. Peter Perdue, *Chinese Environmental History Newsletter*

Li Wenhua and Zhao Xianying 1989. *China's Nature Reserves*. Beijing: Foreign Languages Press

Lim, Jes T. Y. 2003. *Feng Shui for Business and Office*. Toronto, ON: Warwick Publishing

Lin Yun and Rossbach, Sarah 1998. *Feng Shui Design: From History and Landscape to Modern Gardens and Interiors*. New York, NY: Viking Penguin

Linn, Denise 1995. *Sacred Space*. New York, NY: Ballantine Books

Lip, Evelyn 1979. *Chinese Geomancy*. Singapore: Times Books International 1996. *Fengshui: Environments of Power. A Study of Chinese Architecture*. London: Academy Editions

Lutz, Jessie Gregory 1988. *Chinese Politics and Christian Missions: The Anti-Christian Movements of 1920–28 (Church and the World)*, vol. III. Notre Dame, Ind.: Cross Cultural Publications

McCarthy, Terry and Florcruz, Jaime 1999. 'Toxic China', *Time*, 1 March: 16–23

Mak, Michael Y. and Ng, S. Thomas 2005. 'The Art and Science of Feng Shui – A Study on Architects' Perception', *Building and Environment* 40: 427–34

Mao Tse-tung 1982. *Selected Works of Mao Tse-tung*, vol. I. Beijing: Foreign Languages Press

March, Andrew L. 1968. 'An Appreciation of Chinese Geomancy', *Journal of Asian Studies* 27(2): 253–67

McHarg, Ian L. 1969. *Design with Nature*. New York, NY: Doubleday

Monina, A. A. 1983. 'The Missionary Question in Qing Policy (the Zongliyamen Memorandum of February 9, 1871)', in trans. *Manzhou Rule in China*, David Skvirsky. Moscow: Progress Publishers

Morrison, G. E. 1985. *An Australian in China. Being the Narrative of a Quiet Journey across China to British Burma*. Sydney: Angus and Robertson

Myron, Paul 1915. *Our Chinese Chances through Europe's War*. Chicago, Ill.: Linebarger Brothers Publishers

Nakayama, Shigeru and Sivin, Nathan 1973. *Chinese Science: Explorations of an Ancient Tradition*. Cambridge, Mass.: MIT Press

Needham, Joseph 1962. *Science and Civilization in China*, vol. II. Cambridge University Press

  1969. *The Grand Titration: Science and Society in East and West*. London: Allen and Unwin

Needham, Rodney 1972. *Belief, Language and Experience*. University of Chicago Press

Nevius, John 1869. *China and the Chinese*. New York, NY: Harper

Nielsen, Bent 2003. *A Companion to Yi Jing Numerology*. London: RoutledgeCurzon

Ou Yang Yufeng 2004. *Jiaju feng shui shiyong shouce [A Practical Manual for Home Feng Shui]*. Beijing: Zhongguo wenlian chubanshe

Pan Haoyuan and Zhao Chunlan 1997. 'Feng shui and Ancient Chinese Landscape', *International Institute for Asian Studies Newsletter* 13: 34–5

Paper, Jordan 1994. 'Religion', in Dingbo, Wu and Murph, Patrick D. (eds.), *Handbook of Chinese Popular Culture*. Westport, Conn.: Greenwood Press

Paton, Michael 2007. 'Feng shui: A Continuation of the Art of Swindlers?', *Journal of Chinese Philosophy* 34(3): 427–45

Petersen, Marianne L. 2005. *Kom godt i gang med Business Feng Shui* [Get well started with Business Feng Shui]. Silkeborg: Ca'Luna

Potter, Jack M. 1970. 'Wind, Water, Bones and Souls: The Religious World of the Cantonese Peasant', *Journal of Oriental Studies*, 3(1): 139–53

Qi Xing 1988. *Folk Customs at Traditional Chinese Festivities*. Beijing: Foreign Languages Press

Qu Geping and Li Jinchang 1994. *Population and the Environment in China*. London: Paul Chapman

Rawski, Evelyn 1985. 'Introduction', in Johnson, David, Nathan, Andrew J. and Rawski, Evelyn (eds.), *Popular Culture in Late Imperial China*. Berkeley, Calif.: University of California Press

Ricci, Matteo 1953. *China in the Sixteenth Century: The Journals of Matthew Ricci: 1583–1610*, trans. Louis J. Gallagher. New York, NY: Random House

Rossbach, Sarah 1983. *Feng Shui: The Chinese Art of Placement.* New York, NY: E. P. Dutton

Rossbach, Sarah and Lin Yun 1987. *Interior Design with Feng Shui.* New York, NY: E. P. Dutton

1994. *Living Color.* New York, NY: Kodansha

1998. *Feng Shui Design.* New York, NY: Penguin

Schumm, Claudia 2004. *Feng Shui im Krankenhaus: Architektur und Heilung, Räume Für Die Seele* [Feng Shui in the Hospital: Architecture and Healing, Rooms for the Soul]. Austria: Springer Verlag

Sennett, Richard 1998. *The Corrosion of Character: The Consequences of Work in the New Capitalism.* New York, NY: W. W. Norton

2006. *The Culture of the New Capitalism.* London: Yale University Press

Shahar, Meir and Weller, Robert P. (eds.) 1996. *Unruly Gods: Divinity and Society in China.* Honolulu, HI: University of Hawai'i Press

Shapiro, Judith 2001. *Mao's War against Nature: Politics and Environment in Revolutionary China.* Cambridge University Press

Simons, T. Raphael 2001. *The Feng Shui of Love.* New York, NY: Gramercy

Siu, Helen 1989. 'Recycling Rituals. Politics and Popular Culture in Contemporary China', in Link, Perry, Madsen, Richard and Pickowicz, Paul G., *Unofficial China. Popular Culture and Thought in the People's Republic.* London: Westview Press

Skinner, Stephen 1976. *The Living Earth Manual of Feng-Shui: Chinese Geomancy.* London: Routledge & Kegan Paul

1980. *Terrestrial Astrology. Divination by Geomancy.* London: Routledge & Kegan Paul

2000. *Feng Shui for Modern Living.* London: Trafalgar Square Publishing

2003. *Flying Star Feng Shui.* Boston, Mass.: Turtle Publishing

2004. *Feng Shui Style: The Asian Art of Gracious Living.* Singapore: Periplus Editions

2006. *The Water Dragon: From the Classic Ch'ing Dynasty Text,* original author Chang Ping Lin, Feng Shui Classics, vol. I. London: Golden Hoard Press

2008. *Guide to the Feng Shui Compass or Lo P'an.* London: Golden Hoard Press

Smil, Vaclav 1993. *China's Environmental Crisis. An Inquiry into the Limits of National Development.* London: M. E. Sharpe

2005. 'China's Thirsty Future', *Far Eastern Economic Review* (December): 29–35

Smith, Athur H. 1902. *Chinese Proverbs and Common Sayings.* Shanghai: American Presbyterian Mission Press

Smith, Howard 1968. *Chinese Religions.* London: Weidenfeld and Nicolson

Smith, Kidder *et al.* (eds.), *Sung Dynasty Uses of the I Ching.* Princeton University Press

Smith, Richard J. 1991. *Fortune-tellers and Philosophers. Divination in Chinese Society.* Boulder, Colo.: Westview Press

1998. 'The Place of Yi jing (Classic of Changes) in World Culture', *Journal of Chinese Philosophy* (Winter): 391–422

2003. 'The Yi jing (Classic of Changes) in Global Perspective: Some Pedagogical Reflections', *Education About Asia* 8(2): 5–10

Snow, Edgar 1973. *The Long Revolution*. London: Hutchinson

Song, Dachuan 2000. 'Zhongguo chuantong feng shui xueshuo de yuanliu ji shehui yingxiang' [The Origin and Development of Chinese Traditional Feng shui and its Social Influence], *Beijing Wenbo* 1: 51–7.

Spear, William 1995. *Feng Shui Made Easy*. London: Thorsons

Stasney, Sharon 2004a. *Chic Living with Feng Shui*. New York, NY: Main Street

2004b. *Feng Shui Your Work Spaces*. New York, NY: Sterling Publishing

Staunton, George T. (trans.) 1810. *Ta tsing leu lee* [Qing Dynasty Legal Code]. London: T. Cadell and W. Davies

Swetz, Frank 2001. *Legacy of the Luoshu: The Mystical, Mathematical Meaning of the Magic Square of Order Three*. Peru, Ill.: Open Court Publishing

Tam, C. M. *et al.* 1999. 'Feng Shui and Its Impact on Land and Property Development', *Journal of Urban Planning and Development*, 125(4): 152–63

Tambiah, Stanley Jeyaraja 1990. *Magic, Science, Religion, and the Scope of Rationality*. Cambridge University Press

Teiser, Stephen F. 1995. 'Popular Religion', *Journal of Asian Studies* 54(2): 378–95

1999. 'Religions of China in Practice', in Lopez Jr., Donald S., *Asian Religions in Practice*. Princeton University Press

Too, Lillian 1996. *The Complete Illustrated Guide to Feng Shui*. Shaftesbury: Element Books

2000. *Easy-To-Use Feng Shui For Love: 168 Ways to Happiness*. New York, NY: Sterling

2003. *Feng Shui Life Planner*. London: Hamlyn

2004. *Total Feng Shui*. Lewes: Bridgewater Book Company

Toulmin, Stephen 2001. *Return to Reason*. London: Harvard University Press

Tucker, Mary Evelyn and Berthrong, John (eds.) 1998. *Confucianism and Ecology. The Interrelation of Heaven, Earth, and Humans*. Cambridge, Mass.: Harvard University Press

Wagner, Rudolf G. 1992. 'Reading the Chairman Mao Memorial Hall', in Naquin, Susan and Chün-fang Yü, *Pilgrims and Sacred Sites in China*. Berkeley, Calif.: University of California Press

Walters, Derek 1991. *The Feng Shui Handbook*. London: Aquarian

Wang Chunyu (trans.) 1993. 'The Errors of Geomancy', in Ebrey (ed.): 120–2

Wang Qiheng (ed.) 1992. *Fengshui lilun yanjiu* [Theoretical Feng shui Studies]. Tianjin: Tianjin daxue chubanshe

Wang Yude 1991. *Shenmide feng shui* [Mysterious Feng shui]. Nanning: Guangxi renmin chubanshe

Watson, James L. and Rawski, Evelyn S. 1988. *Death Ritual in Late Imperial and Modern China*. Berkeley, Calif.: University of California Press

Watson, Rubie 1995. 'Issues of identity in the 1990s', Association of Asian Studies paper

Weber, Max 1951 [1920]. *The Religion of China: Confucianism and Taoism*. New York, NY: The Free Press

Webster, Richard 1999. *Feng Shui for Love and Romance*. St. Paul, Minn.: Llewellyn Publications

Weller, Robert P. 1987. *Unities and Diversities in Chinese Religion*. Seattle, Wash.: University of Washington Press (see Appendix A: Geomancy)

   2000. 'Divided Market Cultures in China: Gender, Enterprise, and Religion', in Schech, Susanne and Haggis, Jane (eds.), *Culture and Development: A Critical Introduction*. Oxford: Blackwell

Weller, Robert P. and Bol, Peter K. 1998. 'From Heaven-and-Earth to Nature: Chinese Concepts of the Environment and their Influence on Policy Implementation', in Tucker and Berthrong (eds.): 313–41

Welsh, Holmes 1968. *The Buddhist Revival in China*. Cambridge, Mass.: Harvard University Press

   1972. *Buddhism under Mao*. Cambridge, Mass.: Harvard University Press

White J., Lynn 1962. *Medieval Technology and Social Change*. Oxford University Press

Williams, Samuel Wells 1848. *The Middle Kingdom*. New York, NY: Wiley and Putnam

Willoughby-Meade, G. 1928. *Chinese Ghouls and Goblins*. London: Constable & Co.

Wittvogel, Karl 1957. *Oriental Despotism: A Comparative Study of Total Power*. New Haven, Conn.: Yale University Press

Wong, Angi Ma 2002. *Feng Shui Do's and Taboos for Love*. Carlsbad, Calif.: Hay House

Wright, Arthur F. 1977. 'The Cosmology of the Chinese City', in Skinner, G. William (ed.), *The City in Late Imperial China*. Stanford University Press

Xu, P. 1990. 'Feng Shui: A Model for Landscape Analysis'. Ph.D dissertation, Harvard University

Yang, C. K. 1959. *A Chinese Village in Early Communist Transition*. Cambridge, Mass.: MIT Press

   1970 [1961] *Religion in Chinese Society*. Berkeley, Calif.: University of California Press

Yang Guobin 2004. 'Global Environmentalism Hits China', *YaleGlobal*, 4 February

   2005. 'Environmental NGOs and Institutional Dynamics in China'. *The China Quarterly* 181: 46–66

Yang, Mayfair Mei-hui 2000. 'Putting Global Capitalism in Its Place: Economic Hybridity, Bataille, and Ritual Expenditure', *Current Anthropology* 41(4): 477–95

Yang Wenheng 1993. *Zhongguo di feng shui* [Chinese Earth Feng shui]. Beijing: Guoji wenhua chubanshe

Yates, M. T. 1868. 'Ancestor Worship and Fung-Shuy', *Chinese Recorder and Missionary Journal* 1(3): 37–43

Yeji Laozi 1993. *Minsu dili feng shui* [Feng shui as Folk Geography]. Chengdu: Sichuan daxue chubanshe

Yen, Chih-t'ui 1968. *Family Instructions for the Yen Clan*. Leiden: E. J. Brill

Yi Ding, Yu Lu and Hong Yong 1996. *Zhongguo gudai feng shui yu jianzhu xuanzhi* [Ancient Chinese Feng shui and Imperial Construction]. Shijiazhuang: Hebei kexue jishu

Yoon, Hong-key 1976. *Geomantic Relations between Culture and Nature in Korea.* Taipei: The Orient Cultural Service

2006. *The Culture of Fengshui in Korea: An Exploration of East Asian Geomancy.* Lanham: Lexington Books

Yosida, Mitukuni 1973. 'The Chinese Concept of Nature', in Nakayama, Shigeru and Sivin, Nathan, *Chinese Science: Explorations of an Ancient Tradition.* Cambridge, Mass.: MIT Press

Yu Kongjian 1990. 'Exploration of the Deep Meaning of the Ideal Feng-shui Landscape Model', *Exploration of Nature* 9(1): 87–90

1992. 'Keep the Living Qi: Theory and Practice for Sustainable Environment'. (unpublished paper). Landscape Architecture Department, Beijing Forestry University

Yu Xixian and Yu Yong 2005. *Zhongguo gudai feng shui de lilun yu shijian* [Theory and Practice in Ancient Chinese Feng shui]. Beijing: Guangming ribao chubanshe

Zhang Huimin 1993. *Zhongguo feng shui yingyongxue* [Applied Chinese Feng shui]. Beijing: Renmin zhongguo chubanshe

Zhang Juwen 2004. *A Translation of the Ancient Chinese 'The Book of Burial (Zang Shu)' by Guo Pu* (276–324). Lewinston, NY: Edwin Mellen Press

Zhou Wenzheng *et al.* 1993. *Dili zhengzong* [Orthodox geography]. Nanning: Guangxi minzu chubanshe

SOME CHINESE CLASSICS WITH RELEVANCE TO FENG SHUI

Han long jing (*Book of the Moving Dragon*, or *Canon on the Means to set Dragons in Motion*)

Huangdi zhai jing (*The Yellow Emperor's Book on Dwellings*)

Li ji (*Book of Rites*)

Qin ding luo jing jie ding (*Explanation of the Luo Jing Classified by the Imperial Order*)

Qing nang jing (*Book of the Blue-Green Bag*)

Shi jing (*Book of Songs*)

Shu jing (*Book of History*)

Shui long jing (*Book of the Water Dragon*)

Yi jing, or *Zhou yi* (*Book of Changes*)

Yilong jing (*Book of the Doubtful Dragon*)

Zang shu (*Book of Burial, or Book of Interment*)

Zhou li (*Rites of Zhou*)

Index

activism 91, 164
agency, human 3, 49–50, 79
agglomerative tradition 23, 114, 116, 155
agriculture 15, 25, 58, 78, 91, 177, 186
Ahern, Emily 91
amoral explanation 86
ancestor worship 15–18, 23, 48, 50, 51, 55, 67, 76, 79, 84–86, 88, 91, 154, 173, 191, 193
Anderson, E. N. 95, 97
anthropocentrism 76, 175
anthropological fieldwork 84, 85, 93, 158, 176–183
anthropology 85–87, 90, 91
architecture 97–99, 120, 121, 127–129, 134, 136, 139, 146, 155, 170
'armchair' position 180
Asian philosophy 3, 185, 193
astrology 49, 73, 82, 96, 112, 124, 161

bagua 52, 104, 114, 116, 135, 149–151, 160, 165
Bauman, Zygmunt 9, 10, 194
Beck, Ulrich 7, 8
Beijing 33, 41, 44, 118, 171
Berger, Peter 7
biodiversity 186
Book of Burial (Zang shu) 20–22, 28, 67, 93
Book of Changes (Yi jing) 12, 37, 83, 100–106, 116, 122, 193
Book of Dwellings, Yellow Emperor's (Ze jing) 19
Book of Filial Piety (Xiao jing) 18
Book of Rites (Li ji) 16, 101, 107
British authorities in Hong Kong 129, 137
Buddhism 1–2, 20, 23, 94, 119, 125, 132, 136, 153, 154, 168, 188
burial 16, 18, 20, 22, 24, 26, 48, 67–71
business 74, 122–123, 132, 134, 135, 138, 168
business corporations 171–172

Casanova, José 7
causality 104, 193
Chan Wing-tsit 88

Chen Shui-bian 130
Cheng Yi 103
Chiang Kai-shek 131
Chinese Almanac 55–58, 80
Chinese classics 14, 19, 28, 102, 149
Chinese culture 3–5, 85, 93, 101, 119, 135, 138, 146, 156, 158, 188, 191
Chinese festivals 51, 52, 132
Chinese religion 85, 87, 90, 147
Christianity 5–6, 78, 94, 95, 132, 147, 191
clan organization 25, 26, 53
classifications 88, 107, 161
colonialism 44
colour application 155–157, 160–161
complexity 194
competition among brothers 68
competition, social 62, 75, 86, 92
Confucianism 88, 101, 119, 174
Confucius 17–18, 189
cosmological model 89
cosmological resonance 79, 81, 101, 193
couplets 54, 72
Cultural Revolution 70, 87, 119, 188

Daodejing 17
Daoism 11, 17, 19, 109, 119, 132, 149, 154, 165, 188, 193
de Groot, J. J. M. 43, 84, 95, 138, 144, 180
dili 11
divination 11, 14–16, 19, 20, 22, 23, 25, 28, 30, 58, 82–83, 86, 101
dragon, symbol of 12, 16, 90, 92, 111–113

Eberhard, Wolfram 96, 146, 147
ecology 94–97, 134, 147, 157, 159, 173, 176, 187, 193
economic enterprise 51
Economy, Elizabeth 175, 176
Edkins, Joseph 43
education 5, 26, 72, 76, 118, 129, 138, 144, 145

ego-centred universe 89
Eitel, E. J. 12–14, 43, 95, 144, 157
Elvin, Mark 175
emotional value 188
environmental crisis 175, 181
environmentalism 183–190
evangelists 192
evil spirits 54, 61, 132
evolutionary perspective 84
extrasensory perception studies 193

Falungong 48, 120, 127, 188
family altars 51, 53, 132
family organization 53, 59, 64, 67
famine 28
fatalism 77, 79
feng shui associations 171
feng shui compass (*luopan*) 28, 65, 95, 100, 113,
    115–117, 125, 146, 147
feng shui manual authors 168–169
feng shui manuals 9, 29, 100, 115, 136, 156, 159,
    160, 162–164
feng shui trees 180, 188
Feuchtwang, Stephan 88–90, 148
Five Elements 20, 106–108, 140, 161, 165, 167
flora and fauna 175, 179
Forbidden City 15
fragmentation 6, 8, 9, 67, 164, 192
Freedman, Maurice 85–86, 88, 92, 95, 128, 148,
    180
Fujian 119, 121, 180
functionalism 85

garden design 157
Glacken, Clarence 94, 96, 146
globalization 136, 138, 145, 170, 186, 191, 194
gods 50, 78, 132
graves 12, 16–17, 26, 69–71, 77, 84, 111, 119, 131,
    134, 138, 155, 159, 180, 195
Guo Pu 20–22
Guomindang 70

harmony 119, 121, 144, 156, 161, 163, 189, 193
He Xiaoxin 122, 157
health 63, 73, 75, 161, 162, 178, 180
Heaven and Earth 16, 105, 106, 114, 174
hexagrams 104, 105
Hong Kong 56, 92, 98, 116, 129–130, 136–141, 153
Hsu, Francis 88

immanence 101
imperial examinations 34
imperial metaphor 16–17, 53
individualism 6, 172, 192
industrial society 4, 8, 138, 177, 190

intentional design 98, 168
interior design 159–163
International Feng Shui Association 170
internet 1, 70, 140

Japan 149
Jesuits 35–36, 56, 145
Jung, C. G. 94, 103, 193

Kaifeng 32–33
kanyu 11
kitchen position 61
Knapp, Ronald 59
Korea 93, 149
Kunlun Mountains 112

landscape 97, 111, 112, 114, 154, 173
Leibniz, G. W. 37, 103
Lien Chan 130
life-cycle rituals 50, 67
Lin Yun 153–155
lodestone compass 115
love 164–166
Lü Cai 24
Luo Shu 151–152, 161, 163

Mao Zedong 47, 144, 175, 191
March, Andrew 95, 146
mental disorders 73
missionary work 35, 37, 40–42, 44, 45, 79, 137,
    144, 191
modernization 103, 118, 119, 144, 145
monetary compensation 66, 182
morality 103, 185, 189, 194

Nanjing University 121
nationalism 99
nature, concept of 174, 189, 193
Needham, Joseph 95, 108, 146, 157
Neo-Confucianism 12, 25–27, 100, 107, 109–110,
    175
new age 6, 169, 193
NGOs 186–188
numerology 32, 57, 58, 102, 151

obscuritism 109
One Hundred Schools 17–18
oracle bones 14, 56, 102
Oriental Wisdom 12, 98, 156, 193

pagodas 34, 39, 48, 61, 145
palaces 15, 31, 33
perception of reality 16, 102
personality 162, 168, 192
pesticides 178–179

phoenix, symbol of 12
political metaphor 11, 89, 107
political rebellion 44, 90
pollution 181–183, 186
polytheism 87
popular religion 2, 12, 29, 44, 47, 85–87, 90, 128
post-modern architecture 136, 139, 141
post-modern society 4, 145, 159, 193
Potter, Jack 87
pragmatism 121
proverbs 75, 81

qi 27, 31, 34, 59, 60, 62, 75, 108–110, 132, 133, 154, 155, 158–160, 163, 164
Qingming Festival 26, 55
Qu Geping 176

railways 44–46, 137
rationalism, Chinese state 94
rationality 5, 8, 120, 193
Red Guards 91
religious movements 8
Ricci, Matteo 35
Rites of Zhou (*Zhou li*) 31, 32
Rossbach, Sarah 148, 153–156

Schools of feng shui
  Bagua 149–151
  Black Hat Sect 153
  Flying Star 151–153
  Forms 27, 28, 61, 63, 98, 99, 110–113, 127
  Orientations/Directions 28, 64, 65, 98, 113–115
scientific enquiry 194
self-deification 194
Sennett, Richard 8
sha position 125, 135, 139, 167
shamans 15–16, 169
Shanghai 46, 118, 127, 139, 171
Sima Qian 106
single-surname villages 64, 66
skepticism 12, 18, 73, 81, 120, 158
Skinner, Stephen 148
Smil, Vaclav 182
Smith, Richard J. 30
specialization of practitioners 72
stagnation 191

subjective interpretation 3, 114
superstition, concept of 5, 30, 39, 47, 70, 84, 85, 87, 88, 91, 96, 97, 118, 121, 133, 135, 144, 146, 159, 188, 189
synchronicity 104

Taiping rebellion 91
Taiwan 46, 56, 91, 116, 130–136
territorial cults 50, 54
Three Great Learnings 78
tiger, symbol of 12, 16, 90, 91

universities 77, 121, 122, 127, 170, 187
urban culture 118
urban development 170
USA 97, 130, 153

violence 63, 66

Wang Ji 28
Weber, Max 4, 147
westernization 119, 157, 188
White, Lynn 94
women 133, 169, 193
world religions 2
Wright, Arthur F. 32

Xiamen 124, 125, 128, 139

Yan Zhetui 23
Yang C. K. 87, 90
Yang Xin 187
Yang Yunsong 23, 28, 110, 112
Yangshao culture 12
Yellow Emperor 19, 56
Yi jing, see Book of Changes
yin-yang 11, 16, 19, 20, 107–109, 111, 114, 131, 165
Yoon, Hong-key 93, 95–97, 144, 147
Yu Kongjian 158
Yu Xixian 121

Zhang Juwen 93, 158
Zhu Xi 25–27, 29, 103, 109–110